ALL AMERICAN

ALL AMERICAN

Two Young Men, the 2001
ARMY-NAVY GAME
and the War They Fought in Iraq

STEVE EUBANKS

WILLIAM MORROW
An Imprint of HarperCollins*Publishers*

A hardcover edition of this book was published in 2013 by William Morrow, an imprint of HarperCollins Publishers.

FIRST WILLIAM MORROW PAPERBACK EDITION PUBLISHED 2014.

Designed by Jamie Lynn Kerner

Library of Congress Cataloging-in-Publication Data has been applied for.

ISBN 978-0-06-220281-9

14 15 16 17 18   OV/RRD   10 9 8 7 6 5 4 3 2

To the Rangers and Marines who gave it all.
RLTW and Semper Fi.

CONTENTS

CONTENTS

PART THREE: SURVIVORS

PROLOGUE

First and ten at the Army thirty-six-yard line.

Both teams trotted from the south end of the field to the north as whistles announced the end of the first quarter. Had it been the start of the fourth quarter instead of the second, all the players would have sprinted from one end to the other, a tradition meant to display the indefatigable spirit of football men. None of them knew how the tradition started, and now that every high school and college team in the country was doing it, too—some while holding four fingers in the air—it seemed to have lost its luster.

No fingers were lifted for the second quarter, a break in the action that warranted only a light jog as a fresh fifteen minutes flashed on the game clock and sixty-seven thousand fans stood and stretched their legs.

From the field, the movement of the crowd looked like water cascading down the walls of a well. Some of the fans still waved tiny American flags, the ubiquitous pompoms for this contest, while others shed their jackets and sweaters, exposing arms and necks and the occasional coed shoulder. By 1 P.M. the temperature had crept above seventy degrees in Philadelphia, sunbathing weather for the first day of December 2001.

The fans had been in these rigid old stands for hours before kick-off, many arriving at sunrise to watch the cadets of West Point and midshipmen of the United States Naval Academy fall into formation in the parking lot, a spectacle so foreign to most college football fans that they were left shaking their heads in wonder. No one cared that Veterans Stadium sagged under the weight of indifference and looked much older than its thirty years. Built in the late sixties to keep the Phillies from moving to Cherry Hill, New Jersey, and to provide a home to the Philadelphia Eagles, who once played their home games at Franklin Field at the University of Pennsylvania, the Vet had been inadequate from the moment the doors opened in 1971. Even though dual-purpose stadiums were all the rage at the time, with Atlanta, Washington, St. Louis, Cincinnati, and Pittsburgh opening squatty, circular coliseums, the dimensions and requirements of the base-ball diamond and football field were so different that most of them worked well for neither. Early-season football games were played on dirt infields, and fifty-yard-line seats were often as far away from the action as you could get.

Veterans Stadium had all those problems and more. The place was overrun with mice, and many of the creaky seats—soon to be meticulously removed and sold as souvenirs—stuck open or shut. The paint was cracked, and the elevators rumbled and wobbled in ways that made fans want to take the ramps.

On this day no one cared. Veterans Stadium—hard, gritty, and named for veterans of all wars—seemed like the perfect spot for the Army-Navy Game, even though neither academy had anything to do with it being held there. Philadelphia is close to equidistant be-tween West Point, New York, and Annapolis, Maryland, so with few exceptions the game had been played in the City of Brotherly Love since 1932, mostly in the old Municipal Stadium. As for the name, Philadelphia city councilmen voted to call it Veterans Sta-dium in 1968 as both a tribute to those who served their country and a less-than-subtle snub at the Vietnam protesters whose numbers were swelling at that time.

There were no protesters on this day. That would come later. Today, emotions ran high. Many of the spectators had already cried themselves spent. Some hugged, while others made mental notes of every tidbit of history they witnessed. This football game between two losing teams, a meeting that would have no effect on the college football standings, had become a rallying point for the country, a healing salve on a gaping national wound. Fires from the World Trade Center still burned eighty-one days after September 11.

And this was now the most watched college football game in the country. Four million American television sets tuned in early that Saturday afternoon, with another four million sets tuned in overseas.

Army led Navy, 13–0.

The Cadets of the United States Military Academy at West Point had scored on their first two possessions and would have been up 14–0 if not for a missed extra point by kicker Derek Jacobs. That miss gave hope to the U.S. Naval Academy Midshipmen. Army's quarterback, Chad Jenkins, was playing on an injured knee, a condition far more serious than anyone realized at the time, and one that affected his passing accuracy. A brace that looked like something out of the Spanish Inquisition gave him the ability to run on torn ligaments, but if he twisted the wrong way during a throwing motion, the ball could go anywhere and he could end up writhing on the ground.

Army's last possession of the first quarter had ended with Chad throwing an ugly interception, the sort of wobbly "jump ball" that was every quarterback's nightmare. Navy wasn't able to capitalize, but the momentum had shifted to the Mids.

They needed to hold Army on this drive. The difference between two scores and three is far greater than numbers on a board. Comebacks are built on the belief that the mountain is not too high, the time is not too short—the obstacles are not too great. Thirteen points down with three quarters to play was not that big a hole, and both teams knew it.

The players were thrilled to focus solely on football, at least for this day. The cheers, grunts, yelling coaches, and smells, the thick grass wedged in their fingers and soft soil under their cleats were all a welcome reprieve from the knowledge that they would soon be called to do hard things. Even though American football at the turn of the twenty-first century was applauded for its militarism and the way it prepared young men for life in another kind of uniform, the chaos, nuance, strategy, beauty, and violence of this game, with its tradition of rivalry between two branches of the nation's military, allowed these players to push aside all thoughts of war. For three and a half hours, they could focus on a sport they had played since they were children. The gridiron had become the one place in their lives where nothing seemed off-kilter.

Fifty of the players were seniors—twenty-six from Army and twenty-four from Navy—and that meant they were just a few months away from the reality of commanding men in combat. For some of them, the main reason for enrolling in the academies was to get an education on par with those of the best Ivy League schools, plus a guaranteed job out of college. Others were legacies (offspring of career military fathers or mothers). They never expected to see actual conflict. Then there were the men and women who had longed to be soldiers, sailors, or marines since they were old enough to pick up a toy gun. More than a few fell into a category the Army referred to informally as "hooah," a gung-ho catchphrase that meant everything from "Do you understand?" to "Let's take that hill!"

Hooah is the guy obsessed with polishing every buckle and shoe, who wants to be Infantry, Airborne, and Ranger, and who can't imagine a life not spent in uniform. If he wasn't at West Point, the hooah guy would be in the Reserve Officer Training Corps (ROTC) or working his way through the enlisted ranks and applying to Officer Candidate School (OCS). Navy had them as well, although their pronunciations were different. Those heading into the SEALs are "hooyah!," and marines, "oooRAH!," shouted from the back of the throat like the gravelly bark of a bloodhound.

But for all of them, the answer to why they were there eventually came around to the quarter-million-dollar answer: it's free. The grand bargain at the United States Military Academy and United States Naval Academy (and the Air Force Academy as well) is that in exchange for a five-year military commitment, cadets and midshipmen need only show up on campus with underwear and a toothbrush. Everything else—clothes, shoes, food, room, furniture, books, backpacks, and tuition—is paid for and provided by the government of the United States, a value estimated at between $250,000 and $300,000.

The National Collegiate Athletic Association (NCAA) does not allow student-athletes to work during the school year or take money from anyone other than their parents. So, while an athletic scholarship at a nonmilitary college might take care of room and board, things like gas, pizza, logoed sweatshirts, and date money have to come from mom and dad. At West Point and Annapolis, not only are the wardrobe and meals free, the Army and Navy pay cadets and midshipmen a $7,500 annual salary. For a football player who is not quite good enough to play at one of the bigger schools it is a good deal: four years of college football and a five-year job after graduation.

After the five-year service commitment, academy graduates can either re-up and perhaps become "lifers," or they can get out and be at the front of the civilian hiring line. There is no official name for those who get out after the minimum, but unofficially they are known as "five-and-fliers." Less than half of the class from 1991 was still active duty by 2001, but no one blamed them. Recruiters for Fortune 500 companies listed the most sought-after college graduates as those from, in order: West Point, the Naval Academy, the Air Force Academy, Massachusetts Institute of Technology, Harvard, and Yale. Stanford, Brown, Princeton, and, oddly enough, Georgia Tech have slipped in and out of the fifth and sixth slots, but no school has knocked Army and Navy off the top in almost three decades.

The academies get the brightest who, for whatever reason (usually money), don't go Ivy League or advanced tech, and who want the challenge of being part of something greater than themselves. All the cadets and midshipmen say this proudly, but most don't even try to explain what it means. If you aren't part of it, you wouldn't understand.

The fans in Veterans Stadium and at home watching on television did their best to grasp what these young men were about to do. Everyone at the academies trains for combat, but when these football players signed on to play for Army and Navy, war was a distant figure in a rolling fog, out there somewhere but unidentifiable. Many of them had signed up for a chance to play Division I football and be on national television; they really hadn't thought much about what would come after.

All that changed after September 11.

Something was different about this game even before it began. The fans knew this, and so did the players.

President George W. Bush had spoken in both locker rooms before the game. His remarks, while heartfelt, seemed stilted, somber, and somewhat unprepared. "Your opponents today on the football field will be the men you will be serving beside on the battlefield very soon," he said. It was another hard kernel of truth that many of them hadn't fully embraced, or if they had, it had been pushed to the backs of their minds.

The Army players also got a visit from one of their heroes, General Norman Schwarzkopf, the commander of Desert Storm and graduate of the West Point Class of 1956. After 9/11 Stormin' Norman had become an even bigger folk hero at the academy. This was the man who crafted and executed the battle plan that crushed the fourth-largest army in the world and liberated an occupied Arab nation in less than six weeks. The general gave a stem-winder of a speech where he talked about the weeks, months, and years that lay ahead, and about how their conduct this day on the field would mirror their future conduct on another field with another objective.

Then he concluded by saying, "Men, today you are going to battle. You are going to war with Navy. And let me tell you something: the Army does not lose wars. You will prevail. You will win."

Every cadet who heard him had been ready to run through walls to get onto the field.

The speeches in the other locker room were a little more colorful. Senator John McCain, combat aviator and Naval Academy Class of 1958, had surprised the Midshipmen in their locker room. They snapped to attention when McCain walked in and were immediately put at ease. The senator began his talk slowly, mentioning how this group was not playing for the people in the stands at Veterans Stadium, but for the U.S. troops in Kabul and Kandahar, people who were already in the fight and who were looking at this game as a rallying point and as a reminder of why they were there and what they were fighting for.

Then the senator really got revved up, his voice getting higher and louder with each breath. Within moments, the former POW's face turned crimson. Some players worried that he might stroke out right in front of them.

That was when the tirade really started. "You are going to go out there and beat those Army bastards!" McCain yelled. "You are going to knock their asses backward!"

Whoa. Some of the guys looked at each other as if to say, "Is this really happening?" while others smiled and enjoyed the moment. Pregame pep talks were always fiery, but the added celebrity cachet of the speakers and the intense emotions surrounding this game ramped up the intensity to an even higher level. Like their Army counterparts down the hall, all the Navy players ran out of the locker room ready for battle.

Quarterback Chad Jenkins and Navy outside linebacker Brian Stann, two men on the field together for the start of the second quarter, did their best to remain focused on the next play and the next down. Neither could claim to be immersed in the warrior mind-set, not yet anyway. They had both gone to the academies for football. Neither of them had been raised in a military family, and they weren't guys who had dreamed of wearing a military uniform since childhood.

The first time either of them had considered West Point and Annapolis was when they realized the limits of their Division I scholarship options. Both had been outstanding high school athletes, but
despite wanting to play the big time like most seventeen-year-old
males, the cold, hard reality was that neither Chad nor Brian was
big or fast enough to play for the likes of Penn State, Oklahoma,
Ohio State, or the University of Southern California. They could
have played Division II, maybe even been stars at that level, but to be
on the highest plain of their sport, to play on television and compete
against the best, their best bet was to attend one of the academies.
When Army and Navy called, they had both jumped at the chance
to play.

Three months before this game they weren't even thinking about
war, except as it was taught in their classes and field exercises. Service and duty and honor were ingrained in them, to be sure, but war
had always been more theoretical than real. Now they would be the
twenty-first century's first class of officers to lead men in combat.
And neither of them had any idea how they would respond.

John Bond, the thirty-nine-year-old offensive coordinator for
Army, called the first play of the second quarter from the press box.
Bond knew what Chad could and could not do as well as anyone. The
kid had the heart of a lion, but the body of your average computer
science major. He reminded Bond a little of himself at that age, a
similar-sized coach's kid from Arkansas who played quarterback for
Hall of Fame coach Lou Holtz at the University of Arkansas. Like
Bond, who had been able to walk around the Razorback campus in
near-total anonymity, Chad would never have been picked out of
West Point's morning formation as the leader of the football team.
Still, Bond had more faith in Chad than in any other player he'd ever
coached.

The first play of the second quarter was a straight drop, hitch-
and-go with receiver Anthony Miller as the primary target and secondary receiver Brian Bruenton running a hook pattern.

They had practiced this a hundred times, and should have been able to execute it in their sleep. But practice never took place in front of thousands of screaming fans, including the president of the United States or a sideline full of reporters and cameramen. Every player knew this game was being broadcast to every continent, including McMurdo Station, Antarctica. Millions of people were hanging on every play. Coaches couldn't simulate that kind of pressure in practice.

Chad broke the huddle and scanned the Navy defense. The Mids were in a four-three with four down linemen and three linebackers. He saw a mismatch in size and speed. Miller was bigger and faster than the Navy cornerbacks, but even if he wasn't, the play was designed so that the cornerback would come up and inside to cover Bruenton, leaving Miller alone with only a smaller, slower safety to beat. Chad should be able to get this play off for a big gain, assuming his offensive line held.

"Set, blue, twenty-one: blue, twenty-one. Sa-hit!" Chad yelled.

The center snapped the ball and linemen slammed into each other in a cacophony of slapping pads and guttural growls. Chad dropped back and bounced on his toes. Every good quarterback can sense when the offensive line is holding and when his pocket is folding around him. This time he saw the pocket collapsing a second too soon but a sliver of an opening up the middle. The Navy linebackers had scampered backward a couple of steps to cover their passing assignments. With no receiver breaking into his sight, and the memory of the last interception still fresh and raw, Chad tucked the ball and ran up the middle.

Brian reacted perfectly. With no receivers in his zone, he was free to follow the football. Once Chad tucked and leaned into his run, Brian broke toward the line of scrimmage. As one defensive end grabbed Chad from the side, Brian reached him with a shoulder. Chad went down like a dropped bag of sand.

No gain. Second and ten.

The midshipmen, all four thousand of them in the stands near the goal line, went wild. Coaches slapped Brian's helmet and yelled "good job" as he came off the field, yielding his spot to another linebacker. It would be one of the highlights of his Navy football career, one that had started with great promise before enduring numerous transitions. Brian hadn't been recruited to Navy as a linebacker, even though it was a role that suited him like no other. He was one of those all-around good athletes who could have played four or five different positions. But he looked like a linebacker with the squared-off features that graphic novelists gave all their tough guys: hair angling at ninety degrees in the back and chin chiseled at an equally impossible angle in the front.

Brian could have been the model for the original Captain America, the one from the 1942 comic books, not the 2011 movie. As looks went, guys like Dick Butkus had nothing on Brian. And he loved to hit. There was nothing he enjoyed more than lowering his shoulder and popping an opposing runner, which made him perfect for the position he now played.

Chad and Brian had never met before that moment, although they shared a special competitive bond that Army and Navy players had always shared. For more than a century, Cadets and Midshipmen had been going after each other with an old fashioned game-day hate unrivaled in college football. The standard mantra on the West Point campus, no matter what, no matter what season, was "Go Army, beat Navy." And at Annapolis: "Go Navy, beat Army." It was their version of "Roll Tide."

But when the game was over, all the players would hug and cry and wish each other well. They would walk together en masse between sidelines and sing each other's alma maters, a sign of the bond they shared beyond football.

All the players, including Chad and Brian, would do the same after this game, embracing as those before them and those after them had and would, as brothers in arms.

Despite the predictions of their commander in chief that they would serve side by side, Brian and Chad never saw each other in any uniforms other than the ones they wore that day in Philadelphia, even though they fought within a few miles of each other during the toughest days of the Iraq War.

They were players in the most-watched college game of the decade. But it was in the coming years that both men did things that they never imagined possible. It was in those years that they became All Americans.

ALL AMERICAN

PART ONE

PLAYERS

CHAPTER I

I fear all we have done is to awaken a sleeping giant
and fill him with a terrible resolve.
—ADMIRAL ISOROKU YAMAMOTO OF THE JAPANESE
IMPERIAL NAVY, WRITING IN HIS DIARY AFTER THE
ATTACK ON PEARL HARBOR

All they had to do was look up. The hijackers out of Boston used the Hudson River as a visual landmark, which meant they flew right past West Point—"the post," as the cadets who attend the United States Military Academy call their campus. Because of the steep elevation change between the river and the academy's main black-and-gray stone buildings, a hill every plebe learns to hate as he runs up it, the Boeing 767s would have been seen at just above eye level by anyone standing near George Washington's statue on the Plain, the campus parade ground and site of the first Army-Navy Game, which took place in 1890.

The location for the nation's oldest military academy wasn't picked for its beauty or scenery, although both were plentiful. It was a strategic "gift from the Almighty," as General George Washington would later say: the perfect place to defend a wide and unwieldy river from British ships in 1778. The first three years of the Revolutionary

War weren't going that well for the upstart rebels, and Washington's Continental Army had already erected numerous forts along the Hudson, including Fort Washington in Manhattan and Fort Lee in New Jersey. But the most significant one was at West Point. The river makes an S curve around Constitution Island, some forty-nine miles north of Manhattan and one of the only tricky spots to sail on a river that in places spreads a mile wide. The western point of that curve sits like a geological staircase, with sharp inclines leveling off to a series of relatively flat plateaus.

It was like nature's shooting gallery, a spot where artillery could rain down upon encroaching vessels as if they were ducks in a barrel. Washington improved the kill zone by stretching a six-hundred-yard-long series of enormous cast-iron links known as the Great Chain, each link weighing 114 pounds, across the river at the first turn. British vessels could navigate no farther south than West Point, where they were bombarded with cannon fire from above.

In 2001, in an eerie historical coincidence, the enemy came down the Hudson again, only this time they had the high ground.

Chad Jenkins did not see the planes. Like every cadet, even those in the First Class (as the academies called their seniors), he had to be dressed in his uniform and in platoon formation at parade rest outside Grant Hall at 6:55 A.M. Grant is one of several stone dormitories named after former West Point grads—Lee (as in Robert E.), Sherman (William Tecumseh), Bradley (Omar), Eisenhower, and MacArthur—clustered behind Washington Hall, the gigantic dining facility that seats more than four thousand people. The routine was simple: up at 6:00 A.M., shower, dress, and square the quarters away (Army speak for making your bed and cleaning your room, a given at the academies) in forty minutes. That was a virtual vacation considering that in the winter and spring, Chad would have been in the gym at 5:00 A.M. for strength training and conditioning drills. Football season offered at least one break: sleeping until 6:00 A.M. was a treat he didn't take for granted.

Then it was downstairs to breakfast formation at 6:55 A.M., regardless of weather. Not 6:56 A.M. or even 6:55.30 A.M. Punctuality is sacrosanct at the academies, a lesson learned in the first days on post. Plebes, as the academies call their freshmen, take turns standing at attention in their hallways announcing the number of minutes left until their first Accountability, which is West Point–speak for roll call, and also announcing what uniform is to be worn. So as plebes roll out of bed and straighten their barracks, one of their classmates is shouting, "Attention all cadets: there are ten minutes until assembly for breakfast formation. The uniform is 'as-for-class' under gray jacket . . ." Accountability happens like clockwork between 6:55 A.M. and 7:05 A.M., a miserable time in the winter, when cold wind off the Hudson can cut the skin. Wind is often worse than sleet or snow. At least on Tuesday, September 11, the weather was perfect, a clean, crisp late-summer day.

Once everyone called out that Tuesday morning, the entire Corps of Cadets marched together to the dining hall, where they removed their covers (military jargon for hats), stood behind their chairs until ordered to sit, and then devoured their breakfast in less than twenty minutes. There was no slouching, no slurping, and no elbows on the tables. Every cadet sat with his shoulders back, bending forward at the hips at a forty-five-degree angle, chin up, bringing the food to the mouth, not the mouth to the food, a procedure that was drilled into each plebe by his company commander in the first week. Incoming students at West Point were expected to know advanced calculus and the history of the Roman Empire: they were not expected to know how to eat. That and many other disciplines were taught.

Chad had gotten used to inhaling his food, a habit everyone who'd ever refueled in Washington Hall found hard to break, even after having been away from West Point for years.

"My wife can't understand why I can't take my time and enjoy a meal," said Rick Dauch, Class of 1984 and a former defensive back on the Army football team. "I haven't been in the Army in seventeen years, but I still eat every meal in about twenty minutes, and it all goes back to the four years I spent at West Point."

After breakfast, Chad hustled back to his room to gather his books and put them into his standard-issue backpack, as much a part of the uniform of the day as the dark blue worsted wool shirt and dress gray slacks worn by every cadet. His first class started at 8:05 A.M.: systems engineering, his major. The window in his classroom faced away from the river, so he wouldn't have seen the planes even if he had been looking. No one in class was.

West Point was not a place where students stared out the windows during class. In math classes, for example, cadets hung their covers on pegs outside the classroom and stood at parade rest behind their desks until the professor arrived. They were ordered either to sit or go to the blackboards that covered every wall of the room. If they were ordered to the boards, problems would be assigned and each cadet had to work his problem in silence.

After an allotted amount of time—not long in most instances—the professor would say something like "Cadet Jenkins, present your problem." The cadet would then turn and say something like "Sir, the problem presented to me was to find the third standard deviation of x . . ." and so on.

Turning your back on the professor during the presentation was an automatic deduction. In fact, on any given day solving the problem correctly accounted for only half the grade. The other half was based on your ability to explain and present your answer to the class. Everything—every class, lecture, drill, meal, rule in the manual (and there were thousands)—came back to leadership. A math class at West Point was only partially about math. Mostly it was about leadership, with math as the vehicle.

At 8:55 A.M., Chad walked onto the paved area between the Pershing, Eisenhower, and Bradley barracks, a spot any cadet who screws up knows all too well. Fail to dust under your bed or fold your underwear properly and you are standing watch in that courtyard, marching back and forth through rain, sleet, snow, or blistering heat. Cadets who weren't in trouble spent as little time there as possible, so Chad was surprised to see his roommate, Dominic Trippodo, waiting for him.

"You need to turn on the news," Dom said. "A plane just flew into the World Trade Center."

Televisions weren't allowed in the dorms, but there were special cable hookups that allowed cadets to watch certain channels, including CNN, MSNBC, Bloomberg, and Fox News, on their computers. Chad got his computer up just in time to see the second plane. It took a second for him to realize what he had witnessed, but within minutes he knew the country was at war.

Chad's journey to that moment had been winding at best. He hadn't thought about Army until his senior year of high school. He was West Point material from the time he could walk—he and his family just didn't know it. A precocious and handsome boy, he was one of those neighborhood kids who could always be found outside. The youngest of three children and the only boy in his family, Chad was the perfect playmate for his father, Dave, who loved to hunt in the countryside near the family's six-and-a-half-acre homestead in Dublin, Ohio, an upper-middle-class suburb of Columbus. Chad could handle a rifle before he could read, and when he wasn't hunting rabbits and pheasant with his dad, he could be found dribbling or kicking or passing some ball or other.

As young as five, he would climb onto the couch to watch sports with Dave. When he would see an acrobatic play or flashy catch, he'd say, "Dad, let's try that." At the first commercial break, the two would head outside, where Dave would grab a baseball bat and hit pop flies—and then watch Chad stand with his arms at his sides as the ball fell perilously close to his face. Only at the last second would Chad lean forward and catch the ball behind his back. Then Dave would hit grounders to him and Chad would make diving grabs, and throw the ball to the spot in the yard designated as first base. Chad set up targets against walls and trees and would throw pitches for hours, working on a leg kick like the one he'd seen from Goose Gossage or the high delivery he'd seen from Steve Bedrosian.

It wasn't just baseball that drew his attention. When a new sub-division sprang up a few hundred yards behind the Jenkinses' home, Chad went on a reconnaissance mission with a water bottle in one hand and a ball in the other. When he found that the newly constructed homes had hoops out front, he fetched his mother's broom and lowered the backboards so he could get in some practice. The residents hadn't moved in yet, so he felt sure it was fine. When Lee Jenkins missed her son and went on a recon mission of her own, she found Chad doing his best Michael Jordan impression, leading a fast break of imaginary friends, dribbling behind his back, faking one way and stutter-stepping another until he broke free from his defender and hit the winning shot, all the while giving play-by-play commentary.

Chad would play any game, no matter how obscure. When his sisters, Laura and Teri, practiced their field hockey in the yard, Chad would grab one of his golf clubs and join them. They all knew Chad was special, and not just athletically. He had something that everyone around him recognized, but no one could describe, not because they couldn't put their fingers on it, but because there wasn't an English word that thoroughly summed it up.

Two anecdotes from when he was ten years old would be repeated many times in an attempt to describe Chad. The first occurred at Wrightsville Beach in North Carolina during the annual Jenkins vacation getaway. Laura was fifteen and Teri thirteen, both awkward and perpetually mortified by everything their family said or did. Chad was always the quickest to set them off. They hadn't been in North Carolina an hour when he embarrassed them beyond belief. The kids had gone out and discovered some older high school boys, perhaps a college freshman or two, playing volleyball on the beach. Laura and Teri hoped one or more of the young men would catch their eyes, maybe give them a smile or invite them to sit and talk afterward. Of course they would never speak first, or even make eye contact.

But Chad harbored no such inhibitions. He immediately asked if he could join the game, even though he was at least six years younger and eighteen inches shorter than everyone there. If that weren't enough, within minutes Chad had taken over as his team's captain, motioning people to different positions and shouting instructions during the points. At first the older boys chuckled. They got a kick out of his gumption. Then they realized he knew what he was doing.

Laura and Teri were furious with him but not surprised. That was just Chad. He couldn't be any other way.

The second incident happened at a field near their home. In addition to being a hunter, Dave Jenkins loved motorcycles. He had always been fascinated with Harley-Davidsons and, as an adult, had always owned one. Much to Lee's chagrin, Dave took Chad riding from the time he was three years old. By age four Chad had his own Honda 50 cc dirtbike. He also had a best friend named Jeff Schroeder who had become like part of the family. Earlier that school year Jeff and Chad had collided going for the same ball during a kickball game and Jeff's knee broke one of Chad's teeth. Months later, neither of them brought up the broken tooth, but they still argued over who should have caught the fly ball.

This afternoon, Chad had finally agreed to let Jeff ride his bike, but only if the adults were around because Jeff had never operated any vehicle that didn't have pedals and a chain. Dave and Lee came out, as did Jeff's mom, who crossed her arms and tried to calm her racing heart. Jeff strapped on a helmet and revved up the engine to an ear-piercing pitch. He found first gear and quickly got the hang of it. The Honda motored along, much like his bicycle, only without all the pedaling. He kept his hands near the clutch and brake in case of trouble, although none seemed likely.

He never saw the hole. It was large and deep and camouflaged by grass. The front wheel fell hard and Jeff lunged forward. His butt left the seat, but he kept his grip on the handlebars. He countered the lurch by pulling back. In doing so he opened the throttle wide. The rear wheel spun and the bike tilted at an impossible angle. Jeff went to one knee, bouncing off the grass. Somehow he spun the bike upright and came to a stop.

As often happens in such situations, the adults froze, their eyes wide as their brains tried to process what they were seeing. It couldn't have been more than a second or two, just long enough for shock to slap them. But by the time the paralysis faded and the grown-ups could move, Chad was already there. He sprinted to his friend and cut the bike's engine. When Dave and the others reached them, Chad was helping Jeff get his helmet off.

"Man, I told you about that dip," Chad said. "You have to be careful."

That event would stick with everyone there, not because Chad helped his friend, but because of the speed with which he did it. There was no hesitation and no fear. He saw trouble and ran toward it, a curious trait in a ten-year-old, and one that he would never outgrow.

Chad played football for the first time in the sixth grade, and before the first practice ended he was the starting quarterback. Once again imitating moves he'd seen on television, he rolled out and motioned receivers to open spots like Cincinnati Bengals quarterback Boomer Esiason, then tucked the ball and ran, spinning off would-be tacklers like Steve Young. Many afternoons after that first practice Dave would come out of his home office to find Chad throwing to makeshift receivers in the yard.

The trash can became a wide-out, the oak tree a tight end, and the bicycle a running back on a slant pattern across the middle. The lawn mower became a big defensive tackle rushing from his blind side, one he would always manage to avoid. He would go through one play after another, calling out signals to his imaginary teammates before taking a three-step drop and looking for the open man.

Jeff Schroeder played running back behind Chad throughout middle and high school, and as they grew up, both became stars of the Dublin Coffman High School Shamrocks. Chad was the typical high school jock. He loved the spotlight; he loved the nervous giggles from the girls as he walked down the halls, and he loved the rumors of college scouts hiding in the stands at all his games. Despite his size, Chad put up great numbers as a high school quarterback, but it was his quickness and his ability to evade tacklers that had some other high school coaches comparing him with the likes of Doug Flutie, heady stuff for a seventeen-year-old.

He played lacrosse for the first time his junior year and was awarded All-State honors. Like everything else, he worked at the ancient Cherokee game for hours, throwing and catching a ball against the wall of his house, and shooting corner shots in his front yard at a dead sprint. By fall of his senior year more colleges wanted him for lacrosse than football, including Ohio State, where both his sisters went.

But Chad was determined to play college football, even though he blew his chances with one foolish move the summer before his senior season. After a scrimmage, coaches gave the winning team a T-shirt proclaiming their victory. Chad wore his to a party the weekend after the game. When one of the revelers took offense and threw a soda onto the shirt, Chad punched him in the jaw. Chad ended up breaking his hand in three places. Four surgical pins, three wires, a plastic brace, and explicit instructions to avoid contact and not run up the middle later, Chad played every snap of his senior year with a broken hand. He also ignored the advice of his doctors and rushed for more than five hundred yards. He passed for almost two thousand and was named team MVP.

Several Ivy League teams wanted him. He probably could have started right away at Harvard, Yale, or Princeton, and he had been offered preferred walk-on status at Ohio State, where he would probably be moved out of the quarterback spot and into a wide receiver or safety role. Schroeder signed with Bowling Green and urged Chad to go with him. But Chad wanted to keep his Division I options open, so he sent tapes of his games to coaches all over the country, including the three main service academies—Army, Navy, and Air Force—even though he had no real passion for the military other than watching *A Few Good Men* and *Top Gun* scores of times.

Army had gone 10-2 in 1996 during Chad's senior year of high school, and had almost beaten traditional SEC powerhouse Auburn in the Independence Bowl, a game that so shocked the football world that people weren't saying Auburn had a bad team—they were proclaiming that Army had a great one. With that game fresh on his mind, Chad shipped out a tape and a nice letter to West Point in which he gushed about how much he would love to play for Army. In truth, he didn't give the academy a second thought after dropping the tape in the mail.

Folks at Army thought about him, though. Running back coach Mike Dietzel got so many letters and tapes from kids all over the country that, at times, he felt like the good-looking waitress at a Saturday night bar: he had become impervious to the pickup lines. "I would give anything to play for Army," most of the letters read.

Dietzel could spot the form letters the second he opened them. Then there were those players who got their English teachers to write letters for them. No matter how smart a seventeen-year-old boy might be, he did not use the word *subjugate*. Dietzel never even watched those tapes. You had to weed them out somehow, and if a kid couldn't write a cogent letter selling himself to a coach, he didn't stand much of a chance at West Point.

Chad's letter caught his eye. It was well written without being bullshitty, striking just the right tone to get Dietzel to cue up the tape. He liked what he saw. The kid had natural skills and an instinct for the game, but more important, he was a natural-born leader, the kind of high school player with a commanding presence that elevated those around him. Dublin Coffman's offensive line played above their physical abilities because this kid was on the field. That was exactly the kind of player Army needed.

Ohio was Dietzel's recruiting territory, so while he didn't make a special trip to talk to Chad, on his next visit through Columbus he stopped by Dublin Coffman High School to make his pitch. After a few minutes of saying things that no other college recruiter would ever tell a potential signee—"Army isn't for everyone . . . The discipline is tough and the lifestyle is challenging . . . It takes special character to succeed at a place like West Point"—the coach asked Chad if he had any questions.

Chad said, "What part of Indiana is it in?"

A burly man in his early thirties who had put on twenty-five pounds since his All-American days as a defense back at Otterbein, Dietzel cocked his head and blinked, unsure of what to say.

After an awkward couple of seconds, he said, "Son, West Point is in New York."

The coach pulled out brochures and a map. He showed Chad the serpentine bend in the Hudson and the "west point" where the post stood. He told him how it was originally called Fort Arnold, named after Benedict Arnold, and how Arnold had betrayed General Washington and tried to sell West Point to the British for £20,000; how the fort became a training ground for soldiers and then a college. He showed Chad photographs of the hillsides around the Hudson in autumn, the leaves bursting with color against the backdrop of a clean blue sky, and he showed him shots of the Corps of Cadets in formation, and a cheering throng inside Michie Stadium (pronounced "Mikey," like the kid in the Life cereal commercial, and named after Dennis Michie, West Point Class of 1892, who organized the first Army football team in 1890, and who was killed in action in Cuba during the Spanish-American War in 1898).

Then Dietzel, sensing he had found the right candidate, not just for Army football but for the Army way of life, said, "Who knows, Chad? You might be the next General Jenkins."

General Jenkins. Chad said it to himself several times throughout the day and into the night. He liked the way it sounded, and the mental image he painted of himself in a uniform, standing at attention, returning a salute. He had always envied the *Top Gun* guys, or at least the way they were portrayed in the movie. "Tell me one thing: if you had to go into battle, would you want him with you?" He could quote every line, even the cornball ones like Val Kilmer telling Tom Cruise he could be his wingman anytime. The Army had to be the same thing, right? Brotherhood and bonding and really cool, athletic friends who got to see the world and do amazing things. By the time he replayed all of Coach Dietzel's points in his head, he had convinced himself there was nowhere else he could go.

It was March of his senior year. National Signing Day, the day on which all major colleges sign their most sought-after high school recruits, was in February, so Chad was already behind the curve. His options were dwindling, but Army seemed like the perfect fit, at least from Chad's perspective. He didn't even mind that he would have to spend a year in something called the United States Military Academy Preparatory School, in Fort Monmouth, New Jersey. West Point required a congressional recommendation, medical exams, references, and the kind of grades Chad simply didn't have at the time. Prep school was the equivalent of being redshirted, which, once he made the decision, wasn't such a bad thing.

He had it all worked out, at least in his own mind. Then he told his parents. The announcement came at the dinner table. He said, "Mom, Dad, I've decided where I'm going to school."

Dave and Lee sat up straight and gave him their full attention. "Where, son?" his dad asked.

"West Point," he said. "I'm going to Army."

His mother burst into tears. The only words she could get out were "Why would you do that?"

His dad shook his head and wore a hard frown, saying, "You don't want to go to the Army."

Chad couldn't believe it. For two years they had been telling him he needed to choose his own college, just as his sisters had done. Now that he'd made the choice, they weren't just second-guessing him: they were telling him he was flat-out wrong. His mom was crying real tears.

Dave was a veteran, having served two years in Büdingen, Germany, with the 83rd Artillery Division during the height of the Vietnam War. He held the Army in high regard—in fact, he was a civilian contractor now, providing large-scale pumps to the Navy, so he was as pro–armed forces as anyone—but as every parent knows, standards are different when it's your child. When it became obvious that Chad wasn't changing his mind, the Jenkinses embraced the idea as much as they could. How bad could it be? At least he would have a guaranteed job after graduation.

Lee would later tell everyone that "Chad went to Army for all the wrong reasons, but stayed for all the right ones."

That didn't stop her from pulling Chad aside the day she and Dave dropped him off at the prep school in New Jersey. Quietly checking over his shoulder to make sure no one was watching, Lee gave her baby a one-way ticket back home dated three days hence.

"Just in case," she said in a low voice, patting his hand.

Those memories ran through Chad's mind as he watched the towers collapse. Announcements were coming fast and furious. Classes would continue on schedule. Everyone was to report as normal until ordered otherwise. The base was on lockdown. No one could come or go. At the time it wasn't clear if more attacks were on the way, but obviously West Point would be on any terrorists' short list of targets even if no one had intelligence of an imminent threat.

Many of Chad's teammates and friends were still in class. Brian Zickefoose, a linebacker and defensive captain of the football team and one of Chad's closest friends, was on the twelfth floor of the law building taking a Law of War class when an aide knocked on the door and interrupted the instructor, a hard colonel named Patrick Finnegan. Colonel Finnegan suffered fools with all the patience of a career Army lawyer, which was to say he didn't suffer them at all. Interrupting his class for anything less than a full-scale invasion would result in swift and unpleasant corrective measures.

The aide wasted no time telling Colonel Finnegan that the World Trade Center had been hit by a plane, and that if it pleased the colonel, he should turn on the television. Finnegan flipped on the old Zenith in the corner of the room just in time to see United

Airlines Flight 175, a Boeing 767 with fifty-eight passengers and six crew members, crash into the south face of Two World Trade Center at 513 knots.

Zickefoose's classmates broke noise discipline, several going so far as to utter profanities, another infraction that would normally earn a cadet a weekend's restriction. Finnegan let it slide. He watched in silence for five minutes, his big neck tightening the collar of his uniform. Then he turned off the set and returned to his lecture. Laws of war had just gotten a lot more important.

The mood changed throughout the post, but the procedures didn't. Since no one was quite sure what to do, they did what they had always done. Chad went back to class after watching the second plane hit the South Tower. Life continued at West Point with the same precision as always. At 11:30 A.M. he went to the dining hall with his teammates for early lunch. The entire Corps of Cadets eats three squares a day at the same time with one exception: the football team eats the midday meal before everyone else during the season so they can study film and work with their position coaches during standard lunchtime. It is one of the small things that often alienated the football players from the other cadets, a bone of contention shared at all service academies, where uniformity is sacrosanct.

Team lunches weren't better or longer than the ones consumed by the rest of the corps. If anything Chad and his teammates inhaled their food even faster than normal so they could head to their breakout groups. Major General Eric Olson, Class of 1972 and commandant of cadets from 1999 through the end of his term in 2002, spoke to the team in the dining hall. He told them what they already knew: the nation was under attack and West Point was a "target of opportunity." He also informed them that things would go on as scheduled, including football practice that afternoon.

"The Army doesn't stop, no matter what," he said.

They were the only Division I football team to practice that day, a decision Coach Todd Berry reinforced before they took the field with the same message given by General Olson.

"The Army does not stop, ever," he said. "That includes us."

They were 0-1 for the season, having lost a heartbreaker to Cincinnati three days before. But that game now seemed like a dream to Berry. A former quarterback at Tulsa who had never lost his Oklahoma accent, Berry felt a duty to coach at Army even though he wasn't from a military background. His father, Reuben, had been a soldier and a college coach and served a brief stint as a head coach in the Canadian Football League for the Saskatchewan Roughriders, but it was those Saturdays in December with his dad that Berry remembered most. Reuben would buy a bucket of fried chicken and put it on a TV tray so that he and Todd could watch the Army-Navy Game.

"This is the greatest game of them all," Reuben would tell his son. "This is the way it should be played, for the love of the game."

Then, during his time as the offensive coordinator at East Carolina, Todd's wife, Lisa, had made a road trip to West Point when the Pirates played at Michie Stadium. She had been to Memorial Stadium in Lincoln, Nebraska; the Swamp (Ben Hill Griffin Stadium) in Gainesville, Florida; and Neyland Stadium at the University of Tennessee, where 103,000 fans wearing orange sang "Rocky Top" as loud as they could. There were a few she'd missed, but as college football stadiums went, she had seen the most raucous. That Saturday night in West Point she told Todd, "I want you to be the head coach here someday. I want you to coach these men." Now he was doing just that.

Berry had always understood the challenges. Not only was the NFL carrot never a recruiting option, but it took a special kind of kid to want the West Point life. Not that they weren't smart enough or athletic enough—these were the smartest and hardest-working young men he'd ever been around—but their focus was always divided. Now football had tumbled even farther down their list.

Within a few months, some of his players would be fighting in some foreign land, not fighting as the metaphor is often used in football, but with guns and explosives and heavy artillery: real fighting where people died. How was he supposed to get them honed in on Conference USA opponents like Cincinnati, Texas Christian University, and Louisville when they were thinking about Al Qaeda and Osama bin Laden? He couldn't. And more important, he knew he probably shouldn't.

Offensive coordinator John Bond sensed the difference as well. Bond had played for fifteen years in Rogers, Arkansas, where his dad was a high school coach, and at the University of Arkansas for Hall of Fame coach Lou Holtz. He'd spent another fifteen years coaching under Berry at Illinois State and had made the move with him to West Point the previous year. It had been a culture shock. His first day walking the line during stretching drills, he overheard two of his players talking about live-fire exercises with M240 Bravos, heavy, general-purpose machine guns also known as 240s. Bond walked away knowing that in his thirty years in football, he had never, ever heard that kind of talk from football players.

As Bond walked through the line on September 11, the banter was gone. Each man prepared in his own way. Once practice got under way, players flew around the field like it was a national championship game. None of the usual verbal needling or trash-talking could be heard, but half a dozen fights broke out. Linebacker Ben Edgar and offensive guard Steve Schmidt threw the first punches after Schmidt shoved Edgar late and Edgar, a senior from Chattanooga, Tennessee, called Schmidt, a junior from Brookshire, Texas, a "shithead." Coaches let them punch and shove for a few seconds before breaking it up.

Zickefoose got a shove or two in but managed to stay out of the melee. His was a slow burn, the kind that built up in the boiler until the engine was running at full steam. Bond kept an eye on him just in case. You never knew when 'Foose might blow.

Chad shouted signals as if every play was the most important of his life. Bond's mind flashed back to the first time he'd seen his undersize quarterback. Berry and Bond had been brought into Army because of the pro-style offense they ran at Illinois State. The previous regime had run the wishbone, a triple-option offense almost exclusively devoted to the run. Berry and Bond were there to break the wishbone and add some explosive depth to the Army offense. That most likely meant changing quarterbacks, even though the starter in the 1999 season, Joe Gerena, had been the star of the Army-Navy Game, breaking a long run late to beat the Mids. Chad wanted Gerena's job, and when the new coaches arrived in the spring of 2000, the kid from Ohio was the first player in Bond's office.

Bond told Chad what he told all players: every position was up for grabs and everybody was on equal footing. Evaluations would be made during spring practice. Chad had the same chance as every other quarterback on the roster. But Bond didn't give him much of a shot. Chad was a couple inches shorter and a good twenty to twenty-five pounds lighter than Gerena. The arm might be better, but that was only part of the pro-set equation, an offensive scheme with backs lined up side by side behind the quarterback from which multiple run and pass plays can be run. A good pro-set quarterback had to have speed, the ability to read defenses, enough poise to sell the play-fake, and the arm to throw on the run. Gerena had all of these skills.

Then something unexpected happened. The smaller, slower kid worked harder and did better than the veteran. Not only was Chad's passing efficiency better than any other quarterback on the team; his decision making was far superior, especially when it came to learning the new offense and making the right defensive reads. Suddenly Bond had a tough decision on his hands. Gerena was a rising senior, a "firstie," so it was going to be a big deal if he benched him for a junior, or "cow," at West Point.

Bond would spend months learning the nuances of language at Army, like the fact that the term *cow* came from a time when cadets were not given leave until after their sophomore or "yearling" (often shortened to "yuk") year. When they returned to the post for their third year, officers referred to them as "the cows coming home." But those words were more than academy titles. They represented rank. Benching a firstie for a cow would be like sitting a captain and putting a lieutenant in charge.

First Class cadets held leadership positions from first captain to platoon leaders within the brigade, and the underclassmen fell somewhere beneath them with titles like cadet sergeant and cadet corporal. These weren't ceremonial positions at West Point. It was deadly serious stuff. Bond hadn't been around long enough to understand what the off-field repercussions would be if he benched Gerena in favor of Chad, but he had to do what was best for his football team.

It was a close call. Both players had good spring workouts, but Chad gained an edge with his ability to adapt and improvise. He also refused to be denied. During one drill where Bond was alternating quarterbacks, Chad had to go the bathroom, but he was afraid that if he left the field for a quick pee, he would lose a couple of reps and maybe his shot at the starting job. So for the first time in Bond's coaching life, a player wet himself rather than leave the practice field.

Watching Chad run the offense on 9/11, Bond tried to burn every second of this practice into his brain. He never wanted to forget a single detail of this moment or these men.

By sundown Chad had grown antsy. One of his best friends and former teammates, Gary Bartels, who had retired from football after so many shoulder surgeries that he had more scar tissue than skin, lived in the Bradley Barracks and had gone onto the roof to watch the smoke rise from Manhattan while the team practiced. Hearing Bartels talk about it made Chad's heart race. The shock was gone. Now he was pissed. Chad and his roommate, Dominic Trippodo, along with a backup tight end named Mike Schwartz, had all decided they were ready to leave on Wednesday morning and kill the people who did this.

They couldn't wait.

CHAPTER 2

*There are no great men, just great challenges which
ordinary men are forced by circumstances to meet.*
—ADMIRAL WILLIAM F. HALSEY

Brian Stann was waiting to get a haircut when he noticed something
happening. Morning formation at Annapolis started at 6:30 A.M.
sharp outside Bancroft Hall, a mammoth, century-old structure
with 1,700 rooms and thirty-three acres of heated floor space that
serves as the largest dormitory in the world. The entire U.S. Naval
Academy Brigade of Midshipmen lived together, and had since the
building's completion in 1906.

Brian, a junior at the academy, had gotten up early and walked to
morning chow, which was how mids referred to breakfast. At West
Point cadets marched to breakfast together, but at Annapolis the
brigade went to the dining hall on their own after formation. Still,
their days were no less hectic.

Brian's first class started at 7:55 A.M., and he then went from
one classroom to the next, end to end, until 11:05 A.M. Lunch was
at noon, a meal he planned to gobble down in fifteen minutes so he
could meet with his fellow linebackers to go over the drubbing Navy
had just taken at the hands of Georgia Tech. It would be a sorry

subject to relive on such a beautiful Tuesday. The water of the Severn River glistened pure blue, matching the cloudless sky. Nobody had interrupted class or stopped him as he was walking from one room to the next. Ironically, the brigade, men who were months away from being on the front line of America's response to the attacks on the World Trade Center and the Pentagon, were among the last to know what had happened.

After his last class, Brian slipped down to the first floor of Bancroft to get a quick snip in the barber's chair before noon chow, blissfully ignorant of what had gone on just thirty-two miles away at the Pentagon. The Navy football team would play Northwestern on Saturday, and Brian was looking forward to the game. The Georgia Tech score was 70–7, but it might as well have been 100–0. Every player was looking for redemption.

Head football coach Charlie Weatherbie had been getting more anxious by the day. In 2000 he went 1-10, and he lost the first two games of 2001. It was quite a tumble from 1996, when Weatherbie led the Mids to a 9-3 record and a win in the Aloha Bowl. They won seven games a year later, and five in 1999. Navy wasn't expected to have a winning record every year—administrators understood the challenges a football coach faced at the academies—but they could and should win some, and they shouldn't be embarrassed. The Georgia Tech game wasn't a loss: it was a humiliation.

Monday had been a hard-hitting practice, coaches yelling more than normal, drilling hard and doubling the reps, and Tuesday promised to be more of the same. Brian used the haircut as an excuse for a little R&R before "twelve hundred," as he now called noon.

Marine-speak had become his first language. Brian had committed to the Marine Corps early in his tenure as a midshipman, and since then stairways had become ladders; floors were now decks; walls, bulkheads; the bathroom, a head; meals were chow; stuff was gear; 6 A.M. was 0600; and 10:30 P.M., the time Brian normally racked (turned out the light and went to bed), became 2230. Then there was the seemingly endless stream of acronyms decipherable only to other servicemen. The extended-stay hotel on base was a BOQ (bachelor officers quarters, although plenty of married civilians stayed there), and going on a business trip in your own car was being TDY in a POV (temporary duty in a personally owned vehicle). It was like the Pentagon had a department that calculated how much time and confusion could be saved by coming up with two- and three-letter abbreviations for everything, and Brian Stann had memorized it like a child immersed in a second language.

The learning process began for him on I-Day (the abbreviation for Induction Day), a July 1 tradition in which hundreds of kids, most no more than five or six weeks out of high school, take the first step toward becoming naval officers. Brian's mom, Beth, and sister, Alison, had driven him to Annapolis and waited with him in line in front of Alumni Hall as sailboats glided lazily down Dorsey Creek to the Chesapeake Bay, past the magnificent campus: 238 acres of prime real estate on the mouth of the Severn River.

Many of the parents stared in awe at the waterfront views and glistening white buildings while a ragtag bunch of teenagers stood in line like any group of incoming freshmen: anxious, awkward, hands in pockets as the occasional hovering mother straightened her baby's hair. Once the line moved into the hall, the parents gave goodbye pecks and strolled down Stribling Walk to Tecumseh Court, the courtyard enveloped on three sides by Bancroft Hall and guarded by a bust of the Shawnee warrior for which it is named. Others toured "the Yard," as the campus is called.

Like the rest of the incoming plebe class Brian walked through the gymnasium, getting measured by rough men who did not look like tailors. He got socks, shoes, T-shirts, shorts, and sweats stuffed in a duffle bag. Then, as unceremoniously as throwing away an old pair of underwear, Brian and the others shuffled to the barber station where unsmiling men with electric clippers shaved mountains of hair off scalps that had never seen the light of day. Brian didn't know everything that would happen on I-Day, but he knew that the hair was coming off. It surprised him how many kids didn't. One in particular had long, flowing locks dyed white and tipped gunmetal blue. That young man stood in the hair line like he was on the way to a firing squad. He actually whimpered as the barbers sheared him like a yearling lamb.

In the sunlight, all the scalps shined like giant pearls, and hands went to heads as men felt the stubbly prick of hairstyles they would wear for the next decade.

After a couple more stops, where he picked up a canteen and learned how to salute, Brian was herded out to Alumni Hall by upperclassmen yelling for him to move faster. Plebe Hall was separate but within sight of Bancroft both physically and symbolically. "Plebe candidates," as the incoming class is called, lived close to but not with the rest of the brigade until they made it through the six weeks of boot camp called Plebe Summer and run by Marine drill instructors.

He would learn through time that the marines were the men you did not want to cross in Annapolis. Like every institution, the Naval Academy had certain instructors who were tougher and stricter than others. There were no slackers—no dope-smoking English professors or tweed-wearing communists with dandruff in their beards—but some were more low-key than others. The marines were not among those. While a naval officer might calmly correct a cadet who didn't salute quickly or sharply enough, the marines would "jump in your shit with both feet," as Brian would later recall.

On that first day, Brian had no idea what was in store as he lugged his gear up the stairs of Plebe Hall and found his classmates (his "company," another new term) standing shoulder to shoulder at attention in front of the doors. Brian dropped his gear on the floor and tried to joke with the guy next to him by saying, "Man, what a load of shit that was, huh?"

The kid kept his eyes ahead, which Brian initially took as a sign that the kid was either deaf or ignoring him. That analysis proved inaccurate. Within seconds three drill instructors, called detailers, swarmed him, one with his nose a centimeter from Brian's forehead, the other two a couple of inches from each ear. One yelled, "Our first troublemaker! We've found him!" while another said, "Stann! That's your name? What kind of name is that, Stann? It doesn't matter. We know what you are."

Then Brian made the biggest mistake of the day. He made a T with his hands and said, "Hey, time-out, guys, I didn't know we were playing yet."

The response was ferocious and obscene. They screamed at him, ordering him to stand at attention, eyes front, shoulders back, mouth shut, while they insulted everything about him. Brian didn't say another word, but the question running through his mind was the one every plebe, past and present, has asked himself at some point: *What have I done?*

Everyone considers quitting at some point. Pulling extra duty for some minuscule infraction like a crooked belt or wearing your hat too far back on your head; standing at attention in the sleet before sunrise; marching all night with a fifty-pound ruck on your back; getting your ass chewed out for nothing at all while most of your high school classmates are judging wet T-shirt contests in Daytona—there isn't a midshipman or cadet who hasn't seriously thought about going home. Some go as far as to say so openly to a roommate or a parent, people they know will talk them out of it, while others quietly pack their things and slip away. The rules are simple: The first two years are freebies. If you quit, or flunk out, or get booted for lying about how many beers you've had, or if you can't pass a physical fitness test or can't reach proficiency at sailing or swimming or shooting or some other test that no other college student in America has to take, you will be "separated" with no ramifications other than shame.

They don't expel you at the academies. They "separate" you, with all the physical and psychological connotations the word implies. Once you are out, you are gone. There is no hanging out or getting scuttlebutt from your old classmates. They are polite and respectful in the same way a Goldman Sachs trader would be to an old mate who lost his license for insider trading, or the way a district attorney might greet a former colleague who has been disbarred. It can be harsh, and at times cruel, but it is never unfair. Everybody knows the deal going in. The first two years, separation costs nothing. After the beginning of your junior year, however, you are in for the duration. Become separated at that point, and you'll be serving in the enlisted ranks with a six-figure bill due to the government.

Brian gave quitting a thought or two in the early months, but those thoughts were fleeting. He was one of those mids who accepted each of the thousands of regulations as a personal challenge. He was also someone who loved the structure and evenhandedness of academy life. Whether you grew up in a trailer in Alabama or within sight of the Montauk Yacht Club, everyone wore the same uniform, lived under the same roof, and suffered under the same strict rules. Life hadn't always been that way for Brian, and it wouldn't be that way for him in the future. But for those brief years at the academy he lived in a near-perfect meritocracy, and he loved it.

Brian's father, an Air Force officer, abandoned his family when Brian was two years old. It was the second family he had walked away from, which Brian wouldn't learn until later in life, when he found out he had half brothers and sisters. His mother was the second oldest of seven children, so caring for others had been in her nature since she was old enough to walk. When divorce papers arrived in Pennsylvania while her soon-to-be ex was still in Japan, Beth Stann moved forward with the job of caring and feeding Brian and Alison.

They rented a meager house in South Scranton but moved several times. Beth worked as a nurse, but providing was tough. Once when they were going to a department store, she asked Brian if he could wait until the weekend to buy a toy. "If you can wait, you'll get an even better toy," she said. Brian cried and Beth felt so bad she bought him the toy he wanted. Before they reached the checkout line, Alison, who was five years older, pulled him aside and said, "You baby, she can't afford it!"

That stuck with him. He would be a baby no more.

Beth remarried a man named Marty Ceiless, who had a grown son, Martin, who was a cop in Scranton. Brian had a complex relationship with Marty, never fully accepting him as a father while Marty never tried to be the male influence an intense young man so desperately needed. So Brian lived a serious life long before he was old enough to know how. When he was six, a cousin told him he was "over-mature." And in the fourth grade, his history teacher showed a slide show photo of Charles de Gaulle raising his fist and shouting to a crowd and said, "Hey, kids, that's Brian Stann at age twenty."

On the other side were the fights. As a kid who insisted on dressing well and combing his hair in an area where that was seen as pretentious and sissified, Brian was a target for taunts at McNichols Plaza Elementary School, the poorest project-fed school in chronically crime-ridden South Scranton, a place Brian described as "a graffiti-scarred hellhole built sometime after the Second World War."

Kids respond differently to ridicule. Those with a compass at home handle it better than those who are on their own. Without a father to talk him through his problems and set an example, Brian let the insults fuel his naturally hot temper. He learned the natural laws of violence early. Gangs ruled the streets and the school. One evening, when he was in the seventh grade, Brian and his best friend, Jake, were walking Jake's girlfriend home after a church dance they'd attended. The drop-off was a place called Pizza Prince, a storefront hovel with asbestos and grease in the ceiling. The pizzeria was the turf of a gang called the Valley View Terrace Boys (named for the nearby federal housing project). They smoked Marlboros and sold ecstasy in the surrounding blocks. After Jake kissed his girlfriend good night and she ran home, Brian could see they were being sized up by gang members loitering in the parking lot.

The boys didn't make it a block before the gang fanned out and surrounded them. One of the banger girls yelled something obscene at Jake, who made the mistake of answering. It was his second mistake of the evening, his first being kissing his girlfriend in their territory. At age twelve, Brian already understood that you don't date girls from gang neighborhoods, and you sure as hell don't acknowledge taunts. When the banger girl punched Jake in the mouth, busting his lip, the attack began. Classic assault tactics: distract the target with a small frontal strike and then swarm from the flanks.

Brian had several choices: he could fall to the ground, cover up and beg for mercy; he could run and yell for help, hoping for the best; or he could fight an unwinnable battle and take a certain beating. But there really wasn't a choice. The Valley View Terrace Boys were not a merciful bunch—they would beat him more viciously if he begged, and if he ran once, he would be running forever. They would ambush him in the hallways or the school restroom or on his way home after football practice, and he would become the punching bag for every gangbanger in the area.

With Jake getting pummeled on one side, Brian picked what he thought was a weak spot in the line and charged, lowering his shoulder and putting his best linebacker tackle on a beefy kid who seemed just a little hesitant. Brian pushed him through a hedge and pounded him with as many blows as he could land before the rest of the gang caught up. The blows came hard and heavy, but Brian held his ground, adrenaline flooding his body, powering his punches and numbing the blows being landed on him. He would hurt later, but at that moment the fury of the fight shoved the pain back and allowed him to keep pounding away on his target until he drew blood.

That evening Brian learned that the human response to fear can be a wonderful thing. Muscles tighten, senses are sharpened and focused, and energy surges through you. Time slows, and the world becomes smaller as blood flees the extremities and surrounds vital organs. As long as you don't become paralyzed, fear is an asset, transformed in battle from a weight on your chest to a club in your hands.

The whole thing was over in a couple of minutes. A passing motorist stopped and yelled that he was calling the cops. Since most of the Valley View Terrace Boys had juvie records, this beatdown wasn't worth another appearance before a judge. The gang scattered like roaches in the light.

Stiff and bleeding, Brian went home and cleaned up. As he pressed a hot, wet towel to his face, he thought about the exhilaration, the fear, and what it took to overcome it. He realized he had discovered a sense of clarity in the chaos of that street fight, and a sense of honor in doing things beyond yourself for people other than yourself, pushing through the impulse to run, having the courage to stand up to thugs and bullies. That, Brian realized, was why he had been put on earth in this time and place.

The lessons to follow would be painful. Just a few months after taking on the gang from the projects, Brian broke up a group of skateboarding dropouts as they attempted to mug a sixth-grade kid on his way home from school. That altercation didn't come to blows. The "skater punks," as Brian called them, had heard about the Valley View Terrace fight and didn't want a repeat.

One of them threatened, "We're going to get you, Stann."

Brian didn't take it seriously, but a couple of days later, when he was on his way home from school, a white van screeched to a halt in front of him. Two men jumped out of the sliding side door and beat Brian so badly that he suffered a concussion, cracked ribs, and two black eyes. The skater punks had given dope to a couple of eighteen-year-olds in exchange for beating Brian. He was lucky to escape without permanent injury.

On his second day in high school, a kid insulted him, and Brian broke his nose. It wasn't a proportional response, or even a necessary one, but in Brian's mind it was a statement that needed to be made.

Beth realized that her son was not thriving in his current environment, so after two years of public high school, she worked and scraped and did whatever it took to get him into private Scranton Preparatory School, where he would be the starting quarterback and leading candidate for a Division I football scholarship. But he almost blew his chance before it started. Early in the school year, a smaller, younger boy spit on one of his friend's shoes. Brian didn't hesitate. He punched the kid with an overhead blow that dislodged the orb of his eye.

The entire student body was horrified. Only a handful of kids saw it, but they told others who claimed to have been there. It became more monstrous with each telling, not because the punch was particularly vicious, but because private school kids had never seen anything like it. Before the day was out, Brian realized the gravity of what he had done. The kid was small, there was no threat, but he had done it to prove that you didn't mess with Stann or his buddies, a thug move that embarrassed him in hindsight.

The police officer who arrested him accused him of hitting the young man with a bottle. Given the severity of the cut over his eye, the cops assumed Brian had to have used a weapon. For the first time since the melee with the Valley View Terrace Boys, Brian was scared. When his mother cried, the humiliation overwhelmed him. No matter what happened, he decided at that moment that he would never lash out in anger again. He would fight if needed, but it would be against real threats.

One of his teammates' mothers worked in the probation office, and Marty's son Martin was still on the Scranton force, so they worked on Brian's behalf to get him sentenced to six months of probation. After that, his record would be expunged. But nothing could get rid of the shame he felt. Twice a week he had to leave track practice early to meet with his probation officer and pee in a cup. And his schoolmates never looked at him the same again. It was a wake-up call that put him on a different path.

Still, he wasn't sure how to become the man he thought he should be, and he didn't know where to look for guidance. For a while he turned to his high school football coach, Tony Cantafio, but Cantafio was having troubling raising his own son. He could only take

Brian so far. Brian tried to lead his football team, but he wanted to win so badly that he pushed too hard, often alienating his teammates and driving his own numbers down.

College coaches came calling, but they weren't from Penn State or Notre Dame. They were assistants at Harvard and Yale. Brian was perfect for them: great grades, great athleticism, and a working-mom backstory that could be held up as an example of the social and economic diversity of today's Ivy League. There was only one problem: they didn't offer full athletic scholarships. Without a full ride, Brian couldn't go anywhere.

"Boys raised without a father always try to impress every male figure in their lives," Brian said years later. "I always tried to impress Marty, my coaches, my buddies' fathers, everybody. Growing up, I didn't have what those guys had, so I had to find it on my own. I had to be independent."

Then a friend from his high school track team, two years older, named Clint Cornell, came home for the summer from the Naval Academy. Trim, athletic, clean-cut, and exuding a confidence that far exceeded the other graduates who slowly filtered back to Scranton after spring finals, Clint talked about how much he loved Navy: the discipline, the challenges, and the brotherhood of the brigade. All of those things sounded appealing, but what Brian couldn't get over was the aura that seemed to emanate from Clint. He had returned to Scranton stronger, certain, and infinitely more polished than the ordinary high school graduate he had been two years earlier. That was what Brian wanted.

He also didn't have to worry about scholarship money at Navy. Football players did not get a penny more or less than any other student, which appealed to Brian's sense of fairness. After scrounging for enough money to attend high school—the counselor withheld his grades one semester and when Brian went to the office to find out why, he was told he couldn't get a report card until his mom caught up on back tuition—the notion of going to a place where every student got the same deal, no matter what sport they played or who their parents were, tipped the scales for him. Annapolis seemed like the perfect place for a kid who had no money and plenty of heart.

The day he chose to go to the Naval Academy, Brian's relationship with his stepfather changed. Marty looked at him differently, more respectfully. He said, "I'm proud of what you did. You just took a huge burden off of your mother. That was a mature decision. It was a good decision."

As he looked around the barbershop, a hint of a smile crossed his lips. His mother always tried to get him to smile more, to enjoy more of the small moments of happiness each day offered. He still wasn't very good at it, but he tried. Having a couple of minutes free before noon chow and football was one of those moments, so he might as well enjoy as much of it as he could.

Then he noticed the barber wasn't talking, and he wasn't cutting hair. He was putting away the clippers, head down as he walked to the back of the shop. Outside there was a flurry of activity. Mid Store, the campus bookstore, appeared to be closing, and midshipmen were running in various directions as if something important was happening. He saw a classmate on a pay phone and overheard him leaving a message for his father.

"Just calling to see if you're okay," the midshipman said. "Please call and let me know that you're okay."

Brian knew the man's father was stationed at the Pentagon.

Something was definitely happening. Brian trotted back to his room to see what it was.

General John Allen, USMC, the deputy commandant at the Naval Academy (the first marine ever to serve in that post, and the man who would later take over U.S. Central Command from General David Petraeus), addressed the midshipmen at a general assembly at day's end. His remarks were strikingly similar to those given at West Point.

"The nation is now at war," the general said. "But we will not let the enemy enjoy a victory by not having class tomorrow. We will have more security; you will stand more posts; but you will move forward. You will go to class. You will continue with everything."

That included football. The Mids didn't practice on Tuesday, but they planned to get back at it on Wednesday afternoon. Until someone said otherwise, they had a game on Saturday to prepare for.

CHAPTER 3

I want an officer for a secret and dangerous mission.
I want a West Point football player.
—ARMY CHIEF OF STAFF GENERAL
GEORGE C. MARSHALL, 1944

On Wednesday, September 12, 2001, all the games in the country, college and professional, were canceled for the week. Even the Ryder Cup, the biannual golf event between teams from Europe and the United States, which was supposed to be held at the Belfry in Sutton Coldfield, England, on September 20, got moved to the next year. Army's game against Buffalo, originally scheduled for September 15, was shuffled to their off week, November 10, meaning Chad's next game would be against the University of Alabama at Birmingham, in Birmingham on September 22.

Coach Berry did everything he could to keep his players focused on football, but it was impossible, at least in those early days. West Point was on Threatcon Delta, the highest alert it had been on in its history. Around the campus, gates that had been manned like entrances to national parks were suddenly impenetrable, with sandbags and M985 HEMTT tactical trucks blocking all ingress and egress.

On September 10, visitors could drive through the main gate, park at the Thayer Hotel or the visitor's lot, stroll the grounds, take pictures in front of the statues of Douglas MacArthur (known on post as MacStatue), Dwight Eisenhower, or George Washington on his horse, or reach out and touch a link of the Great Chain, which spanned the Hudson during the original British blockade. Tourists could stroll through the West Point cemetery, where they could see the granite obelisk marking the resting place of Major General George Armstrong Custer, who finished last in his class at West Point, kept the official photographer waiting so that he could run to his room and grab a pistol, and, according to the inscription on the stone, was "Killed with his entire command at the Battle of Little Big Horn, June 25th, 1876." They could walk up the hill to Michie Stadium and the reservoir, or drive to the post golf course and faculty housing. Those options were now gone and would never return. Time would scab many of the open wounds of this week, but some things would remain changed forever.

The post was safe but not immune from the damage that had already been done. Some of the cadets had lost friends and family in the attack. Second Class Cadet Joseph Quinn's brother worked at the financial services firm Cantor Fitzgerald, in the North Tower, where one of the planes hit. James Francis Quinn was only twenty-three years old.

First Class Cadet Dave McCracken, who played defensive end beside Zickefoose and was scheduled to graduate in December, just a couple of weeks after the Army-Navy Game, had a harrowing close call. His mother was scheduled to fly United from Newark to San Francisco on Monday, September 10. The flight was delayed for maintenance, so the airline gave passengers the option of waiting it out or taking the first flight out the next morning. Dave's mom chose to wait at the airport and leave on Monday. Had she made the other choice she would have been on United Flight 93.

There were others: firefighters and cops and servicemen stationed at the Pentagon. Those who didn't know someone knew someone who knew someone. Scores of cadets asked to resign so they could enlist and head to the fight immediately, but academy superintendent General William J. Lennox Jr. quashed that by telling everyone they must practice "battlefield patience," one of the most difficult disciplines they would ever have to master.

Instructors handled it well, given that West Point was still thought to have been a secondary target. Knocking out four thousand future second lieutenants would have been a heck of a strategic coup. Still, professors and staff conducted business with remarkable calm. Captain Todd Green, who taught constitutional law in Thayer Hall, had his students put their books under their desks for several days and just talk, a serious departure from protocol, which dictated that every cadet was to have his book on his desk and opened when Green entered the room.

"It's apparent that it just got very real for you," Captain Green told his class on the Wednesday after the attacks. "The intensity is ramped up now and it's going to remain ramped up. This is no longer a peacetime Army. This is no longer about you going into the garrison and to your training mission. You are going to be leading the sons and daughters of America. That isn't what you expected when you arrived here. But that's the way it is now."

Green's words hit Gary Bartels like a hammer between the eyes. Nine-eleven was Bartels's birthday, so a morning that had started out with well-wishes had become a day he would never celebrate again. He had been looking forward to spending that evening with his best friends and former teammates, Chad, Zickefoose, and Clint Dodson, a big tight end from Fogelsville, Pennsylvania. On the field those guys were the three amigos, but Bartels was the fourth member of the gang, the one who had walked away from football because of injuries and grades. On the day he left the team, Chad came to his room and begged him to reconsider. Finally Bartels had to tell Chad about how he'd been struggling academically. Later that night, when Bartels called his mom and told her his football career was over, she said, "Did anyone try to talk you out of it?"

"Yeah, one guy: Chad," he said.

"That doesn't surprise me in the least," she said. "That sounds just like him."

But something else Chad said that night stuck with Bartels now. "You know I'll do anything for you," he'd said. "We're brothers forever, no matter what."

"No matter what" had just taken on a whole new meaning.

The Tuesday, September 11, football practice, including the fights, had been cathartic, but once it was announced that they wouldn't be playing against Buffalo, the team took Wednesday off and did what everyone else on post did: grieve, talk, and generally feel helpless. Even though the administration volunteered the services of all four thousand able-bodied men and women at West Point to help with search and rescue, the only things the cadets had that crews at Ground Zero needed were socks. Firemen had plenty of standard-issue gear, but they were on their own when it came to socks. A sock drive was organized with every company attacking the campaign as if it were the Berlin Airlift.

By Thursday emotions on the post had hardened, and the men were already looking ahead to the strategy and tactics they would employ to kill the enemy. Rumors swirled that the First Class would be graduated early so they could join the fight immediately. Not a one of them objected. Chad and Zickefoose talked about how quickly they could get through Ranger School so they could be a part of the first wave, while the team's long-snap center, Reid "Huck" Finn, told anyone who would listen that he would be in-theater by Christmas if that's what it took.

Finn didn't realize it at the time, but by Christmas he would be on the short list of invitees to the New York Giants training camp, the only player from Army invited by any NFL team. He would have an agent and an offer before graduation, but that got tamped down quickly. The Army made it perfectly clear that it planned to hold Finn to his five-year service commitment, which was a relief, in some ways. In the days immediately following 9/11, Finn was just as eager to kill bad guys as every other cadet, and those feelings became mixed when the Giants came calling. When the NFL option was taken off the table, he refocused and was as committed as ever to the fight.

Parents were not so gung ho. All the cadets called home, and all of their family members expressed some level of concern about what lay ahead. They'd sent their kids off to West Point with the same expectations their children had—a good education plus five years of service at a military base—but few had really planned on seeing their sons and daughters off to war. Dave Jenkins tried to be as cool as possible and asked Chad for whatever facts and whatever rumors his son had heard. But Dave's halting speech gave him away, just as the quiver in Lee's voice said far more than words.

"Nothing is happening right away," Chad told them. "We'll take it easy the rest of the week and get back to practice on Monday."

Standard off weeks, what the week of September 11 turned out to be, were different from the normal in-season practice routine. Coaches tried to rest guys, heal injuries, and study film of the next opponent. It was a time to recharge. But this was no ordinary week off. A memorial service for the victims of the attacks, one of thousands held across the country that week, was scheduled for Friday, September 14, in Eisenhower Hall, a grand auditorium, windowless on three sides and large enough to seat all the cadets and a few guests. On the same day that President George W. Bush would speak before a packed house at the Washington National Cathedral and later make his famous "bullhorn" visit to Ground Zero, the entire West Point corps marched in silence down the hill from the Plain.

Once inside the lobby, they passed the "Wall of Generals," a pictorial display of all the West Point graduates who reached the rank of general, from Ulysses Grant, Class of 1843, to Douglas MacArthur, Class of 1903, to Norman Schwarzkopf, Class of 1956, to men whose names were not yet familiar to the public, like David Petraeus, Class of 1974, and Ray Odierno, Class of 1976, who played tight end on the football team. Also on the wall was the man who spoke at the assembly, General Lennox, Class of 1971, and current superintendent at West Point. After graduation, Lennox, a balding, trim Texan with an easy smile and an evangelical heart, had earned a doctorate in literature from Princeton. He would later serve as professor emeritus of speech at Princeton Theological Seminary. This day, he put his skills to good use by delivering one of the most eloquent speeches Chad and his fellow cadets had ever heard.

"The God of heaven has welcomed many of our brothers and sisters to their eternal home," he said. "Those who remain share the task of remembering and honoring them while comforting the living, whose grief is early and immeasurable. And it is we who remain who bear the burden of writing their legacies with our actions. That task begins from this moment forward."

There was no rule against crying, but in a testosterone-rich environment where even female cadets were treated like the guys, weeping was rarely greeted with a lot of "there, there" sympathy. Your best friends would tell you to Ranger up, while the rest of your company would either give you a hard time or, worse, ignore you. That changed after General Lennox's speech. Almost no one walked out of Eisenhower Hall with dry eyes, and not a soul said a thing about it.

The week after the attacks, President Bush told Americans to get back to their lives, and, as they were trained to do, the cadets saluted smartly and said, "Yes, sir," although it was no easy feat. Every class at the academy had become a crash course on terrorism, terrorists, and how to win a war against an undefined enemy with no country and an ambiguous command-and-control structure. Who were you supposed to kill? How did you fight? What would the rules of engagement be? How would you obtain actionable intelligence when your sources lived in caves? What were the objectives? And what constituted victory? The dynamic of daily life at West Point evolved with the nature of the war they were most likely going to fight. The brass with Vietnam experience became sages, with cadets flocking to hear tales of guerrilla warfare, the Vietcong, and how platoon leaders adapted on the fly. These were not just cool combat stories anymore; it was the reality they now faced.

Cadets started looking around and judging the men in their chain of command not by the insignia on their uniforms but by a new standard: "Would I want to entrust my life to that guy in a firefight?" Sometimes the answer was yes, but there were some classmates and some officers on duty at West Point who were universally reviled. One of those was the brigade tactical officer, Colonel Joseph W. Adamczyk, known affectionately among the cadets as "Skeletor" for his gaunt features and sunken, dead eyes. Adamczyk was, in Chad's words, "a dick," and that was one of the nicer descriptions. It wasn't that he was hard or demanding—this was a group that thrived on toughness and longed for trainers who would push them and correct them and teach them how to lead in the hardest of circumstances— but Skeletor seemed to enjoy meanness for its own sake, without any underlying lessons.

During the four amigos' yuk year, when Bartels was still juggling a heavy class load as well as football, the big Texan hustled out of class and was walking briskly to football practice when Adamczyk barked orders for him to stop.

"Where are you headed, Bartels?"

"Football practice, sir."

"And do you know your left from your right, Bartels?"

"Yes, sir."

"Then what shoulder are you carrying that pack on?"

Bartels was carrying his backpack on his right shoulder, because he'd had a five-hour surgery on the left, but that didn't matter. One of the rules stated that all cadets were to carry their packs on both shoulders so they were uniformly positioned in the center of the back and the right arm was always free to salute. Bartels made an initial attempt to explain his circumstances, but Adamczyk was not interested. He could have chewed Bartels out and left it at that, but that was not the Skeletor way. Adamczyk had Bartels retrace his steps all the way back to his room, put his pack on his bed, pick it back up and put it on both shoulders correctly, and then walk to practice, a one-mile, twenty-minute detour that made Bartels late for practice and had him running sprints afterward.

"There were only two cadets that liked Adamczyk, and they were his kids," Bartels said. "And to be honest with you, I'm not too sure how they felt."

The good news was that Adamczyk steered clear of the football field. That was Coach Berry's domain, so for a couple of hours every afternoon Chad and his teammates were under the guidance of a civilian who was one of the least demanding men they faced. Like all firsties, Chad had already done his tactical field training at the academy's nearby Camp Buckner with some of the hard-ass Rangers he would hopefully join soon. He continued to study engineering in the morning and undergo dress inspections where he marched onto a parade ground and had an officer stand in his face and ask him to describe his uniform.

"Sir, this uniform is called dress gray over white under arms. It consists of a gray coat, white gloves, white sash . . ."

Football was a break.

The game had become a rallying point, a familiar reminder of the American way of life. Fans across the country flocked to football in the weeks following 9/11, not because of their passion for the game, but because they needed camaraderie and escapism, as well as a safe place to release their emotions. Nobody thought twice about screaming and crying at a football game. Screaming and crying in the grocery store was another matter. Americans needed to scream and cry in the fall of 2001. Football gave them that outlet.

At this point, Chad hadn't given any thought to how the public at large would see this year's Army football team. All he and his teammates looked forward to was the certainty of the game. The gridiron was like their childhood bedrooms: a place where they felt at home, where they knew every inch of the landscape and every rule. Once practice resumed, he fell back into his normal routine: study film of the upcoming opponent to find weaknesses in their defense, game-plan with Coach Bond, and then drill in practice until they could execute to perfection.

The Cincinnati game four days before the attack had been a nail-biter, the kind of outing every Army player and coach thought they should have won. Leading 7–3 going into the fourth quarter, the defense ran a blitz at the wrong time and Bearcat quarterback Gino Guidugli rolled out and completed a twenty-five-yard pass to Jon Olinger for a touchdown. After that the floodgates opened, and it was one touchdown drive after another. With 11:10 left, Chad dropped straight back and found Aris Comeaux on a slant pattern for a touchdown to put Army up 14–10. Then Guidugli orchestrated a drive for Cincinnati, hitting Tye Keith for a touchdown to put the Bearcats back up.

With time ticking away, Chad managed another drive, picking apart the Cincinnati defense with one pass after another. On second down at the Cincinnati thirty-eight, he took the snap and handed the ball off to Omari Thompson, Army's best all-purpose back and the fastest man on the field for either team. Thompson broke through the line, and Chad immediately knew he was gone. Once Omari beat the linebackers, nobody could touch him. Touchdown. The moment he crossed the goal line, Chad threw his arms skyward, but a sinking feeling hit him in the gut. "Too much time," he said.

Guidugli had two minutes and forty-three seconds, about the length of time it took Chad to sing an off-key rendition of his favorite George Strait song, but an eternity for an efficient quarterback. Sure enough, after marching the Bearcats down the field, Guidugli plunged the dagger in for the kill, finding Keith on a fade route for a twelve-yard touchdown as time expired. The final was Cincinnati 24, Army 21.

Chad had put up good numbers, completing nineteen passes for

203 yards, including one touchdown and one interception, but Guidugli threw for 333 yards and had no picks. Good hadn't been good enough.

Now that game seemed like it had taken place in ancient history.

The trip to Alabama on September 22 for the University of Alabama at Birmingham game was the first time any of them had left the post since 9/11, and it was a welcome relief. No Army team had ever played in the state of Alabama, but Chad didn't care where they were. Just seeing people in civilian clothes eating hot dogs brought a smile to his face. Cadet life made you appreciate simple pleasures like kissing a girl in public or wearing Mardi Gras beads to a game, things that did not happen at West Point before 9/11 and certainly didn't take place in the days immediately after. The first time Chad's sisters visited the post for a game, they walked around speechless as cadets in uniform saluted passing officers and snapped to attention on command. Finally Teri said, "Chad's college life is going to be a lot different than ours."

UAB played at Legend Field in downtown Birmingham, about three miles from campus in one of the seedier sections of Alabama's largest city, so the cadets didn't get to gaze at rollicking fraternity parties as they rode the bus into the stadium. The Blazers had only been playing football for ten years, but that was long enough. This was not a state where anyone took college football lightly. Beyond the University of Alabama with their Bear Bryant legacy and all those national championships, there was Auburn, another SEC powerhouse, and Troy, a small school that had won two Division II national championships. Then there was Jacksonville State, a tiny college between Oxford and Anniston with nine Gulf South Conference championships and one Division II national championship.

UAB was a long way from winning a national title, but they were still a good football team, one that Chad had done his best to prepare for, given all the distractions. Emotions ran high in the locker room beforehand. Coach Berry tried to keep his players focused, but he knew that a moment of silence was planned and that his starting center, Dustin Plumadore, would be carrying a large American flag out of the tunnel when the team ran onto the field. How fans would react was anybody's guess.

No one could have anticipated the strange and wonderful thing that would happen that afternoon at Legion Field. Custom dictated that the home team took the field first, so UAB ran out of their locker room to a rousing ovation from the crowd. One of their players also carried an American flag, which was not customary, but had become part of the post-9/11 ritual at most sporting events. As for Army, the academy had fans everywhere, but they were not a large contingent at away games, especially 990 miles from West Point. Yet when the cadets ran out of their tunnel toward their sideline, the cheers didn't turn to boos, as often happened in college football: the ovation grew louder, reverberating off the steel and echoing back onto the field. Those who weren't already standing leaped to their feet and roared as Plumadore led the team out of the tunnel, his four-foot flag whipping behind him. The cheering didn't stop, even as 'Foose and Clint Dodson walked out to midfield for the coin toss. At first the cadets didn't know how to take it. Had they come out too soon? Was the crowd still cheering for the home team?

It dawned on all of them slowly. Chad was so focused on the game and the first series of offensive plays he was about to run, he didn't realize the fans were still on their feet. He had already run to the sideline and picked up a ball for a few more warm-up tosses prior to kickoff when it occurred to him that something wasn't right. The noise was growing louder. That was when he stopped and looked around the stadium. Most of the crowd wore red, white, and blue clothing rather than the traditional UAB colors of green and gold, and they were still on their feet in full-throated exuberance, cheering the visiting Army team.

At that moment Chad realized that he was part of something much larger than a football game. He and his team had become a symbol of hope for a lot of Americans who felt lost in grief and despair. Chad and his teammates were being cheered at an away game, not for what they would do on the football field, but for what they represented.

He dropped the ball at his feet. His cheeks tightened and his vision blurred with emotion. He had to take a couple of deep breaths to steady himself and get ready to play.

The game turned into a rout. Chad and his offense couldn't move the ball at all, and Zickefoose and the defense couldn't stop anybody. The Blazers could have run the water boy off left tackle and won by three touchdowns. UAB quarterback Jeff Aaron threw for 220 yards to go with the 239 the Blazers rushed. UAB blocked a punt, and Chad threw four interceptions, all of which led to Blazer touchdowns. The final score was 55–3, but it might as well have been 90–0.

Still, the reception was overwhelming. At halftime, parachutists from the Alabama Army National Guard dropped into the stadium carrying American flags to chants of "U-S-A, U-S-A" from the crowd. And afterward, the UAB players stayed on the field to hug and thank the cadets they had just beaten. Usually postgame greetings were short and sweet, a quick slap on the pads or handshake followed by someone saying "good game." This time the players wanted to talk, to say things to the cadets like "God bless you, man," or to relay their own families' histories with the Army. As difficult as it was to lose, especially by such an embarrassing margin, Chad and rest of the cadets stayed on the field and spoke to every UAB player and coach for as long as they wanted.

The pregame scene was repeated at Boston College on September 29, when Army players ran onto the field at Alumni Stadium to thunderous applause. It was BC's first home game since 9/11, and while Boston hadn't been a target of the attacks, the two hijacked planes that hit the World Trade Center originated out of Logan International Airport. Most of the passengers on those doomed flights were from the area. This time the reception started early with hundreds of people lining the bus route to the stadium. Young children waved flags, accompanied by fathers wiping tears from their eyes as they applauded the bus carrying the Army players. They passed an old man wearing a VFW hat, standing as close to attention as his stooped body would allow. With gnarled fingers that would no longer straighten, the man held a dignified salute as the bus rolled past. That was when one of the players in the front of the bus said, "Holy shit, this is unbelievable."

It got better once they took the field. Tens of thousands of flags waved as fans spent most of the game on their feet. By then chants of "U-S-A" had become commonplace at every high school and college football game and in every baseball park in the country. None of the Army players knew that the spontaneous chorus had originated upstate from West Point in Lake Placid, New York, at the 1980 Winter Olympic Games, when the U.S. hockey team upset the heavily favored Soviets, the game known as the "miracle on ice." But the history of the thing didn't matter. The passion and conviction of forty-four thousand fans screaming "U-S-A, U-S-A" as if it were a battle cry continued to overwhelm them. Chad felt chills as the chants grew louder when he and his teammates ran onto the field. Then, after they stood at attention and saluted during the National Anthem, he felt them again as fans resumed their chanting.

Unfortunately for Chad, the support didn't translate into great play. Army received the opening kickoff and after a running play that went nowhere, Chad dropped back to pass on second and ten. For an instant he saw Clint Dodson open, but the second he released the ball he wanted to reel it back in. Like an accident you can't stop, Chad saw Boston College linebacker Scott Bradley break into the flat just after the ball was out of his hands. He knew what was coming, but could do nothing about it. Bradley intercepted the pass and ran in untouched for touchdown. Barely sixty-eight seconds gone in the game and Army was down 7–0.

Boston College led 14–0 eight minutes later after quarterback Brian St. Pierre threw a touchdown pass to Dedrick Dewalt. A late first-quarter field goal by the Eagles made it 17–0 and all the energy went out of the Army sideline.

Chad connected with his fastest receiver, Omari Thompson, in the third quarter on a surprise fourth-down play that went thirty-nine yards for Army's only touchdown. The final was 31–10, making the first two weeks back after 9/11 the worst two consecutive losses for Army football since 1973.

Dejected, Chad went through the ritual of speaking to all the Boston College players again, as he had done in Birmingham. This time, however, things were more orchestrated. Both teams gathered in the south end zone, where BC offensive lineman John Richardson took a microphone and sang "God Bless America." Then all the players from both squads knelt in prayer before exiting to the renewed cheers of an appreciative crowd.

They were 0-3 when they finally beat Houston, 24–14, in a packed Michie Stadium. Coming home felt great, even after the warm welcomes they had received on the road. There was nothing like the pageantry of game day at West Point with the entire corps marching in and sitting together and alumni, who filled the Thayer Hotel, wearing the colors and cheering from the perspective of men who had stood where these players were now standing. The gates of the academy had reopened about the same time as America's airports resumed service, but, like at the airports, security was much different. Rather than alumni wheeling in and parking wherever they wished, every vehicle entering the gates was searched and logged and every visitor had to have identification on them at all times. Still, once inside, the fans were as passionate about their football as ever.

In the Houston game, Zickefoose played like a man possessed, racking up twelve individual tackles. "Coming home had big meaning," 'Foose said. "It was our first home game in four weeks. The emotion was there. The old grads were back and the emotion here was unbelievable. Looking around in the locker room, you could see guys could not wait to get out there and bust some heads."

But Clint Dodson summed it up best when he said, "In life, you take one day at a time. Our responsibility as Army football players is to play football for the fans, for the corps, and for the Army. Football is a rallying point right now. I've gotten e-mails from people all over the world saying: 'We are looking at you guys and we are looking up to you.' I think by us coming out, showing emotion, and playing as hard as we are, it has become a rallying point for the whole Army."

The rallying points continued even though the victories did not. The cadets lost to East Carolina and TCU at Amon Carter Stadium in Fort Worth, where purple was replaced by red, white, and blue and Texans greeted the Army team like conquering heroes from the moment they arrived in town . . . until the Horned Frogs beat them 38–20.

Chad began racking up decent numbers, but not enough wins. He orchestrated 427 yards of total offense against Houston and completed sixty percent of his passes without throwing a single interception. Then he threw for another 289 yards against East Carolina, including one passing touchdown and another touchdown where Chad tucked the ball and ran into the end zone. But he also gave up a costly interception for a touchdown against East Carolina, and the Pirates scored on a fumble return and a kickoff return. That final was 49–26. The fact that it was the first loss at home since 9/11 made it more even more painful. The disappointment on the faces of the alumni as they headed for the exits was hard to watch, but Chad made himself look at them. He wanted to remember this feeling so that he could dig deeper inside himself the next time to avoid it.

Army beat Tulane in Michie Stadium on a crisp afternoon just three days before Halloween. That victory gave fans another afternoon to cheer, but the next week the cadets fell to Air Force in the snows of Colorado Springs, which was a tough loss. Though it was not as heated or historic a rivalry as the Army-Navy Game, playing the Air Force Academy was still different from going up against Memphis or Cincinnati. The Cadet Wing, as the men and women of the Air Force Academy were called, had signed up under the same college plan as the cadets of West Point and midshipmen of Annapolis. And while Army and Navy players joked about the "future flyboys" in their royal blue "bus driver" uniforms, Air Force graduates would head to the same fight as their counterparts at West Point and Annapolis.

There was also the Commander-in-Chief Trophy at stake. Since 1972, the first year Air Force played both Army and Navy as part of their regular-season schedule, the team with the best record against the other two academies won a large three-sided trophy, often presented by the president in a White House ceremony. Losing to Air Force meant that, once again, the future flyboys would take the CAC Trophy, leaving Army and Navy to play for pride.

Ensured of another losing season, Chad hoped to salvage a couple of late wins starting at home against Buffalo and then in Memphis. Army needed to build some momentum before the Army-Navy Game. He looked to be on his way, with a decent opening half against the Bulls, completing eleven passes for eighty-six yards, most of them to Clint Dodson. But Army still trailed in a game Chad thought they should be winning by three touchdowns. So, on the opening drive of the second half, he dropped back to pass. Finding all of his receivers covered, but seeing a slight opening downfield, Chad tucked the ball and ran. He got past the linebackers and into the secondary. The free safety was closing, but if he could make one athletic move and get to the corner, he could at least pick up the first down if not more.

The hits came from both sides. A cornerback running at full speed hit him from the right, while the strong safety came from across the field to hit him from the left. Chad's knee buckled with a sickening pop, the nightmarish sound every athlete knows and fears. He went down and immediately grabbed his leg.

From the press box where he called the plays, John Bond said, "Get up, Chad," as if his quarterback could hear him.

Chad tried to get up, but the knee wouldn't hold. Trainers hustled onto the field and he put his arms around their shoulders and hobbled off to the cheers of the home crowd. On the sideline he thought he might be okay. The pain was like a hot fireplace iron behind his kneecap, but he could put some weight on his leg. Unfortunately, when he attempted to walk, he buckled.

That was it, he thought. A knee injury was feared like the plague, especially among backs. While his teammates came over and offered words of encouragement on the sideline, Chad couldn't shake the idea that his football career might be over. He tried to push those thoughts aside, telling himself that he could run it off and be back in no time, but the support from the joint just wasn't there.

Chad forced himself to stand and watch the rest of the Buffalo game. He cheered and raised his arms to the sky when his backup, Curtis Zervic, threw a fourth-quarter touchdown pass to Aris Comeaux to put Army up for the first time in the game. But he had to sit down before Buffalo came back to score the go-ahead touchdown with just over nine minutes left in the game. He hobbled through the locker room on crutches after the heartbreaking 26–19 loss, wondering if he had taken his last snap as a quarterback.

Once the game ended, Chad went to Keller Army Community Hospital with the team trainer for X-rays. His spirits lifted when the initial film didn't identify any damage. He was out for the entire second week of November and missed the Memphis game, which Army lost 42–10, but with nothing showing up on the X-rays, Chad felt certain that this was just a sprain and he would be back in no time. After a week of rest, he suited up and tried to get back on the practice field, not realizing that he had torn the posterior cruciate ligament (PCL). A far less common injury than a torn anterior cruciate ligament (ACL), a PCL tear allows the patient to move in certain directions, but not others. As long as he was walking or running forward, Chad was fine, but if he tried to make the slightest lateral move, the knee would buckle.

He hobbled through practice the week before Thanksgiving, trying to shut out the pain as trainer Tim Kelly kept saying, "Chad, I don't think you'll be ready for Army-Navy."

He wasn't about to miss that game. "I'll be ready," he told Kelly at a time when he couldn't even jog, much less run an offense. But he believed he would be back. He had gutted through pain before, and he would do it again. Chad would fake it if he had to, but he was going to do whatever it took to play. Army-Navy was the last football game he would ever start in his life. Chad was going to suit up in Philadelphia if he had to wear a prosthetic. Nothing else was acceptable.

CHAPTER 4

*The Marines I have seen around the world have
the cleanest bodies, the filthiest minds, the highest
morale, and the lowest morals of any group of animals
I have ever seen. Thank God for the United States
Marine Corps!*

—ELEANOR ROOSEVELT, 1945

During Charlie Weatherbie's first team meeting as Navy head coach in Mitscher Hall in 1995, the then forty-year-old Oklahoman dropped to a knee, like any good evangelist would, and said, "Men, take a hand next to you and let's begin with prayer."

It wasn't a one-time show. Weatherbie prayed morning, noon, and night, blessing every meal, often taking the hands of total strangers at banquets or luncheons to bond with them while speaking with God. And there weren't many Bible verses he couldn't cite chapter and verse, either. But his Christian heart didn't make him a pushover. Two minutes after the opening prayer with his new team, fullback Omar Nelson slipped into the room and took a seat near the back. Weatherbie stared at him quietly and coldly, and then, in a tone that was softer than the one he'd used to pray, he said, "Son,

I want to tell you something: To be early is to be on time. To be on time is to be late. And to be late is to be forgotten." Then he looked around the room and said, "All of you need to remember that."

Weatherbie came into Annapolis in 1995 with a mission to turn around a failing program, and in the early years he did just that, winning nine games in 1996 and beating the University of California Bears in the Aloha Bowl. The Midshipmen then finished the season 7-4 in 1997. In addition to improving the team's record, Weatherbie brought a different philosophy to Navy, one that used football as a positive, uplifting break in the otherwise tough regimen of academy life. And over the years, Weatherbie never changed his reputation for being punctual, calm, disciplined, and godly, even though his teams slid toward mediocrity. In 1998, the Midshipmen went 3-8, but that didn't dampen Weatherbie's disposition. In 1999, Brian Stann's freshman year, Weatherbie met with his new players during Plebe Summer and the first words out of his mouth were "Gentlemen, it is a great day to play by the bay! Let's take a knee and say an opening prayer."

After the "Amen," Weatherbie gave his pep talk to the plebes. "I know you are wondering why you came here to endure this," he said. "Trust me: you have made a great decision. Stick with it. Plebe Summer ends in a few weeks. There is light at the end of the tunnel. Soon it will be football season and you will all be doing what you love to do. Remember that in the days ahead."

No other coach in America would tell his players to hang on; two-a-days were coming. But then no ordinary Division I football team would survive Plebe Summer and the detailers who ran it. Those mornings, the plebes were awakened by marines throwing tire irons down the hallways, clanging metal off tile to jar everyone out of bed. Ten minutes later, after shaving, making their beds, and getting dressed with detailers yelling in their ears, the plebes were running, and running, and running, followed by jumping jacks, flutter kicks, sit-ups, and push-ups. Then came class work and learning to sail.

To miss one question was to fail, and punishment included, among other things, writing the eleven General Orders of a Sentry—"To take charge of this post and all government property in view . . . To walk my post in a military manner, keeping always on the alert, and observing everything that takes place within sight or hearing . . ."— and on and on.

Then it was two and a half hours of rifle drills, followed by two hours of lectures. If anyone fell asleep, the detailers would punish the entire squad with more push-ups and sit-ups, so most plebes had bruised ribs from being punched by their buddies to stay awake. At 2200 (10 P.M.) they were given twenty minutes of free time to clean up and straighten their rooms before collapsing into their beds at 2230. No football practice could ever top that.

Most head coaches had to deal with new recruits showing up overweight and out of shape after a summer of hometown congratulations for signing on to play big-time college football. Some kids became local celebrities. They even gave press conferences. National Signing Day, the day when high school recruits sign scholarship commitment papers, was carried live on ESPN with seventeen-year-old seniors playing up the drama until the last minute before donning the cap of the college of their choosing. Many of them then spent the summer eating, drinking, and getting out of shape. Outsized egos and oversized bellies were not problems at Navy. The "freshman fifteen," a phrase normally applied to the pounds that students, especially girls, gain in their first year of college, did not apply to plebes. Most cadets lost weight their first semester, despite consuming between four and five thousand calories a day. The physical rigors coupled with the stress of academy life kept the pounds off. But even though he consistently had the fittest, brightest, and most disciplined incoming freshman class year after year, Weatherbie's wins continued to trend downward. In 1999, Navy went 5-7 and in 2000 the team had only one win. That was against Army, so Weatherbie earned a temporary reprieve from the fate that normally befalls a college coach who goes 1-10.

The win against Army gave him a final chance to right the ship in 2001, but his job was on the line every week. Throw in the added pressure (and scrutiny) of playing post-9/11 with the eyes of the world on the Naval Academy, and football in Annapolis became a grind. Weatherbie's Christian values never wavered, but his patience was tested every day. The new wrinkles around his eyes showed it.

He had a higher voice than expected from a still-fit football man, and his Ozark twang, which came out when he got upset, could set your teeth on edge like an out-of-tune fiddle. He never swore, but that didn't stop him from making his points. One drill after another would be followed by the sound of Weatherbie's voice: "No, again: do it again!" Despite his volume, he was still able to throw in a Bible verse or two, and one of his favorites in the fall of 2001 came from the first chapter of the book of James: "Consider it a pure joy, my brothers, whenever you face trials of many kinds, because you know that the testing of your faith develops perseverance. And perseverance must finish its work for you to be mature and complete."

Weatherbie had been hired by Jack Lengyel, the Navy athletics director since 1988 and a man who knew a thing or two about perseverance and the testing of faith. Lengyel had been a head football coach, so he understood the rigors of the job, but he understood how to lead men through crisis as well. In 1971, Lengyel took a job no one else wanted: head football coach at Marshall University, the West Virginia school that had just endured the worst tragedy in NCAA history when, in November 1970, thirty-seven football players, eight coaches, and twenty-five boosters were killed in a plane crash while returning from a game in North Carolina. Somehow, Lengyel cobbled together a team of nonscholarship athletes as well as basketball and lacrosse players who had not come to college with the intent of playing football. They didn't pick up many wins, but the fact that Lengyel kept a program and a community together, coaching them through their grief as much as he coached them on the football field, made him legendary in college sports circles.

After Marshall, Lengyel went into the private sector for a while before returning to college sports as an administrator, first at Missouri, then at Fresno State, and finally at Navy, where he spent a dozen successful years. No one could have shepherded the Navy football program through the aftermath of 9/11 better than Lengyel. Who better to strike the perfect balance between athletics and the emotional turmoil of academy life post-9/11 than someone who had done it before? But the timing didn't work out. Lengyel retired from Navy with the graduating class of 2001. He said his goodbyes in the summer and went back to the private sector as a consultant and vice president of business development for a software firm.

With Lengyel gone, Coach Weatherbie had no institutional allies left. Everyone who had been a party to hiring him had either moved on to another job or retired. The only way for him to win new support was through winning.

That season was one of the few times Brian Stann didn't envy the starters. Those guys felt the brunt of the pressure, and were on the receiving end of the hurt and disappointment when things didn't go well. Brian hadn't made the depth chart as a quarterback, and his high school coach had told Weatherbie they would probably want to play him at another position. At the time that didn't sit well. Brian had always elevated his game when needed, always risen to the occasion, and when someone told him he couldn't do something, he shifted into another gear. But while he had been an accurate passer with decent speed, he wasn't a breakaway runner, which was what Navy needed.

It surprised him a little that he didn't at least get a shot, especially given Weatherbie's own history. The coach had been a passing quarterback for the Cowboys of Oklahoma State, playing three seasons and coming off a shoulder and collarbone injury his junior year to lead the Cowboys to an upset win over Oklahoma in his senior season. Then he made the journeyman rounds in the professional ranks, playing here and there for the Ottawa Rough Riders and the

Hamilton Tiger-Cats of the Canadian Football League. Weatherbie had also roamed through NFL training camps in San Diego and Houston and Cleveland before settling in as an assistant at the University of Wyoming, where he coached quarterbacks.

But his longest assistant coaching stint, and the one that would ultimately differentiate him enough for him to land the Navy job, was the six years he coached quarterbacks and fullbacks at the Air Force Academy. More than his two years as an assistant at Arkansas or the three seasons he spent as head coach at Utah State, where he won one Big West Conference title and one bowl game, the time he spent in Colorado Springs working for Fisher DeBerry swayed Lengyel to hire him. The Navy job required the gift of understanding, not just football but the commitment and kind of men who wanted a military life. Weatherbie had personally recruited Brian when he was the run-and-shoot quarterback at Scranton Prep, so he of all people should have given him a shot, or so Brian thought.

During the early days, Brian realized there were some guys on the roster who had better arms. One was a six-three, 215-pound, blue-eyed kid from Pasadena named J. P. Blecksmith, a stud in the backfield who looked to Brian like he was ready for the NFL. It was a long shot, but it had happened before. Roger Staubach was a Navy graduate. The Dallas Cowboys had taken him in the 1964 draft and waited while he served his commitment; he began playing for Dallas in 1969. No Navy quarterback since had gone to the NFL, but others had made it. Max Lane, an offensive lineman in the Class of 1994, had been drafted in the sixth round by the New England Patriots. Wide receiver Phil McConkey, Class of 1989, served his five as a helicopter pilot before winning a spot as an undrafted walk-on with the New York Giants. And defensive tackle Bob Kuberski was drafted by the Green Bay Packers. As far as Brian could tell, Blecksmith could be the next Staubach. On every snap the big kid hurled the ball on a tight spiral and hit his receiver in open stride. The balls he threw got to their targets faster and straighter than those hoisted by the other quarterback hopefuls: no wobbles or wounded ducks when Blecksmith dropped back into the pocket.

Even with J.P. setting a high bar, Brian felt good about his first couple practices at quarterback. A kid named Garrett Cox, who had gone to the Naval Academy Prep School, lined up at receiver and ran an inside curl pattern. Brian took a three-step drop and Cox broke free from the defender. Brian timed the throw perfectly, hitting him in the hands as though they'd been practicing together for years.

"Hey, we made each other look good," Cox said when he got back to the huddle. "Let's keep it up."

They did just that, throwing and catching one pass after another. Buttonhooks, corner fades, fly patterns: there wasn't a pattern Cox could run where Brian couldn't find him. They had fleeting thoughts of being the star tandem on Saturdays at Navy–Marine Corps Memorial Stadium: Stann to Cox—touchdown!

Then they stepped aside and saw J. P. Blecksmith throw a forty-yard pass that looked like it had been fired from a cannon. He made it look so effortless and had such a quick release that he reminded Brian of Dan Marino. It was at once beautiful and depressing to watch. Blecksmith, Brian decided, would surely be Navy's next starter.

But those thoughts were dashed the next day after coaches had all the incoming recruits run the triple option, the offense Coach Weatherbie preferred and one where Brian and Blecksmith and all the other pure passers had no shot. The triple option was, as the name implied, a run-centered offense where the quarterback reads the defense at the line and either hands the ball off to a lead running back, keeps the ball and runs himself, or pitches the ball to a trailing back. It was a tough offense to defend, and one that, when run effectively, controlled the clock, but the quarterback was little more than a glorified scatback who could toss the occasional dump pass over the middle.

You had to be quick and a bruising runner to thrive in that kind of system, not a pro-set or run-and-shoot quarterback, as Brian and Blecksmith were. Brian had okay speed, but certainly not good enough to start at quarterback against the likes of Boston College, Rutgers, and Notre Dame.

He and Blecksmith both came to the early realization that, despite being recruited by a former pro quarterback, neither of them was the kind of quarterback Weatherbie wanted.

Late in his sophomore year, Brian began to understand that he would never call another offensive play or take another snap. It was tough to accept, but he loved football and wanted desperately to be a part of the team, so he made the move to linebacker, a position he had played off and on growing up, and one that was a better fit for his personality than any other position in the game.

Quarterbacks are pretty: Joe Namath, Joe Montana, Phil Simms, Peyton Manning, and Tom Brady, the guys who do cologne commercials and wear hair gel. Linebackers are the guys who make your voice quiver, the ones you slide away from at the lunch table, and the ones you stand behind if a fight breaks out: guys like Dick Butkus, Lawrence Taylor, Ray Lewis, and Brian Urlacher. They are game wreckers, the kind of men who shave their heads and scream like conquering gladiators after they drive runners into the ground. Brian was that sort of guy. Once he made the switch, linebacker fit him as if he'd been born to play it.

During spring practice of 2000, he earned a spot as a backup linebacker as well as a sprint man on the kickoff and punt teams. He was the man directly to the right of the football during kickoff formation, the guy whose job was to fire down the field with reckless abandon to hit any ballcarrier with the temerity to attempt an up-the-middle return. It was another role that fit him like a dress white uniform. He wasn't the contain man or the one-tackle-a-season guy positioned near the outside: he was the tip of the special team's spear, the guy who got there first and wreaked as much havoc as possible.

By 2001, J. P. Blecksmith had become a receiver and Brian was defense and special teams. That turned out to be a good thing, as Coach Weatherbie had recruited a kid named Brian Madden to play quarterback. Madden, a six-one, 225-pounder from Lawton, Oklahoma, was the best athlete Navy would field on either side of the ball and one of the best the academy had produced since the glory days of Staubach.

Unfortunately for Madden, and Blecksmith, and Brian, who grew to love his role more than he could have ever imagined, the team simply wasn't very good. They were 0-2 and coming off the embarrassment of losing by sixty-three points to Georgia Tech before 9/11. Those previous losses didn't do much for their popularity on campus. If anything, their on-field performance aggravated a rift that existed between the football team and the rest of the brigade.

At all the academies, there is a friction between the football team and the rest of the students, but one that is different than the normal jealousies found at most institutions. Many of the mids felt they were on par physically with the football players, and they weren't wrong. From boxing to swimming, running to push-ups and sit-ups, every midshipman was an athlete. They all went through physical training, or PT, as every serviceman calls it, and they were expected to be able to maneuver through obstacle courses and go on road marches without falling out. Football players weren't treated like demigods in Annapolis the way they were in other college towns. No one stopped the Navy quarterback at the bookstore and asked for an autograph or a picture, and mids didn't brag about sitting next to the star linebacker in history class.

Away from the field, there was no "looking the other way" when it came to football players, a fact of life Brian found out the hard way in December 2000, toward the end of first-semester finals in his sophomore year. He was lying in his bed with his headphones on while six other guys, including his roommate, poured brass polish inside pumpkins, lit them on fire, and threw them out the window of Bancroft Hall.

"[Cutting loose] didn't happen often, but it did happen, especially after finals," Brian said.

Young men doing stupid things after finals was something that every college experienced, but something that the academies didn't tolerate. The mids in Brian's room then set a phone book on fire and threw it out the window. Once they were out of things to burn, they poured the brass polish, a sticky goo with the consistency of maple syrup, onto the windowsill and lit it. The building was stone and nothing would burn, but globs of flaming brass cleaner dripped down to the lower levels like tiny firebombs.

Brian stopped paying attention to the shenanigans. He put his headset on, cranked up the volume, and rolled over in an attempt to catch a little sleep—until the pounding on his door jolted him upright. It was regimental command, and they were in his face. "You stupid SOB! Do you have any idea how much trouble you're in?"

Only then did Brian look around and realize he was alone. His roommate and the rest of the crew had vanished.

To his credit, Brian's roommate came back and admitted to being part of the fun and games, but that honesty and Brian's status as an athlete did not save them. Their company commander, Captain Richard L. Gannon, a lean, no-nonsense marine from Escondido, California, made it abundantly clear that they were in deep trouble. But when time came for the actions to be adjudicated—and all such actions are adjudicated at the academies; nothing is ever just "let go"—Captain Gannon stood before General Allen, outlined what the men in Brian's room had done, and said, "Sir, I remember my marines and I did some pretty stupid things in our younger years. I believe this falls into that category." They received thirty days' restriction during the summer.

Six years later, on April 17, 2004, Captain Richard Gannon was killed in Anbar Province in Iraq during ground operations with 3rd Battalion, 7th Marine Regiment. He was thirty-one years old.

At the time of the pumpkin toss, it never occurred to anyone that Brian would be treated any better or worse because of being on the football team. The great thing about the academy was its blanket justice. Everyone was the same. That was one of the main reasons they had come to Annapolis in the first place. If, as an athlete, you wanted to live under rarefied rules, you went somewhere else.

The only unique reward Navy football players were afforded was the fact that the entire student body saw them play every home game. No matter what their status, grade, or gender, every midshipman filed into Navy–Marine Corps Memorial Stadium on home-game Saturdays and stood from the opening kickoff until the final seconds ticked off the clock.

And that was where the friction arose. It was one thing to tailgate at a Maryland or UVa game, where the music was loud, the barbecue plentiful, and the girls friendly; it was quite another to put on your uniform, your overcoat, your gloves, your scarf, and your cover, and stand for three hours to watch your team get drubbed. Also, at other schools, football was optional. If you wanted to go to a game, tickets were cheap and parties were everywhere, but if you weren't interested in football or big crowds, you could go to the library or the Laundromat or almost any other place on campus during game time. That was not the case at Annapolis, where attending games was a requirement. Free time was precious, so home games were not something most mids looked forward to in the best of times. When the team couldn't beat anyone, it was more than some could bear. More than once, Brian would be walking to class after a big loss and have a classmate say, "Enjoyed the game on Saturday. Thanks for that."

He was hearing it after the Georgia Tech loss, but for weeks after the attacks, wins and losses didn't mean much, even to the mids who had to suffer through the games. On September 22, the first game after 9/11, the Midshipmen hosted Boston College at Navy–Marine Corps Memorial Stadium, a traditional rivalry that normally would have been all about the quarterback matchups and which defense would step up. This time, the 30,064 who filed into the stadium had only a passing interest in the outcome. As was the case throughout most of the country, this was about gathering together as Americans on a Saturday afternoon and regaining some sense of what was normal.

The Brigade of Midshipmen marched in together to thunderous applause, which was not unusual. The tears were new. When the teams ran onto the field, the place reverberated with cheers, which quickly died down to solemn quiet as everyone observed a moment of silence for the victims, including fifteen former midshipmen who died in the attack on the Pentagon. Then both teams saluted while Midshipman First Class Gary Roznovsky sang a moving rendition of the National Anthem. All the players remained at attention, or as close to attention as the Boston College kids knew how to stand, while four F-5 fighters out of the naval air station in Fallon, Nevada, flew directly over the field.

Once the game got under way, the spectators settled in and became football fans again. It appeared as though they would be treated to a great game as the Midshipmen hung with the Eagles for the first half, primarily because of the quarterback, Madden. He could throw a football sixty yards and run faster than most receivers, but he was also the size of a typical defensive end. The fact that he was often the leading rusher in a game spoke volumes for his athletic gifts. He was the nation's leading rushing quarterback in 1999, his sophomore season, but he blew out a knee during the 2000 spring scrimmage game and missed his entire junior year. He also missed the first two games of 2001, not because of an injury, but due to a suspension. During a madcap night out in Baltimore during one of his precious breaks from academy life and football, Madden had helped a teammate, defensive end Michael Wagoner, load a parking meter into the back of a pickup truck. The fact that Madden hadn't been a party to dislodging the meter from the street was the only thing that saved him from being kicked off the team and possibly separated from the brigade for good.

He did voluntarily resign as team captain and sat out the first two games, which was one of the reasons the Mids were so thoroughly trounced in their first two outings of 2001.

In the first quarter of the BC game, Madden threw a forty-nine-yard bomb to receiver Jeff Gaddy in the corner of the end zone, and just like that the Midshipmen looked as though they might have found their footing.

Brian Stann was out for the kickoff immediately following the touchdown, fired up and ready to keep the momentum going. The kickoff team stopped the return, but unfortunately for Navy, the defense couldn't stop the Eagles. Boston College tied it up quickly with a touchdown pass of their own.

Then the teams traded touchdowns in the second quarter, with Madden providing almost all of Navy's offense. Even so, it looked to the casual observer like this might be a close game until the end. But the players and coaches knew better. Those who were on the field understood that Navy was holding it close with emotion, intensity, and Madden. Physically the Mids were outmatched at almost every position. Fans loved the romantic notion of games being won on heart and desire, but the truth was: size and talent ruled the day more often than not, and Navy had very little of either.

BC's coach, Tom O'Brien, knew the strengths and weaknesses of his opponent better than most. O'Brien was a 1971 Navy graduate who served nine years in the Marine Corps, during which time he acted as an assistant coach for Navy's plebe team back in the days when freshmen were forbidden by the NCAA from playing varsity sports. From 1975 to 1982, O'Brien coached tackles and tight ends at Navy under head coach George Welsh while finishing his reservist duty in the Marines. When Welsh took a job at the University of Virginia, O'Brien, followed him and remained on staff at UVa for fifteen years, first as offensive line coach and later as offensive coordinator. He took the Boston College job in 1997 knowing that he would be coaching against his alma mater, although he never thought it was to be under circumstances such as these.

"I think it was tough on everyone," O'Brien said right after the 2001 game. "We knew what we were getting into by coming here to play."

Sentimentality took a backseat once Navy scored their first points. Boston College quarterback Brian St. Pierre gave the Eagles the lead with 7:23 left in the first half when he found receiver Ryan Read for a twenty-five-yard touchdown, and he stretched the lead just a few minutes later when he hit William Green on a hitch-and-go pattern for forty-nine yards and another touchdown.

St. Pierre completed four touchdown passes that afternoon in Annapolis. Madden threw a couple of interceptions, but also completed 124 yards' worth of passes and rushed for another 106. On the strength of their quarterback the Midshipmen put up twenty-one points against Boston College. Unfortunately, they gave up thirty-eight.

In a press conference afterward that had very little to do with football, Madden said, "An incident like [9/11] puts things in perspective as to why we are really here. We are here to eventually keep our country safe."

Coach Weatherbie was thinking about football, however. He had to. His job depended on it. "Our players are expected to perform at a higher level because they are at the academy—on the football field, in the classroom, and in public," he said after the Boston College loss. "They are held to excellence."

Unfortunately for Weatherbie and his players, excellence on the field was in short supply. They had another break after the BC game, which gave them two weeks to get ready to play the Air Force Academy, but much of that time was spent focusing on the new realities of life. "We all stood post and pulled more duty," Brian Stann said. "We were told that this would be the new normal, but we would continue to go to class and conduct our business the way we always had. Nothing would stop."

Business as usual was easier said than done, especially for football players who had the added pressure of playing for a cause that was greater than the game. With people who had never set foot on a military installation rooting for Navy, it would have been nice if they could win a few games. The option-based offense was okay with Madden under center, but Brian's defensive teammates had a hard time stopping anybody.

On October 6, the Mids played their first post-9/11 game outside of Navy–Marine Corps Memorial Stadium, although technically it was still a home game. The Air Force game was the first meeting between service academies after the attacks, and it was held at FedEx-Field in Landover, Maryland, home of the Washington Redskins, a stadium that was only twenty-five miles from Annapolis and another thirteen miles from the still-smoldering Pentagon.

The pregame ceremonies were just as raucous and patriotic as they had been for the BC game. And once again Madden and Navy struck first, this time with a fifty-four-yard touchdown pass to Tony Lane. But as had become the norm, the defense struggled. Air Force's quarterback, Keith Boyea, rushed for 118 yards and the other runners in their backfield tacked on an additional 175. Madden kept it close by barreling into the end zone for a touchdown late, but the Mids lost to Air Force 24–18.

Just like that Navy was 0-4, and grumblings about Coach Weatherbie's future grew louder. Weatherbie didn't lose his faith—he continued to lead a prayer before every practice and after every loss—but he did feel the pressure. His assistant coaches had much shorter fuses in practice. When one of Brian's fellow linebackers missed a read in practice in early October, one of the assistants threw his hat and ripped into the entire defensive backfield as if they had just blown a national championship.

Brian loved the added intensity. It fit his nature. The losses, unfortunately, did not. He understood, like most of his teammates, that he wasn't going to go undefeated at Navy and he wasn't going to contend for national championships, but he had come to Annapolis believing that his team could win more games than they lost. Like most college football players, he had hoped to play in a bowl game or two. But on October 13, with the nation still pulling for them, the Midshipmen gave up twenty-one points and 378 yards of total offense to Rice University. By the time the clock hit zero, Navy was 0-5 and had the worst rushing defense in the nation.

While technically the Air Force game at FedExField was away from campus, the first real post-9/11 road trip was to Piscataway, New Jersey, to play Rutgers on October 20. By then word had filtered back to Annapolis about the reception Army was receiving at away stadiums, so the Mids expected a hearty round of applause from their hosts. The game was also being televised on ESPN, a late pickup for the network, but one where the symbolism was too much to resist. Rutgers was a short train ride from Ground Zero. If the wind shifted you could smell the remnants of the still-burning metal. Having future wartime Navy and Marine Corps officers playing so close to the site of the New York attacks was the story of the day. The New Jersey crowd did not disappoint, waving tens of thousands of flags and giving the visiting team a five-minute standing ovation.

What no one expected, and what overwhelmed Brian and his teammates more than the cheers from the fans, was the reaction of the Rutgers players. Home teams always ran onto the field and rallied on their sidelines prior to kickoff, jumping and slapping helmets and revving up the energy. This time, the Scarlet Raiders lined up on their sideline and applauded their opponents as Navy ran out of the visitors' tunnel. Brian had to swallow twice and grab a cup of water to get the lump out of his throat.

The applause didn't stop the Raiders from whipping up on the Mids. Rutgers beat Navy 23–17. Once again the Midshipmen defense simply could not stop their opponent.

After one more road loss, to the University of Toledo on October 27, the inevitable became real: Charlie Weatherbie, the man who had won twenty-one games and lost thirteen in his first three seasons at Navy and logged a bowl victory for the Mids, was told that the program would be going in a different direction. He was thanked for his service and sent away. Ever the Christian servant, Weatherbie didn't leave before saying a closing prayer with his players, during which he wished them all the blessings of the Almighty in the service they were about to perform for their nation. It was a moment they would remember long after their football careers came to a close.

For the last three games of the 2001 season, including Army-Navy, Brian and his teammates played for Rick Lantz, the defensive coordinator, who was given the interim head coaching job. At any other school this would have been the talk of the campus, but at the Naval Academy, it was a passing reference. Operations in Afghanistan launched on October 7. The midshipmen had far more pressing things on their minds.

CHAPTER 5

This is not a regular game and everyone involved knows it.

—Roger Staubach, Navy quarterback,
Class of 1964

Bonnie Bernstein had expected to do her on-the-field interviewing for CBS Sports during the Dolphins game that weekend in Miami. The network was sending its lead crew, which included Dick Enberg and Dan Dierdorf in the booth and Bonnie on the sidelines. But ten days out, Bonnie got the call that they had been shifted to the Army-Navy Game in Philadelphia

It was impossible to tell who was more excited, the fans or the media. The players were accustomed to Army-Navy being televised, but this year the network's top stars were wandering around their campuses during game week, interviewing, watching, filming, and becoming emotionally wrapped in the rituals and discipline of the academies. For Bonnie, it was a chance to go back to West Point, a place she had admired since her early days as a college gymnast at the University of Maryland. She had been to a couple of formals there, when she was invited by a high school friend who became a cadet.

"I was always so in awe of those men and women, what they were

doing and what they would do," Bonnie said. "So, as I was prepping for that [Army-Navy] game, all my personal memories of Nine/
Eleven came back. It was really emotional. I read a quote and it's
right: that game is the one chance, for three hours, to see the future
of our country and to feel good about it."

Bonnie had graduated magna cum laude in sports journalism
and, at age thirty-one and in her fourth year with CBS, had earned
a reputation as the sharpest sideline reporter in the business. Comparisons to Leslie Visser came early, which was as good as it got
in the sports world. Visser had been a sportswriter for the *Boston
Globe* for fourteen years before moving to CBS to do NFL analysis
as well as the Final Four, the tennis U.S. Open, and other network
telecasts.

Bonnie had never written on deadline for a major paper, but
she had a newspaperman's nose for a story and worked harder than
anyone to ask the right question at the right time. This game was her
biggest challenge. Even though Enberg would later call this 2001
Army-Navy Game "the most important" of his storied broadcast
career, Bonnie and her director, Mike Arnold, were the only two
native New Yorkers working the game, and Bonnie was the only one
who had been in the city on September 11.

"I was watching *SportsCenter* when a friend called and said,
'Turn on the news, I think we're being attacked,'" she said. Within
an hour her phones were down and she couldn't reach her parents
or a friend who was supposed to have a meeting in the South Tower
that morning. "You can feel for people, and you can empathize, and
hurt for people, but unless you were there, you have no idea what
it was like." Bonnie had been there, so she understood the special
significance this game had for all Americans, but especially for New
Yorkers. "It took on a new meaning," she said. "It gave a heightened
sense of purpose to the game."

She arrived at West Point on Tuesday of game week and spent
most of the day walking around, taking in the sights and sounds of
campus, and immediately noticed the heightened security since her

last visit. Still, the game was at the forefront of campus life. Every salute was followed by "Go Army, beat Navy." Bonnie knew the same thing was happening in Annapolis. This might be the only game she would ever cover where the symbolism was far more important than the outcome. It isn't often that you recognize the historical impact of something as it is happening, but this was one of those times. Bonnie made mental notes of everything she saw and heard that week, including every player she interviewed.

Chad was one of the guys she spoke with. He tried not to let all the media hype become a distraction, which was tough because he had to answer scores of questions about his knee. Like most savvy athletes, he had become adept at the clichéd sound bite. "It's good. The knee's good. I'm good. We're good. Obviously a big game. We're ready. Can't wait to take on Navy." It looked and sounded great in five-second television clips and meant absolutely nothing.

He told Bonnie about being offered a graduate assistant's job for the next season, a plum assignment and a resume enhancer for later in your military career. Chad had accepted the job, but after the attacks he backed out. "I want to get to Ranger School as quickly as possible, so I can get over there and get the job done," he said.

Then Bonnie asked about the knee again, not letting Chad slip away with an answer she knew was a dodge.

"Yeah, it's good," he said. "This is the biggest game we have, and I'm a hundred percent ready for it."

The truth was, he didn't know how the knee was going to hold up. He'd practiced with the biggest, most cumbersome knee brace he'd ever seen: "The equivalent of a cast, only heavier," he said. The knee was tender and even though he'd never been the most mobile quarterback in the world, he had great field vision and could anticipate where defenders were going to be, which allowed him to scramble. Now, he could run a straight line without any problem, but cutting and turning were iffy at best. At any moment the knee could buckle and he would go down without warning. In practice, he "juked the jive," as he called it, and snookered coaches into believing he was fine. "No way was I missing Army-Navy my last year. That just wasn't going to happen."

Coach Berry and Coach Bond watched every movement, every detail. One twinge, one limp, and he could be pulled. Even the CBS guys thought Chad would be out. Dierdorf, who was a six-time Pro Bowler, said Chad was "done."

Chad wanted to show them he was far from done, so he picked a fight in the Thursday practice before they were to leave for Philly. This was just a run-through, no contact, simply executing the plays in shorts to keep everybody sharp. During one series, Chad went with the team's long snap count, "on long" as they called it. It was their attempt to draw the defenders offsides. A normal snap count would be "Blue, eighty-two, blue eighty-two, sa-hit!" and the ball would be snapped. The long count went "Blue, eighty-two, sa-hit! Sa-hit! Hit!" If the defense didn't bite and everyone remained onside, Chad would reset and go with the regular count. During this particular "on long" play, one of his own linemen, a big tackle, jumped offside. In the game that would have been a five-yard penalty. Such things, while maddening, were not uncommon, even at the end of a season.

Chad saw this mistake as an opportunity to show the coaches how ready he was to lead this team. He grabbed the tackle by the jersey despite being outweighed by sixty pounds. This was no small gamble. If the lineman had pushed back, Chad's knee would have folded like a soggy piece of bread. Instead the tackle took it, knowing he had screwed up and knowing Chad was right to shove him around.

"You need to lock in!" Chad yelled. "Pay attention. This is Army-Navy! If you're not ready, don't go. We can't afford any stupid mistakes."

Berry and Bond stood stone-faced a few yards away. Trainer Tim Kelly knew how much Chad was faking it, but he kept his mouth shut. Kelly had told Chad they would have a better knee brace by game time, a state-of-the-art titanium model that was lighter and stronger and would give him more mobility. But when Chad approached him in the taping area of the locker room before the final practice at West Point, Tim shook his head. That meant they had to leave for Philadelphia with a brace that looked like something out of a polio museum. But at least Chad would make the trip. That was all he cared about at the moment.

Friday after dark, with players itching to get on the bus for Philly, the entire Corps of Cadets marched to the rugby field for a pep rally, CBS crew in tow. That was when it hit Chad that this game was different than any he had ever played. His three previous Army-Navy pep rallies had started with an intramural football game where the plebes (freshmen) and yuks (sophomores) played the cows (juniors) and firsties (seniors). Not flag football or two-hand touch: the players, while not on the football team, suited up in pads and hit each other, often harder and with more intensity than some of the four-year starters who would play in Veterans Stadium in less than forty-eight hours.

The academy had plenty of athletes who weren't on varsity teams. Everyone was required to engage in some form of athletic competition. Those who didn't compete on NCAA teams played club league sports like rugby, and all the men had to strap on boxing gloves and learn their way around a ring, even the football players. This was, after all, an institution where the criteria for graduation included running two miles in under fifteen minutes, performing a hundred push-ups and a hundred sit-ups, and swimming the length of an Olympic-sized pool in full gear, including boots, while holding a rubber M4 above the water.

The corps's overall athleticism was often hard to quantify, but the superintendent did a good job of illustrating how special the kids who made it into West Point were. His prepared address to an earlier incoming plebe class and their parents in Eisenhower Hall was one such occasion. The ritual of Reception Day, or "R-Day," is the first experience many of the new cadets have with the traditions of West

Point. This opening ceremony, in a basic training period known at West Point as Beast, starts in the theater in Eisenhower Hall and concludes on the Plain, where parents fill bleachers for the parade and oath ceremony. In between those two events, new cadets get their hair shaved, part with their cell phones, learn to stand at attention and salute, and undergo grilling by their fellow cadets. But before any of that begins, everyone sits indoors in the Ike with all the parents on one side of the theater and the new cadets on the other.

"You have all heard that this institution attracts the best of the best, but today I'm going to quantify that for you," the superintendent said to this particular group. Then, to the new cadets, he said, "If you were in the top ten percent of your high school graduating class, please stand up."

Every one of the incoming plebes stood.

"If you were valedictorian at your high school, remain standing," the superintendent said.

Only half the kids sat down, meaning that at least half the incoming plebes had finished at the very top of their high school graduating classes.

"Now, if you have a varsity letter in any sport, please remain standing."

Only a handful of plebes sat. Hundreds remained on their feet.

"And"—the superintendent paused for effect—"if you had nine or more high school varsity letters, please remain standing."

About half of the kids left standing sat down. Audible gasps went out among the parents as the magnitude of what they were seeing sank in. Fully a quarter of the incoming plebe class had graduated from high school as valedictorians with nine or more varsity letters.

Chad was not in that incoming class, nor would he have been one of those still standing at the end of the superintendent's remarks if he had been. He had been a decent student in high school, but certainly not the best. That was one of the reasons he'd attended the academy prep school. He had certainly gotten smarter and more dedicated as his time at West Point went on. As he prepared for the last football game he would ever play, he couldn't help smiling at the thought of his first year at USMAPS—the United States Military Academy Preparatory School, more commonly known as the prep school—and just how ignorant he had been of Army life and all that went with it. That first day, Chad and his new buddies, including Gary Bartels, were milling around the hallway of their dorm when a captain walked onto the hall.

"Attention," Chad yelled, "there's an officer on deck!"

It was a perfect line from *A Few Good Men*, delivered with just the right amount of enthusiasm. There was only one problem: *A Few Good Men* was about the Marine Corps and the Navy. The captain was in his face in a second.

"On deck?" he said. "Jenkins, what the hell are you talking about, 'on deck'? This ain't the Navy. And I sure as hell don't see any boats, do you?"

It was a first-day mistake, one of hundreds made every year by new cadets. Some plebes forgot how to speak after being sheared by the post's barbers, dressed in gray T-shirts and black gym shorts and instructed in firm voices on how to carry a backpack, how to march, and how to address and respond to their fellow cadets. Wide-eyed eighteen-year-olds were told to report to the "cadet with the red sash," which was where many of them encountered their first corrections. Some didn't know what a sash was, while others froze when the upperclassman said, "New cadet: step up to my line; not on my line; not behind my line, not in front of my line." Half of them botched that, and another third either screwed up the salute or the phrasing they were to use when reporting as ordered. Some became so rattled they called male cadets "ma'am." A few forgot their own names.

Prep school didn't have R-Day or Beast, the summer field training for plebes. It was like military community college, a way to get students academically and emotionally ready for the real thing. The upside was that they were ready for plebe year when it finally arrived;

the downside was that they knew going in that they would spend five years in military college. Chad and his classmates went through the same rigors as the rest of the plebes, but they did so with a year of military preparatory experience.

Their first day together in prep school was like every kid's first moments away from home. Just a few hours after the "officer on deck" mishap, Chad heard a knock on his door. Zickefoose walked in and introduced himself, and the two made small talk, mostly about hometowns and football. Chad had a photo of himself and his girlfriend on his desk. 'Foose, attempting to make new-friend conversation, said, "That's a good picture."

Chad flashed his million-dollar smile and said, "Yeah, don't I look good in that picture?"

'Foose paused for a moment to see if he was kidding. When he realized that Chad was serious, 'Foose simply said, "Dude." They had been best friends ever since. Now, five football seasons later, they were prepping for their final outing as athletes, but they knew they would remain friends forever.

The intramural game had been scrapped from the pep rally, not because of security or even out of respect for 9/11, but because the last thing the Army needed at that moment was a bunch of incoming officers being unfit for duty due to injuries sustained at a pickup football game. West Point dealt with enough injuries as it was. By the first of December numerous cadets walked around campus on crutches or in slings. Drilling took its toll. No one on the team knew who decided to cancel the intramural game, but everyone suspected that the orders came from Washington.

That wasn't the only thing missing from the pre-Army-Navy festivities, either. In previous pep rallies, the corps had gathered at the south end of the field, where, earlier in the week, plebes had built a wooden ship with NAVY painted on the side. Then the lights went out and they heard it: the unmistakable whir of helicopter rotor blades thumping through the night air. Two Chinooks and two Black Hawks from the 160th Special Operations Aviation Regiment (SOAR) out of Fort Campbell, Kentucky, would rise off the Hudson like monsters from the sea. They were blacked out, their pilots flying with night vision, which only added to the allure. Then a platoon of Rangers would fast-rope onto the field and assault the wooden Navy ship, setting it on fire.

This was the high point of the football season for most cadets, an experience that made all the shouting and marching and early-morning formations worth it. As the Rangers lit the bonfire, the helicopter pilots would land on the opposite end of the rugby field. Cadets could look at the choppers, talk to the Rangers, and examine their gear. Heady stuff for a pep rally.

Chad looked around at the 2001 pep rally and saw the boat and the entire Corps of Cadets, but no Rangers or Chinooks or Black Hawks, no fast-roping or show-and-tells with cool gear. Those guys couldn't come this year because they were already in the fight in Afghanistan. Special Operations forces, as always, were first in, and the 160th SOAR were the chariots that delivered them to the enemy's doorstep.

Two hundred and sixty-three miles away from the West Point rugby field, the week had been memorable in Annapolis as well, but for different reasons. The Midshipmen football team was in meltdown as the strain between the football players and the rest of the student body grew downright hostile. Both student bodies would travel, in full, to Philadelphia for the game. Both would stand in formation outside Veterans Stadium for hours as fans strolled by and took their photos like they were exhibits in a zoo. They would smell the food cooking on grills at tailgate parties just a few feet away, but they wouldn't be allowed to partake. And not a single drop of alcohol would be consumed by any student from Annapolis or West Point. Once inside the stadium, they would be free to visit the concession stands before the game and at halftime, but when play was under way, unless they were going to the head ("latrine" for the Army cadets and "restroom" to the rest of the world: another subtlety of language that separated the two branches from each other and separated both from civilians), they would stand and watch every down.

Most college students loved rivalry games. Nobody turned down Iron Bowl tickets (the annual Alabama-Auburn game, considered one of college football's fiercest rivalries) just as every fan in Ann Arbor wanted to be in the stands for Ohio State–Michigan. But if those kids had to load onto buses at 0400 and stand all day until the bus ride home, they might not be so gung ho about football Saturdays. Both Navy and Army struggled with a similar problem: the rest of the students often resented the imposition.

The Naval Academy's pep rally before heading out was also more muted than in previous years. As Brian prepared to head to Philly for the game, he thought about what a win at Veterans Stadium would mean for the morale of the academy. The team was fracturing, and the rest of the midshipmen would rather be somewhere, anywhere, other than in the stadium for yet another beating, especially by Army. Interim coach Rick Lantz, a sixty-two-year-old former marine, stuck with many of the Weatherbie schemes, including a four-three defense that relied heavily on great play from the linebackers.

But the Navy defensive linemen and linebackers were undersized and outmanned, and the triple-option offense, while great for ball control and clock management, was not a fast-strike, high-scoring threat. Unless they could come up with a miracle, the Midshipmen had little hope of winning. But they'd pulled out a victory over Army a season earlier after losing every other game, so anything was possible.

Veterans Stadium was so dilapidated and rickety that when CBS producers approached the White House about having President Bush in the broadcast booth during the game, the Secret Service quashed the idea because they didn't trust the elevators.

But Chad thought it was the most beautiful stadium he'd ever seen, even more so now than in previous years. During the pregame walk-through, when the team went out in T-shirts and shorts (a nice change for December), he told 'Foose and Clint Dodson, "Take a good look." This would be the last time they would ever have that view.

As kickoff grew closer, Chad grew quiet. Coach Bond approached him in the locker room when everyone was resting before putting on their pads. "Chad, they're going to want you to say a few words," Bond said. "I've seen a lot of seniors get so worked up and emotional during these 'last game' speeches that it takes them nearly a quarter to lock in and get their focus back. You can't do that. Keep it brief. Say a few words, but I need you locked in."

"Locked in," Chad repeated. He got it.

Coach Berry had prepared them for the president's visit in the locker room. George W. Bush had put the Army-Navy Game on his schedule before 9/11. After the attacks he thought it was even more important that he be there to speak to the players. Everyone knew the president was coming. General Norman Schwarzkopf was a surprise. When Stormin' Norman walked into the locker room, everyone jumped to their feet even before Zickefoose called them to attention. Schwarzkopf quickly told them to relax. But that was impossible with a legend in the room.

The general's speech, especially the part where he said, "the Army does not lose . . . You will prevail! You will win!" sent tingles up Chad's spine. He was ready to run out the door right then, and he might have, if President Bush hadn't walked in. Once more the cadets were called to attention. The president wasn't there for a stem-winder. He was much more conversational, shaking hands and asking cadets their names and where they were from.

"Soon you will be the men who lead our troops in combat," the president said, a sobering acknowledgment of what every man there knew to be true. "Those of you who end up in whatever theater you end up in, I want to assure you that the cause is just. It is right. And we will win. There is no doubt in my mind that we'll win. Thanks for your commitment to your country. It is a fabulous country. And may God bless you all."

Once the president and all the photographers exited, Coach Berry asked Zickefoose, Clint Dodson, and Chad to say a few words. None of them had much to say.

Chad, remembering Coach Bond's advice, said, "Hey, a lot of guys, especially seniors, get all nostalgic and sentimental and forget that they've got a game to play. So, let's cut this shit and go win."

With that they broke, grabbed their helmets, and headed for the tunnel.

Down the hall in the Navy locker room, players were wide-eyed and slack-jawed listening to Senator John McCain's colorful remarks, especially when the F-bombs flew. It was one thing to hear a Navy or Marine officer cut loose in a profane tirade—they didn't call it cursing like a sailor for nothing—but to hear a famous U.S. senator going off in such a manner caught most of them by surprise. Some bit their lips to fight back smiles while others were happy that evangelical Charlie Weatherbie wasn't there to hear it.

McCain chuckled when recalling the day. "It was a bleak time for Navy," the senator said. "They asked me if I would go down and say a few words, and, well, with the emotion of everything surrounding the game, I got a little emotional myself. The game does have an effect on morale of the midshipmen as well as the cadets."

He did his best to look them all in the eye and shake as many hands as he could once he finished and his face returned to its normal color. "I was proud and honored to speak to those young men who were about to go off and serve in combat," McCain said. "I was aware of what they were about to face and aware that some of them might not be as fortunate as I was [to come home alive]. Sadly, that turned out to be the case."

Both student bodies marched onto the field separately by company, their formations looking like a collection of blue and then gray human rectangles stretching from one end zone to the next. The Naval Academy's entire battalion went out at 9:00 A.M. and the cadets followed at 9:30 A.M. Once set, they saluted the fans who were already filling the seats.

"Every one of them has chosen to answer the call to duty," Veterans Stadium public address announcer Dom Alagia said. "With their salute, they recognize and honor your show of support. These men and women today will lead America's sons and daughters tomorrow in defense of our great nation."

The applause went on for five minutes.

Bonnie Bernstein saw her cameraman, Jimmy Kimmons, in the end zone talking to some important-looking person with an earpiece in his ear. Sensing that she needed to be a part of the conversation, she slipped over and introduced herself to Reed Dickens, the president's young, blond assistant press secretary, who looked like he could suit up and play for either team.

After a second of pleasantries, Bonnie said, "Hey, I know there's some reticence about putting the president in the booth, but since he's doing the coin toss, any chance we can get him for a second?"

Dickens smiled and said, "Sure."

Momentarily stunned by how easy that was, Bonnie cued her mike and called producer Lance Barrow, a portly West Texan who was the czar of CBS's big sporting events. "Lance, I have the president," Bonnie said. "Do you want him?"

Lance's twang got sharper. "Well . . . ah . . . where you gonna do it? You gonna do it live?"

They had to make the decision quickly. Dickens motioned Bonnie into the tunnel where the Secret Service had set up a perimeter. The president wouldn't be far behind. Barrow called down to Bonnie, "Do it there. Do it live."

President Bush walked out, and Bonnie was once again faced

with a dilemma. There were a few seconds before Lance would be ready for her, but what do you say to a sitting president as an ice-breaker? She had interviewed Jimmy Carter at the U.S. Open in Flushing Meadow, Queens, but he had been out of office for twenty years. This was the leader of the free world and the commander in chief of a nation at war. "Hi, Mr. President, nice to meet you" wasn't going to cut it. Then she remembered that Jim Nantz, the face of CBS Sports, always talked about his relationship with the Bushes.

"Mr. President, it's a pleasure to meet you," she said. "I hear Jim Nantz is a close friend of the family. If you concede that, it'll be the first time I actually believe him."

The president smiled and said, "Oh, yeah, Jimmy is a good friend."

Then she asked about the Texas Rangers, the baseball team the president once owned, and what off-season moves he expected. Baseball was still fresh on his mind, and he offered a few tidbits, but nothing substantive. Just five weeks prior, President Bush has thrown out the first pitch of game three of the World Series at Yankee Stadium, a moment that had brought many to tears. This coin toss wasn't expected to be as dramatic.

"Cue Bonnie," Barrow said.

As if the idea had just occurred to him, Dick Enberg said, "[The president] is standing by live with our own Bonnie Bernstein."

"Mr. President, how much is your presence at events like this about helping the nation feel safe?" she asked.

"I hope a lot of it is," the president said. "I have no fear coming to the game. What I'm really here to do is to say to the country how proud I am of our military folks. As I told the players, I'm at the game, I'm looking forward to it, I love football, but my mind isn't here. My mind is in Afghanistan in a theater in which we are fighting evil. I want the nation to know how proud I am of our men and women in uniform who are representing our country."

"In light of what's going on in Afghanistan and the War on

Terror, how do you think people in the nation and all over the world will view this game?" Bonnie asked.

The president seemed ready for that one. "I think they will view it differently, of course, because a lot of the young men on the playing field will end up in a theater, whether it be in Afghanistan or somewhere else. When they learn about the lives of these Navy and Army graduates, they will learn that we have some of the finest citizens in our country going to our military academies."

No one was sure what he meant by "somewhere else" at the time. The Iraq War would not begin for another fifteen months.

Navy won the toss and elected to receive, but they all but gave up the first possession by keeping their best athlete on the sidelines. Quarterback Brian Madden was the key to any chance the Mids had, but Coach Lantz wanted to reward senior captain Ed Malinowski by giving him a start. Malinowski ran one series where he threw two incompletions and rushed for a two-yard loss.

Navy punted, and Chad trotted onto the field.

His first incompletion was the most memorable. Coach Bond wanted to go big right away, so they practiced a fly route, a downfield bomb to one of their speedy receivers, Anthony Miller, as the first offensive play they would run. The hope was to catch the Navy defense flat-footed. If the receiver was covered, Chad had several other options, including Clint Dodson, the leading receiver on the season and the biggest target on the field. Dodson was running a crossing route and another receiver, Omari Thompson, ran a hook and go. Bond had counseled Chad before the game, "If it's not there, it's not there. Don't force it. Take your drop down. You'll be fine."

Miller wasn't open, but Chad threw it up anyway. He wanted the ball back the moment it left his fingers, and he breathed a sigh of relief when it fell incomplete. He also knew what he was going to hear when he got back on the sideline. Omari Thompson, the third receiver in his check-down, was wide open. If he'd gone through his progressions instead of trying to force the big play, they would have had an easy first down, maybe more.

He made up for that mistake on the third play, though. After a pump fake that froze the linebackers, Chad scrambled to his right. Running out of time and room, he threw the ball down the sideline one step before going out of bounds. Miller grabbed the ball just inches from the sideline for a first down.

The completion brought the crowd to its feet, but it almost brought Chad to his knees. He had tweaked his knee on the scramble. Thankfully the next play was a toss to Ardell Daniels, so Chad didn't have to plant and throw. Daniels went nowhere, bringing up second down and ten, a perfect down for another play-action pass, assuming the quarterback could roll out of the pocket.

He didn't visibly show relief when Coach Bond called a draw to Daniels, who was to run off the block of right tackle Craig Cunningham and hopefully weave his way past the linebackers for ten or so, but Chad couldn't have been happier with the play.

He was even more thrilled after they ran it. Cunningham opened a huge hole, which Daniels plowed through for five yards, but when Chad looked up he saw that the linebackers had charged the line of scrimmage. They were out of position and Daniels was already behind them. A cut back across the field to the left and Daniels was off to the races. The only player he had to beat was the safety who was running from across the field.

Chad sprinted behind him the whole way yelling, "Go Ardell, go!" Sixty yards later, Chad caught Daniels in the end zone as they celebrated Army's first touchdown.

The crowd roared, and Chad ran off the field with his hands in the air. The euphoria lasted about a minute. Once he put on the headset to talk to Bond, who was upstairs in the coach's booth, he heard, "Good job. Good execution. But what did I tell you about that first pass? If you had hit your drop-down that guy would still be running."

Coach Bond could not see Chad smiling on the sideline. "No matter what you do," he thought.

Chad's knee recovered from the initial tweak. Either that or it went numb from all the adrenaline pumping through his veins. He continued to hand the ball to Daniels on their second possession, sucking the Navy linebackers ever closer with each down. Then, on second and ten, Chad threw a quick out to Miller that hit the receiver in the numbers. But Miller dropped the ball. He slapped his hands in disgust on his way back to the huddle, but Chad was already checking the sideline for the next play, another crucial third down and ten yards to go from the Navy forty-two-yard line.

From the shotgun, Chad had several receiver options again, his first being to Brian Bruenton deep over the middle. Once more the receiver appeared to be covered, and once more Chad threw the ball anyway. This time, though, the bullet pass flew right through the hands of the defenders and into Bruenton's outstretched palms. The receiver turned and had a clear shot into the end zone.

Once again Chad was the first to greet him as Army celebrated their second touchdown in as many possessions. Just like that, it was 13–0.

The thing about throwing passes into tight coverage, especially when defenders are breaking on the ball, is that you look like John Elway when it's successful. When it's not, you rack up a fair number of interceptions. Chad got lucky on the first play of the game throwing a deep ball that could have been picked. He caught another break on the Bruenton touchdown with a ball that sailed right through the defender's hands. Then, on the next Army offensive series, he dodged a third bullet when he underthrew a pass to Aris Comeaux that free safety Paul Clarkson grabbed for the interception but then dropped. Had he been given time to reflect on his good fortune, Chad might have realized he needed to be more cautious, but in the heat of the Army-Navy Game, it was impossible to think that way.

The play immediately after the near interception was another handoff to Daniels, which didn't end well. After a three-yard gain, three Navy defenders fell on Daniels's left leg, twisting his knee at an odd angle. The trainers ran out in a flash, bending over Daniels, who writhed and grabbed his knee in a pain Chad knew all too well. With a trainer under each arm, Daniels hobbled off the field without putting any weight on his left leg. It was not a good sign for the plebe running back, or for the offense. Daniels had averaged almost eleven yards a carry in the first quarter. Now it was up to Chad.

From the shotgun with an empty backfield—three receivers split wide to his right and one to his left—Chad checked the right side and then stepped up. One of the linebackers blitzed late and he had to get rid of the ball quickly, so he heaved it downfield for Miller. It was the first time he had tried to throw deep on the run, a feat that requires tremendous leg action and two good knees. The ball flew five yards short. This time Clarkson had no trouble with the interception.

Unfortunately for Navy, their offense didn't have enough size or talent to move the chains or run the clock. Other than Madden, who for at least the first five games of the season was the best athlete on the field, the Mids were outmuscled up front and outrun in the secondary. Madden threw two incompletions and was thrown for a loss on an option sweep, forcing Navy to punt again after controlling the ball for less than a minute.

Offenses always have an advantage when it comes to the clock. An offensive coordinator can substitute personnel to keep fresh legs on the field, and he can adjust the play calling to allow his guys to catch their breath when needed. Defensive players fly around, fighting off blocks and reacting on every play. That is why defenses wear out when their teammates on offense can't click off enough first downs to run a few minutes off the clock and give them a rest.

Army owned the time of possession, so Coach Lantz tried to run in some fresh defensive players to give his starters a second or two to regroup. That was how Brian got on the field at the beginning of the second quarter as Chad broke the huddle for the first time after throwing a very bad interception. Navy had three good starting linebackers. Dan Ryno was one, a senior with two older brothers who had also been mids and were, at that moment, deployed in theater, one as a naval aviator and the other as a SEAL. Ryno was the leader of the linebacker corps, but the teammates next to him at middle and strong-side linebacker, plebes Dustin Elliott and Ryan Hamilton, were bigger and faster. Brian was in for Ryno.

Chad took no chances. He grabbed the snap from the shotgun formation and checked his first two receivers. When he found nobody open, he sensed some weak-side pressure from a charging defensive end. His tackle, Paul Henderson, picked up a key block, but Chad knew his time was running out. He tucked the ball and charged ahead, only to be caught around the ankles by Navy defensive end Paul Beuttenmuller. Brian and Josh Brindel met him as he was going down.

Navy didn't move the ball into Army territory until late in the second quarter, and only then because Zickefoose got called for a personal foul. "It happens," he would later say of the late shove that earned a rare dead-ball penalty. That led to Navy's first points, a forty-four-yard field goal from kicker David Hills.

Other than that, Army dominated. With thirteen seconds left in the first half, adding insult to insufferable injury for the Mids, Army blocked a Navy punt at the twenty-one-yard line, giving the Cadets one final chance to score before halftime, which they did with a field goal. The scoreboard said 16–3, but it felt much worse. The way the Mids had been pushed around, Navy coaches and players had to feel relieved going into the break trailing by only thirteen points.

* * *

Brian lined up right next to kicker David Hills to start the second
half. He leaned over and stretched his hamstrings as Hills put the
ball on the tee. The kick was high and Brian sprinted after it. This
was where he could shine, hurling himself at a ballcarrier and, perhaps, changing the momentum of the game.

Omari Thompson was deep for Army. At only five feet seven
inches and 165 pounds, Thompson was both the shortest and the
fastest man for either side, with an explosive quickness that caught
more than a few defenders off guard. His sister was on the sideline wearing an Army cheerleader uniform. Raised in Miami, the
Thompson siblings were West Point bound from the moment their
mother saw the campus when they were young kids. "My mother
put the word out at that moment that 'my kids will go to the United
States Military Academy,'" Thompson would later recall. He and his
sister would graduate together that spring.

Brian led the charge downfield as Thompson caught the ball
and made a move to his right. It appeared as though Army was
running a reverse. The up-back was cutting across the field and
Thompson was holding the ball out for a handoff.

Brian secured the middle of the field, but once it became evident
the reverse was a fake, he tried to adjust his containment. That was
when he was held. There was no doubt about it. One of the Army
blockers had two fists full of Brian's jersey, arms fully extended. He
wasn't even trying to hide it. But the officials never saw it, despite
Brian throwing a hand in the air as if to say, "What are you doing?
Can you not see I'm being mauled here?"

Like everyone else in the Vet, the officials were watching
Thompson, who broke one tackle and then turned on the afterburners. No one touched him after he crossed midfield. It was a
ninety-four-yard touchdown run, and a blow to the solar plexus of
every Navy player.

* * *

The Army sideline went nuts, including the man Bonnie was supposed to interview when he came out after halftime, General Norman Schwarzkopf. The plan had been for Navy to kick off and Bonnie to interview the general while the kick team ran off and Chad and the offensive unit ran on. Thompson's return threw that timing off, but Schwarzkopf didn't mind. He had his arms in the air and was yelling, "That's what I'm talking about! Yeah!"

Bonnie got to Schwarzkopf immediately after the touchdown, but Barrow was telling her, "Vamp, just vamp for a couple of minutes."

The plan was to go live with the interview after the Army kickoff, but that got fouled up as well. Todd Berry pulled some more trickery, calling an onside kick, which the cadets recovered. Within the first thirty seconds of the second half, Army had scored a touchdown and recovered an onside kick.

So, Bonnie stayed close to the general's side as he whooped and cheered Army's early second-half dominance. Then, when things quieted for a second, she talked to him about the Tampa Bay Buccaneers, vamping with all she had until things on the field returned to normal. Then Barrow cued her to go live.

"This is the game," Schwarzkopf said. "I distinctly remember the Army-Navy Game my senior year. Navy was ahead six to nothing at halftime and I knew we were going to win. And we did."

Bonnie asked, "There are one hundred forty thousand troops listening to this game on Armed Forces Radio or television. How significant is this game to them?"

"It means everything," the general said. "This is our way of life. They are serving our country to protect our way of life. We need to demonstrate that that way of life is the greatest anywhere in the world. So, I want to say thank you to every single soldier, sailor, airman, marine, and coast guardsman out there defending our country."

When it was over, Bonnie would rank this day as one of her best. "I knew that if my career ended right there, I would be okay with what I had done," she said. "And I would have to say that outside of covering my first Super Bowl—the Giants and the Ravens, and I had grown up a Giants fan—and other than covering every game en route to my alma mater Maryland's 2002 national championship, that Army-Navy Game was the best of my journalistic career."

While the general and Bonnie were chatting on the sideline, Chad threw a pass up for grabs, knowing that Clint Dodson would go up and get it. Dodson fought off two Navy defenders to pull down the reception. Army was on the move again.

First and ten on the Navy fifteen-yard line, one more touchdown would put this one out of reach. But after a run play that went no-where, and an incomplete pass where Chad threw the ball away on the sideline to avoid a sack, he dropped back to attempt a pass over the middle. Only this time, a Navy defensive tackle got a big hand up at exactly the right moment. The ball tipped and wobbled right into the hands of Dustin Elliott, the best of Navy's plebe linebackers.

It was Chad's second interception, and it kept the Army lead at twenty—comfortable but not out of reach.

He got his third pick in the next series, when defensive tackle Nate Chase jumped just as Chad threw. The ball hit Chase in the face mask before he corralled it and charged ahead. Chad charged as well, lowering his head to make the tackle on a man who was four inches taller and ninety pounds heavier than he. That interception led to another David Hills field goal for Navy.

The Mids scored another field goal at the end of the third quarter to cut the lead to fourteen, which was as close as they would get until late in the fourth.

Army put up a field goal in the fourth quarter to extend the lead to seventeen with time slipping away. Chad threw one more interception to end the day with four, but it didn't matter. With a couple minutes remaining, Coach Lantz emptied the benches and made sure that every senior got a chance to play. J. P. Blecksmith, the man who would be starting at quarterback and handing the ball off to Madden at the fullback spot if Navy ran a pro-style offense, caught a pass for a fifteen-yard gain with less than a minute to play. That catch led to Navy's only touchdown, a four-yard completion to Steve Mercer with twenty-three seconds left to go in the game.

Army recovered the attempted onside kick, and the game was all but over. Chad had thrown for 119 yards, with one touchdown and four interceptions; not a great statistical day, but one of the greatest days of his playing career as far as he was concerned.

"Gutsiest player I've ever coached," John Bond would say later. "Chad was the kind of football player you wish you had every year, but that you only get once in a coaching lifetime, if you're lucky."

The final score was 26–17, a result made official when Chad, on the last football play he would ever run, took the snap and knelt down to run out the clock: "the victory formation," as he called it.

"Nothing feels better," he said.

CHAPTER 6

Upon the fields of friendly strife are sown the seeds that upon other fields, on other days, will bear the fruits of victory.

—GENERAL OF THE ARMY DOUGLAS MACARTHUR

As it has done since the days of George Washington, the U.S. military adapted to the new threat quickly and made adjustments on the fly. Special Forces had saddles airdropped into Kandahar, Afghanistan, so they could ride horses through the mountains, and a sergeant realized that standard Home Depot bathroom caulk made better breaching adhesive on desert sandstone than the billion-dollar Pentagon-issued stuff. American servicemen learned while doing and changed the things that needed to be changed.

That has always been one of America's biggest advantages in times of war. Her leaders learn from mistakes. While other countries' generals and presidents try to rewrite history to make their blunders look like successes, U.S. commanders drill down into every error, examining every miscue and detailing every misfire. They look at every asset positioned in the wrong place at the wrong time, every tidbit of intelligence that is inaccurate or misunderstood, and every strategic assumption that proves to be erroneous. Students at Annapolis and

West Point study Cold Harbor, Pickett's Charge, and the Battle of Little Bighorn. They are conditioned to give full accounts of what works, what doesn't, and why. No foot soldier faces a firing squad for delivering bad news. From General Washington to General James Mattis, former head of the Central Command, U.S. military leaders have always shown an unblinking obsession with their mistakes, and especially with fixing them.

The same was true at the academies. In the aftermath of the attacks, the live-fire target cutouts at West Point were shifted from burly Russian-looking dudes to masked terrorists, and in a flash, field exercises started including encounters with Farsi-speaking civilians laced with a bad guy or two. Almost immediately, engineers began modifying their procedures to fit the new battlefield, and everyone started learning the history and evolution of the improvised explosive device (IED).

Academy brass also had to rethink how cadets and midshipmen picked their branches, an event that occurred in September of their firstie year (their last). Branch selection was by far the most important decision a senior made after signing the papers to come to the academies. It defined what kind of soldier or sailor he or she was going to be, and what job he or she would have for the next five years. It was one of the many trade-offs academy grads made compared to their civilian counterparts: Nobody came out of West Point or Annapolis unemployed or saddled with student loans, but newly commissioned officers couldn't change careers after nine months just because the industry wasn't what they expected. Firsties had to decide how they wanted to spend the next five years of their lives (and in some instances, longer than that) before the first leaves of autumn fell in their final academic year.

For some, the choice was easy. If you wanted to be a lawyer, you branched JAG (Judge Advocate General's Corps); if you had always dreamed of flying helicopters, you branched Aviation; if you'd always loved tanks, Armor. Those planning ahead for civilian careers, especially the five-and-fliers, usually branched Engineering, Communications, or Intelligence, but the options also included the Chaplain, Medical, Dental, Veterinary, Chemical, or Finance corps for anyone who wanted the government to train them for a lifelong profession.

Hooahs branched Infantry. In the minds of those who served there, the infantry was the *real* Army, the boots on the ground and the "tip of the spear," as Chad and others called it. Everyone else was just support. Sure, the Army needed men who could engineer bridges and clean teeth, but when it came to night patrols and kill-or-capture missions—the reason the Army exists in many people's minds—they needed infantry officers, men who understood that their military skills have very few civilian applications. As one infantry captain put it, "Sniper kill from six hundred yards is not something you can put on a civilian resume."

Prior to September 11, the cadets had little trouble with their branching decisions. If they were smart enough to get into medical school, they branched Medical with no worries. If they aspired to be pilots, as long as they passed all the skill and proficiency tests, Aviation would accept them and they were off to flight school. The biggest concern wasn't getting a branch: it was the first deployment. In the old days, the cream posts for infantry were Italy, Hawaii, and Germany—and after that came the okay posts like Fort Carson, Colorado, a beautiful place with plenty of things to keep a young soldier occupied. Korea was considered awful, as was Fort Sill, Oklahoma, where tumbleweeds outnumbered the civilian population. Nobody wanted Fort Polk, Louisiana, where the mosquitoes were the size of your hand, or Fort Hood, in middle-of-nowhere Killeen, Texas. But now, posts were not a priority. Everyone was going to combat.

The problem this time was the number of infantry requests. West Point normally got 180 slots for Infantry each year. With a graduating class of about one thousand, and seventeen available branches for incoming second lieutenants, there were usually a few infantry spots left over, but not this time. Three weeks after 9/11, West Point had 230 applications for Infantry. More loud "Hooahs" rang out on campus than ever before. That created a minor political dilemma.

Nobody wanted to be known as the commander who denied West Point graduates a chance to lead an infantry platoon. Fudging the number of spots by three or four had never been a problem, as empty positions could be filled from ROTC programs around the country. But exceeding the allotted spots by fifty percent required some restructuring. In the end, the Department of Defense had to get Congress to pass a resolution taking spots away from ROTC and Officer Candidate School so all the West Point cadets who wanted infantry would get into the infantry.

Chad was one of those. He had decided on infantry between his second and third years when he went to air assault school, a three-week course with the 101st Airborne. "Those guys were a cut above," he said. "Their professionalism and confidence: that was what I wanted." He would have to wait, though, not because there wasn't a slot for him but because his knee injury turned out to be a lot more serious than previously diagnosed. Another MRI in the spring showed the tear in the PCL. Surgery would soon follow, which meant that even though he would graduate on time with the rest of his class, he would not be off to basic training and Ranger School until the knee healed. He went back to Coach Berry and Coach Bond about the graduate assistant position he had originally been offered, and they were more than happy to have him, especially John Bond, who had developed a deep affinity with Chad.

"Really loved that guy," Bond would say years later. "Of all the young men I've coached, Chad is at the top."

It was a little frustrating. Chad had gone to the prep school, so he was behind a number of his high school classmates who graduated in four years and were already in the workforce. Now the rest of his West Point class would be heading off to basic, and he was stuck. The surgery would throw him at least another six months behind, meaning he wouldn't be ready to deploy until sometime in early 2003. With no other means to blow off steam, he rented a Winnebago with Zickefoose, Dodson, and Bartels and drove to Panama City Beach, Florida, for spring break in March 2002. With a cowboy hat on his head and camouflage flip-flops on his feet, Chad drove 1,216 miles from West Point to the Gulf of Mexico, singing Madonna's greatest hits off-key for most of the nineteen hours. "Come on, vogue . . ."

"Dude, that's pretty fucked up right there," Zickefoose said.

Chad couldn't care less. This was his final break before becoming an Army officer. He wasn't going to waste a second of it.

"We tried to drink every drop of beer in Panama City," Bartels said. "Of course, Chad found the prettiest girl on the beach and charmed her. She was ready to go back to West Point and marry him, but after three days, we couldn't drink another drop, so we pulled up stakes and drove out. I think that girl showed up later where the RV had been parked, and we were gone."

In Annapolis, Brian also felt the effects of change, but in a different way. In the cold winter of 2002, Navy cleaned out its coaching staff. Rick Lantz had faint hopes he might assume the reins, but he was told that a full and complete change was in order. He thanked the team and was gone by New Year's Day. The brass hired Charlie Weatherbie's old offensive coordinator, Paul Johnson, the guy who had called the plays when the Mids went to the Aloha Bowl in 1996 and beat Cal 43–38. It was heralded in the sports world as a great hire, and a bold move: one of the last by outgoing Naval Academy superintendent Vice Admiral John Ryan, and one of the first by new athletic director Chet Gladchuk.

Johnson had begun his college coaching career when Georgia Southern University, in the tiny southern town of Statesboro, took up football again after a forty-year hiatus. It was the perfect convergence of time and place, as Johnson, who had never played college football and whose only job in the game had been as an assistant high school coach in North Carolina, joined the staff of legendary coach Erk Russell. A defensive guru known for butting heads with his players without a helmet until his bald head bled, Russell was quite content to let Johnson handle the offense, especially after the

Eagles fielded a triple-option running game that became almost un-stoppable. In 1985 and 1986, just three years after starting a football program with no stadium and a crop of misfit walk-ons, Georgia Southern won back-to-back NCAA Division I-AA national championships with Paul Johnson as offensive coordinator.

Johnson went to the University of Hawaii as offensive coordinator in 1987 and stayed seven years, during which time the Rainbow Warriors went to their first major bowl and won their first WAC Conference Championship. Anxious to get back to the mainland, he signed on as Weatherbie's first offensive coordinator at Navy in 1995. It didn't go unnoticed that the best seasons Charlie had as head coach were the ones with Johnson calling the plays.

Georgia Southern lured Johnson back by offering him his first head coaching job in 1997. Just as he had done everywhere else, he won almost immediately. The Eagles lost in the national championship game in 1998 and then won back-to-back national titles in 1999 and 2000. A lot of Navy alumni wanted Johnson to be offered the head coaching job after the abysmal 2000 season in Annapolis, but with Jack Lengyel retiring and Weatherbie beating Army for his lone millennial win, the decision was made to give it one more year.

Now Johnson had agreed to move back to Navy as head coach. He started showing how different things would be from day one. If Weatherbie had been the sunny bright spot in the Mids' day, Johnson was a winter midnight. From the first team meeting, where he eyed each player with the dispassionate gaze of a butcher visiting a hog farm, Johnson brought an intensity to the football field that had been missing at Navy for many years. In his first week as head coach in January 2002, he brought the team in for strength and conditioning. During the workout, Johnson yelled, "Goddamnit, you are all pussies! I don't know how the hell you're going to be officers. You're not in good enough shape to be football players!"

Change began at that moment.

* * *

On Saturday, June 1, 2002, Chad graduated in Michie Stadium in full dress gray over white uniform. President Bush spoke again, this time to the entire class and a stadium filled with proud parents and alumni. The Jenkins clan drove up from Dublin and, like a lot of parents, they had to fight back emotions as the president said, "You walk in the tradition of Eisenhower and MacArthur, Patton and Bradley, the commanders who saved a civilization. And you walk in the tradition of second lieutenants who did the same, by fighting and dying on distant battlefields. Graduates of this academy have brought creativity and courage to every field of endeavor. West Point produced the chief engineer of the Panama Canal, the mind behind the Manhattan Project, the first American to walk in space. This fine institution gave us the man they say invented baseball and other young men over the years who perfected the game of football."

Chad couldn't help chuckling at that line. They had been far from perfect, but they had beaten Navy. That was enough perfection for him and many others.

"Every West Point class is commissioned to the armed forces," President Bush continued. "Some West Point classes are also commissioned by history to take part in a great new calling for their country. Speaking here to the Class of 1942, six months after Pearl Harbor, General Marshall said, 'We're determined that before the sun sets on this terrible struggle, our flag will be recognized throughout the world as a symbol of freedom on the one hand, and of overwhelming power on the other.'

"Officers graduating that year helped fulfill that mission, defeating Japan and Germany, and then reconstructing those nations as allies. West Point graduates of the 1940s saw the rise of a deadly new challenge, the challenge of imperial communism, and opposed it from Korea to Berlin, to Vietnam, and in the Cold War, from beginning to end. And as the sun set on their struggle, many of those West Point officers lived to see a world transformed.

"History has also issued its call to your generation."

Caps flew up and tears flowed down after the ceremony. The graduates all received commissions as second lieutenants on the spot, and all swore to "support and defend the Constitution of the United States against all enemies, foreign and domestic; and bear true faith and allegiance to the same . . ."

By the next morning, Chad was cruising the streets of Dublin, Ohio, in his four-wheel-drive truck, enjoying the summer and resting his knee. He attended house parties and caught up with old friends. Still a star in his hometown, he accepted congratulations from people who had seen him beat Navy, and he received good-luck wishes from those who knew he would end up going into combat.

One girl he had known off and on since middle school caught his eye again at a neighborhood gathering of young adults. Emily Kiehborth had been a year behind Chad throughout school, which meant they had graduated from college at the same time. A cheerleader at Penn State, Emily had known Chad enough to nod and say hello but little more. Chad had always been the star quarterback and she the bashful younger girl.

"If he'd spoken to me back when we were in high school I probably would have run off giggling with my girlfriends," Emily said.

But now, at age twenty-two, she had grown past the giggles and insecurities of youth, and when she kept running into Chad at house parties throughout the summer, they would talk. One night at a friend's house, Chad walked by Emily and said, "Hey, I really like your dainty purse."

She laughed and said, "Did you just use the word *dainty*?"

Three days later, he picked her up in his truck for their first date. They went to the Brazenhead, a crowded Irish bar in Columbus that was a favorite spot for Ohio State kids. Chad was a perfect gentleman, and Emily found herself curiously smitten, although she didn't know why. She was not from an Army family and didn't have any close friends who had been in the military. Going on a couple of dates with a guy like Chad was one thing, but to develop a relationship with him would require work. She'd never had to work especially hard at relationships. "We had no idea what we were doing," she would say later.

Emily had taken a job with GlaxoSmithKline and would be training in pharmaceutical sales throughout the fall in Philadelphia. Chad would be working at West Point as a graduate assistant until his knee was at full strength. They agreed to see each other when they could, which they did, with Chad driving down on his days off to surprise her, and she working her schedule to be with him when he could break free. It wasn't the most convenient way to get to know each other, but the more they were together the more they wanted to be together. Somehow, they believed they could make it work, even with Chad's deployment looming just over the horizon.

In the summer of 2002, two-a-day practices in Annapolis started at 0445, a time of the morning so black that the bugs were still asleep. The only sounds piercing the crisp Maryland air were the river waters lapping against nearby docks and men grunting and panting like horses as they ran. Every so often a "come on, we got this" would come out of one Midshipman encouraging another.

Then the hitting started: the slaps of pads followed by guttural expulsions somewhere between growls and moans. And there were whistles, loud and high and short. The entire team was on the field, sprinting, rolling, working agility and reaction drills, hitting sleds, and high stepping through obstacles. No one was spared. When a starting receiver went down with a ghost injury after getting hit on a crossing pattern, Coach Johnson watched dispassionately as the doctor checked him out. When no discernible injury was discovered, Johnson demoted the player on the spot.

The coach yelled, cursed, and threatened, proving to anyone who had missed the message in the spring that he was the anti-Weatherbie. Football practice would no longer be one of the easiest parts of a Midshipman's day. Johnson made them run when they broke the huddle too slow; he yelled and made them run when they jumped offside, when they hung their heads, and when they stopped playing before the stinging sound of the whistle hit them like a ball-peen hammer. Johnson didn't care if you had started every game since you arrived on base; he didn't care if you were a star recruit with world-class speed; and he didn't care what your statistics were in the months or years before he arrived.

"You were oh-and-eleven, how good could your stats be?" he would ask, not expecting an answer.

Throughout the mornings, the Mids would hear only one voice: Johnson's. "No wonder you pussies went oh-and-eleven!" he screamed. "Half of Bancroft could outrun your sorry asses. Now move!"

Brian was next to his friend, defensive tackle Pete Beuttenmuller, during one of the few breaks in the morning action. "Why do I get the sense that football is going to suck this year?" Brian said.

And he was right. The Mids got off to a promising start, winning on the road in Dallas against Southern Methodist University. It was Navy's first victory in eighteen months, and it felt great. Craig Candeto, the quarterback who replaced Brian Madden, threw for 106 yards and rushed for 153 and three touchdowns, and the entire team enjoyed the moment, especially since it was an emphatic 38–7 romp. Perhaps this signaled good things to come.

That turned out to be wishful thinking. Despite all the hard work and all the intense conditioning Coach Johnson employed, Navy still wasn't very good.

"We just didn't have enough athletes," Johnson would say later. "They were outstanding men, every one of them. I'm honored to have coached them and gotten to know them, and I'm in awe of their bravery, but we simply didn't have enough talent out there to win football games."

That became painfully evident on September 7, 2002. As people throughout the country braced themselves for the feelings that would accompany the first anniversary of 9/11, Navy hosted the twenty-first-ranked team in the country: the Wolfpack of North Carolina

State, led by a superstar quarterback named Philip Rivers. All the positive energy the Mids had drawn from their win in Dallas quickly evaporated as Rivers picked them apart.

On the third play of the game Rivers hit Wolfpack receiver Bryan Peterson in perfect stride over the middle for a sixty-four-yard touchdown. That was okay. One touchdown was not insurmountable. Brian and his teammates were still encouraging each other on the sideline. Then Navy fumbled the ensuing kickoff and Lamont Reid, a member of NC State's kickoff team, scooped the ball up and ran thirty yards for another score. Just like that, the lead was fourteen points.

Three plays later, the Mids fumbled again, giving Rivers the ball on the twenty-eight-yard line. Five plays after that he threw an eighteen-yard touchdown strike and the rout was in full swing. As the game got out of hand, Navy players slinked away from Coach Johnson. Losing was something the upperclassmen were accustomed to, but their coach did not handle it well. Once the NC State lead leaped above twenty points, players fled from Johnson like he was contagious, leaving the coach to walk in a zone of privacy on the sideline. The final score was 65–19, an embarrassing home defeat that quashed any fantasies the Mids had that they might have turned things around.

After a week off, Navy lost another home game on September 21, to Northwestern. This one was a lot closer, though. Candeto threw for 212 yards and rushed for another 138 as the offense put up a total of forty points. When the quarterback scored on a one-yard touchdown run in the fourth quarter, the Mids took a three-point lead. But the defense was still getting pushed around. Northwestern scored two late touchdowns to win 49–40.

"I'm not used to losing," Johnson said. "I'm out of these speeches. I don't have any more left. They've used all of mine. We just need to play."

Brian continued to play intermittently throughout his senior season, contributing at linebacker and continuing to be the suicide man on kickoffs. He was a warrior at both spots, but at six-one and two hundred pounds, he was outsized by every blocker he faced and most of the runners he tried to tackle. By his senior year he had grown wise enough to realize where he stood in the pecking order of football. His love of the game would never make him four inches taller, thirty pounds heavier, or two seconds faster. Heart would carry a man only so far in the game.

Coach Johnson knew it as well, but he refused to let his players stop believing they could win. "Brian was a great man and a dedicated player who would do whatever was asked of him at a hundred percent," Johnson said later. "But he was outsized. I wish we'd had five or six other guys like Brian. Unfortunately we had forty like him."

On September 28, 2002, Navy lost its third game in a row at home when they fell to Duke 43–17. As was required, the entire Brigade of Midshipmen stood and watched every painful down. Afterward the football players received a lot of cold shoulders and hostile stares from their fellow mids. By then, fifty-four weeks after the 9/11 attacks, casual fans weren't as emotionally invested in Navy football as they had been the year before. Wins and losses mattered again, and the Midshipmen looked to be as far from winning as a team could get.

Things got worse after the Duke game. Coach Johnson began pulling seniors and other veteran players and going with underclassmen in the hopes of finding someone who could get the job done. It didn't work, at least not in the short run. Navy lost by forty-one points to Air Force in Colorado Springs the first Saturday in October, and they lost again to Rice at home in Annapolis a week later.

Boston College beat them by twenty-five points in a game that could have been much more lopsided if the Eagles had wanted to run up the score. Then Tulane quarterback J. P. Losman threw a season-high five touchdown passes against Brian and his defensive teammates in New Orleans. Once again the Navy offense gained yardage and put up points, scoring thirty against the Green Wave, but the Midshipmen gave up fifty-one.

"We have to play perfect," Johnson told the team afterward. "You don't have enough talent to win on talent, so you have to play flawlessly every time you go out. I know that's a tough thing to do. I'm frustrated and you're frustrated, but we have to continue to execute and hope we can put together that flawless game."

They came close on November 4. Playing in Baltimore in front of a raucous sellout crowd at Ravens Stadium, the Midshipmen played as near to perfect as they could against the ninth-ranked team in the country. Navy led Notre Dame by eight points in the fourth quarter, but the defense gave up two late scores, the final one coming when the Fighting Irish quarterback, Carlyle Holiday, threw a sixty-seven-yard touchdown pass to Omar Jenkins with two minutes left in the game. The final score was 30–23.

But there were signs of good things on the horizon. The silver lining in the eight-game losing streak was the offense, which continued to put up good numbers and show improved blocking and ball control each week. Notre Dame ranked eighth in rush defense, yet the Midshipmen were able to gain two hundred yards on the ground. The season was lost for this team, and for seniors like Brian Stann, their football careers were destined to end in ways they would rather forget, but Coach Johnson seemed to be moving the program in the right direction.

They lost badly to Connecticut the second week in November, but then, the week before Thanksgiving 2002, Navy led Wake Forest by four points with a minute to play. Once again the offense had put up good numbers, rushing for an impressive 444 yards and scoring twenty-seven points. But once again the defense couldn't make tackles when they were needed most. Running back Fabian Davis gave the Demon Deacons the lead with fifty-three seconds left in the game when he ran in from five yards for a touchdown.

The score was 30–27. Navy would head to their final game
year, the 2002 Army-Navy Game, having lost ten in a row.

It was no consolation to Brian or his teammates that the Army team
was no better. With Chad in the press box keeping stats and helping John Bond with personnel changes, the cadets lost their first
nine games. Todd Berry was no Paul Johnson. He couldn't threaten
and run and drill more wins out of his players. He was demanding,
but not over-the-top. Like Johnson, Berry simply didn't have enough
athletes, and with the recruiting problems that came post-9/11, he
wasn't likely to get many more.

"You could see it when you were in [the recruits'] houses," Bond
said. "You would give the pitch about all the great things West Point
had to offer: the lifestyle, the discipline, the character it took to be
a cadet and what it would mean to you for the rest of your life, and
the kids would be sold. They would be ready to sign. But then the
mama would get involved, and when the mama figured out that her
son would be going to war after college, we never heard from them
again."

The Conference USA schedule didn't help, either. When Army
was an independent, which it had been prior to 1998, coaches could
always mix in some easier games to go with the traditional rivalries.
But once the cadets joined a conference, it was one tough game after
another. After an opening loss at Holy Cross, they had Rutgers (a
44–0 rout), Louisville (45–14), Southern Miss (27–6), East Carolina
(59–24), TCU (46–27), Houston (56–42), UAB (29–26), and Air
Force (49–30).

The cadets finally won at Tulane on November 16, week ten of
one of the longest seasons of Todd Berry's career.

"I hurt for Coach Berry and Coach Bond," Chad said. "I was just
there helping out, it didn't even feel like work, but you could see that
they were concerned for their livelihoods. They felt like they weren't

oing to be there much longer, and as the losses kept coming, those
elings grew."

The workload didn't slow down, though. Chad was up before
dawn getting ready for the day's practice, helping Bond game-plan
and break down film of the upcoming opponent. Then they had practice, and then a post-practice debriefing. After that it was recruiting
calls. Chad had California, so he was on the phones to kids on the
West Coast until midnight.

That level of effort made the losses hurt even more, especially
from Chad's perspective. He was still close enough to the players
that he understood what they were going through and what they
were thinking, but he was also seeing the program from a new angle.
Now he understood how much coaches gave of themselves, and
how their livelihoods hinged on what kind of Saturday afternoon
a twenty-one-year-old college kid had on the football field. It was a
sobering realization, one he would never forget.

A loss to Memphis, the final Conference USA opponent of the
year, cast a pall over the team. They had one more shot to salvage the
year and perhaps Coach Berry's job. They needed to beat Navy again.

This time the Army-Navy Game was at Giants Stadium in East
Rutherford, New Jersey, one of the few times it had been moved out
of Philadelphia. The people of New York, less than ten miles away,
were thrilled, and seventy-nine thousand filled the place to cheer,
even though there wasn't much drama after the first couple of minutes. The offense that Paul Johnson had been forging through fire
all year finally clicked and put together that perfect, flawless game.
Navy scored touchdowns on their first eight possessions. Candeto,
who had taken the brunt of much of Johnson's wrath throughout the
year, set a school record with six rushing touchdowns. The Midshipmen racked up 508 total yards of offense in a game that set records
for lopsidedness.

Brian got more playing time than he had in two seasons during the final game of his career, in part because Navy kicked off so many times, but also because every player on the team got onto the field before the final whistle. The Midshipmen annihilated the Cadets by a score of 58–12, the biggest rout since 1973 and the most points scored by one side in the game's history. Just like Chad, Brian went out a winner in the most important football game of his life: the last one he ever played.

Emily had driven up to New York for the game, and she and Chad gave Coach Bond a ride back to West Point from East Rutherford. The trip was one of the quietest Chad could remember. He wanted to say something, anything, to ease the pain over Army's loss, but no words seemed adequate. After the game, Coach Berry said, "I've been around the game for a while. This has to be the toughest one I've ever experienced." All Chad could do was empathize and get on with his life. He had Infantry Officer Basic Course (IOBC) and Ranger School ahead of him. Football was something he had to put on a shelf forever. As far as he was concerned, it would never be missed.

The next fall, Coach Todd Berry was released halfway through the 2003 regular season after Army went 0-6. He would leave West Point, the place his wife had dreamed of having him coach, with a record of 5-35. But he found a home quickly, taking a job as offensive coordinator at the University of Louisiana–Monroe.

The head coach who hired him was Charlie Weatherbie.

PART TWO

WARRIORS

CHAPTER 7

People sleep peaceably in their beds at night only because rough men stand ready to do violence on their behalf.

—GEORGE ORWELL

Long before Chad arrived at Army IOBC in Fort Benning, Georgia, the drill instructors had heard that they needed to watch out for the West Point guys. They were the ones most likely to get too drunk, too loud, too carried away at nights and on weekends, far more so than the OCS or ROTC candidates. The reason was the West Point regimen.

Other officers had gotten the drinking and carousing out of their systems in their early college years or during some transition period right out of high school. Cadets hadn't had that opportunity. Every second of their college lives had been planned and every action scrutinized. While other eighteen- to twenty-two-year-olds were going to parties and maturing in their relationships with the opposite sex, West Point cadets were going out for field artillery exercises, lining up for morning formation, and sneaking kisses from female cadets whenever they could, with a constant fear of violating some fraternization rule.

To other recruits, basic training was the most challenging environment they had ever experienced; to West Point graduates it was like gaining their freedom.

Chad did not fall victim to the party scene, in part because he didn't know any of the people in his Officer Basic Class. If he had gone to IOBC immediately after graduation, he would have been there with his West Point classmates, and it might have been like the spring break Winnebago trip, but the six-month delay eliminated a lot of temptation. By January 2003, when he drove through the gates at Fort Benning, he was the only academy graduate there. He had no desire to drink and carouse with strangers. IOBC was going to be tough enough without any added distractions.

The first thing he noticed when driving in was the jump towers extending above the treetops. They looked like partially constructed amusement park rides, with vertical scaffolding rising 250 feet and supporting crossbeam platforms. From any angle, they looked like a series of giant T's overlooking several single-story, nondescript buildings and a lot of open fields. It would be weeks before he strapped on a parachute and was pulled to the top of one of those arms, where, on the count of three, he would be released to float back to earth. Just the thought of it made his knee hurt in those early days.

IOBC was a sixteen-week training course that started with physical fitness. Road marches of up to twelve miles at 0400 with full rucks were just the start. After a quick morning chow, new commissioned officers began with chin-ups and sit-ups and all manner of calisthenics. Then it was off to the obstacle course, where men crawled on their bellies and backs beneath barbed wire, climbed ropes and walls, and shimmied across logs; they maneuvered up and down thirty-foot posts connected by four-by-fours spaced five feet apart, and climbed headfirst down ladderlike structures before high stepping over hurtles. Immediately after completing the course they would be asked questions or instructed to read and plot coordinates on a grid. An officer's ability to reason, solve problems, and make decisions while exhausted was fundamental, so it was tested often.

Chad did well in all these areas. He had been working with obstacles for five years at the academy and had been making decisions under physical and mental stress since he took his first snap as quarterback. But one of the obstacles in the course, island hopping, was a concern. That particular obstacle required the soldier to hop from one post to another without falling. The posts looked like stumps, large telephone poles buried so that just a few feet protruded aboveground, nothing that would cause any serious damage if the officer fell—unless, of course, that officer was recovering from a torn PCL. Chad worried that if he hit one of the islands wrong, the knee could buckle, and he might end up face-first in the hard Georgia clay. It was one thing to push your legs in rehab, but this would be a test of his ability to perform in the field.

One deep breath, and he leaped onto the first island, and then the second, and the third. It was a test of speed, agility, and balance, things Chad had been expert at since boyhood on two good legs. The knee felt perfect. He jumped again, and it held. By the end of the obstacle, all residual doubt had vanished. He knew he was at full strength.

Almost the entire sixteen weeks were devoted to field training. Chad earned proficiencies on every infantry weapon, including live-fire exercises in the dark with night-vision goggles, where the challenge was always the loss of depth perception. He learned about communication equipment and how to give orders to a platoon over a radio in the middle of a firefight; he learned about voice discipline and how the tone used by a commanding officer was at least as important and sometimes more so than the words he used. He also learned when and how to call in artillery and air support so that he wouldn't get his own men killed by friendly fire.

He learned how to repair a vehicle and secure a perimeter; he learned grappling techniques for close-quarter hand-to-hand combat. There were also courses on how to defend against a nuclear, biological, or chemical attack. And he had to master land navigation, a specialty that was variously maddening and thrilling. Instructors would plot several landmark coordinates on a map and instruct the officers to make their way from point A to point B by way of points C, D, E, and F. The trick was to do so in dense pine thickets with nothing more than a compass and a map. And, in some cases, he was out there after being up for eighteen hours and having run five miles, marched another ten, and undergone all manner of other drills throughout the day.

There were drills on urban combat. Benning had an area filled with empty concrete-block buildings that resembled small towns everywhere from Kosovo to Kandahar. Soldiers drilled on everything from breaching and clearing a multistory structure to finding their way out of a smoke-filled firefight. As part of the drills, Chad and his classmates would have to lead a platoon into and out of urban settings where they couldn't see five feet in front of them while taking fire from areas they couldn't identify.

And they learned how to blow things up. Walls, gates, roadblocks, vehicles: if it got in the way or needed destroying, an infantry officer needed to know how to get rid of it.

After sixteen weeks of basic, where he qualified in every discipline, Chad moved on to Jump School, where the towers came in. Soldiers are introduced to jumps easily but quickly. They start at a small platform from which they slide to a landing on a zip line. Then they move a little higher and then higher still until they are ready for the towers. There they are hauled up by their parachutes and dropped from 250 feet. The physical demands weren't as tough as overcoming millions of years of evolution reminding Chad that he couldn't fly. Even though he knew intellectually that the chute was there and that if he went through his steps he was going to float to the ground without any problem, his body and mind still had an almost overwhelming desire to flee. It's the same instinct that makes riding a roller coaster exciting. Even though he knew he was safe, humans are hardwired to fear falling.

Chad's heart raced, and his head swam. Everyone's did the first couple of times. When it came time to jump out of an airplane, the chutes were initially tethered to a static line inside the C-130, which was a good thing given the shock to his system when the rear hatch opened and the sky rushed in like an intruder. His first jumpmaster instructor waved a fist in the air and yelled "Go! Go! Go!" as one soldier after another tumbled out into the cold blue air. Third in line, he didn't have time to be scared before he was flying.

For nineteen weeks, Emily Kiehborth had been dating her new boyfriend mostly over the phone. A new sales associate with GlaxoSmithKline, Emily was based in Findlay, Ohio, a nice midwestern town without much for a new college graduate to do other than order takeout pizza and watch television in her apartment. She still wasn't sure what to make of her relationship with Chad, except that she missed him when he wasn't around, and when he was, it was like he had never left.

Every weekend Chad had free during his five months of IOBC and Airborne School, they would meet. He would leave Fort Benning and drive north on I-75 every Friday afternoon, and she would leave Findlay and drive south. Their meeting spot was Knoxville, Tennessee. Without traffic, Emily could make it in six hours. Chad always had traffic through Atlanta and Chattanooga, but he could still drive it in just over five. They would spend all day Saturday together, going out on the town with the University of Tennessee students, and then stay together until midafternoon on Sunday, when they would jump back in their vehicles and head in opposite directions.

"I was focusing on my career, but I was also thinking about him and what I was doing with him," she said. "Chad David Jenkins messed up my whole life plan, but it turned out to be in a great way, a way that I needed."

They did the long-distance thing from January until June 2003. Then Chad went to Ranger School and the weekend meetings and phone calls stopped. The only communication for the next sixty-two days was through letters, hers penned from the comfort of her apartment and his scribbled in pencil from a dark barracks or while lying on the brick-hard ground.

Up until that moment, Chad only thought he had been challenged. Ranger School showed him that everything he had experienced to that point—Beast during his plebe year at West Point, two-a-day football practices, summer training, and IOBC—was like a pleasant jog through a springtime park.

"Ranger School sucks," Chad said. "It's a sixty-two-day gut check where you are constantly sleep-deprived, food-deprived, and mentally and physically exhausted, really beyond the point that you think you can make it. It teaches you that the mind and body can overcome a lot more than you think they can. Ranger training prepares you to be in situations the average person doesn't think a human being can survive."

Adding to the intensity was the fact that at 9:34 P.M. EST on March 19, 2003, ten weeks before Chad graduated from Jump School and began Ranger training, coalition forces, including the U.S. Army 3rd Infantry Division, the 101st Airborne, and the 15th Marine Expeditionary Unit, invaded Iraq. Now, for the first time since World War II, the United States Army was fighting on two major fronts, one an urban war in a blistering desert and the other a tribal conflict in the mountains of Afghanistan.

Chad longed to get through training and join the fight. The next step in that process was Phase I of Ranger School at Fort Benning's Camp Rogers, a peaceful pine-tree-laden area near the Alabama border where 60 percent of Ranger candidates were dropped because they couldn't pass the physical fitness tests. In the first hour of day one, Chad was told to drop and start reeling off push-ups. He had remained in good shape from football, even though it had been more than a year since he'd taken a snap, so he was certain that this would not be that tough. He soon found out how wrong he was. The initial Ranger Assessment Phase (RAP) requires candidates to do forty perfect push-ups in two minutes, nose to the ground, palms flat and shoulder width apart, and zero bend in the torso. Then, with no rest, the candidate must do a minimum of fifty-nine full bent-knee sit-ups in two minutes. From there the candidate must do six chin-ups from a dead hang with no lower-body movement. Chad struggled to get through the chin-ups, but he made it.

The candidate behind him was not as fortunate. After reeling off the push-ups and sit-ups without a hitch, the candidate grabbed the chin-up bar, his feet hanging perfectly still a foot above the ground. He pulled himself up. One. Then a struggle and hesitant pull, but the chin made the bar. Two. At that point the men in line behind him were cheering, chanting his name and yelling words of motivation and encouragement. The soldier's arms quivered and the veins in his neck bulged as he pulled, stuttering and stopping a couple of times before his chin finally reached the bar. Three. After a few deep breaths and more shouts from his buddies, he pulled again. His face, neck, and arms turned crimson as his progress slowed. Halfway up, his muscles failed, and he dropped to the ground. It was over. He was out of the Ranger course in the first five minutes.

"There is no room for anything less than excellence," Chad said when describing the Rangers. "It's one of the only places left where you can say there are no slack employees. You can go into any organization, even the FBI, and there is a bottom fifteen percent that doesn't meet the standards everyone else sets. They're not bad people or terrible employees, but they just don't merit excellence. Teachers, cops, businesspeople: they all have them, the employees that do enough, but just enough, to get by. That doesn't exist in the Rangers. If you don't cut it, you're gone. Immediately."

Ranger history permeates every corner of Fort Benning. The National Infantry Museum, located just outside the gates, has a special Ranger section, and the acronym RLTW can be found on signs and buildings and even on the signature lines of most of the Ranger officers' e-mails. It stands for "Rangers Lead the Way," a motto dating

back to D-Day and the assault on the Dog White section of Omaha
Beach. During the battle to inch inland, Brigadier General Norman
Cota, the assistant commanding officer of the 29th Infantry Division
at the time, approached a major named Max Schneider.

"What outfit is this?" Cote asked.

Schneider shouted, "Fifth Rangers, sir!"

Taken by the gutsy enthusiasm of Schneider and his men, Cota
said, "Well, goddamnit, Rangers, lead the way!"

Six miles west of Omaha Beach on D-Day, the 2nd Rangers
were doing just that, leading an assault against a battery of 155 mm
German guns atop the cliffs of Pointe du Hoc. Cut off and outnumbered, the Rangers destroyed the guns and then fought off counter-
attacks for two days until help arrived. A memorial in the shape of a
bayonet sits atop the cliffs of Pointe du Hoc today to commemorate
the event.

A similarly shaped memorial sits in the shade of two oak trees
between Running Avenue and 1st Battalion Drive at Fort Benning.
The Ranger Memorial at Benning is slightly less weathered than the
one on the French coast, and to the average civilian, the giant obelisk that is the centerpiece for 4,700 polished marble stones memo-
rializing fallen Rangers does resemble a bayonet. It is actually the
likeness of a Fairbairn-Sykes fighting knife, designed by the British
and given to the Rangers while they were training in Scotland. The
individual stones at the base do not show the ranks of the men they
memorialize, only the word *Ranger*, which, to those who are part of
that fraternity, is far more important.

"You don't wear rank at Ranger School," Chad said. "You wear
your name and 'U.S. Army.' That's it. My first Ranger buddy in the
Benning phase was a Bat Boy [a name given to the enlisted men
in the Ranger Battalion] who had already been overseas fighting in
Afghanistan as a private. Now, he was in Ranger School with me.
Talk about humbling. He was nineteen years old, I was twenty-two,
and I was looking up to him. That opened my eyes to a whole new
perspective of military life."

The training also brought a new perspective. Passing the RAP required candidates to run five miles in under forty minutes after the push-ups, sit-ups, and chin-ups. Then they swam for fifty meters with one arm in and one arm out of the water while wearing full combat gear. Prospective Rangers were then dropped from a high-dive platform while blindfolded and told to swim ashore. Once those tasks were either passed or failed (and failure resulted in immediate dismissal from the program; no points for effort), soldiers were submerged and told to get rid of all their weight-bearing gear before swimming to the surface.

The water drills were conducted at Victory Pond, a murky green pool near the Chattahoochee River, the kind of place where no parent would ever let their kids swim, for fear of what disease they might catch. Bacteria and earaches were the least of the Ranger candidates' concerns. After the water survival tests, they had to go through something called the Water Confidence Test, a three-phased drill designed to make sure the men could overcome a fear of heights and water while stressed and exhausted. First, Chad and his fellow candidates had to walk across a log that was thirty feet above the water. You couldn't run or crawl or even hesitate. The assessment, which again was pass or fail, was whether you could "calmly" navigate the obstacle.

Once across the log, Chad had to crawl on a rope, again suspended thirty feet above the water, touching a Ranger placard at the other end. Then he dropped into the pond, a plunge equivalent to an Olympic platform dive. Once in the water again, he shed his gear and swam to a ladder where he climbed seventy feet to a zip-line platform. With no safety harnesses and exhaustion so profound that many candidates could not see the cable or even their own hands, Chad secured a pulley to the line and slid down to a lower altitude where he once again plunged into the drink.

Fear or hesitation or simply slipping and falling meant immediate dismissal. The water phase weeded out a healthy portion of the class.

Then came more land navigation, this time at night with no flashlights and no talking: just a map, a compass, and several landmarks you had to visit before sunrise. Speaking or violating "light discipline" sent a few more candidates packing.

Once daylight broke, Chad and his buddies lit out on a three-mile terrain run in full gear. Chad was in good shape: better than most, or so he thought. He had run up and down stadium steps during summer football camps, gone through agility training, done bounding jumps where he ran the length of the football field, taking the largest strides possible, and then ran that length again backward. He had tied a rope to his waist and pulled a truck tire as fast as possible for forty yards. By civilian standards he came to Ranger School already an elite athlete. But RAP almost killed him.

After the three-mile run over hill and dale, through pine forests and gnarly hay fields, Chad faced the Malvesti Field Obstacle Course, which bore a remarkable resemblance to a Georgia hog farm. The obstacle everyone dreaded was the "worm pit," a series of shallow twenty-five-meter-long ditches watered down into mud holes and covered at knee height with barbed wire. Chad and the other students had to low- and high-crawl through those mud-filled trenches in full gear first on their bellies and again on their backs.

After a full day of nonstop action, Chad adjourned to barracks, where he fell into the sleep of the dead. It wasn't long, though. Three hours later, instructors were banging metal against metal, waking everybody up and getting them out into formation in what Chad figured had to be the middle of the night.

Three hours of sleep was standard. Five was a blessing from heaven. Even after the initial fitness phase, candidates struggled through sleep and food deprivation. Chad had figured he could breeze through the airborne refresher phase, especially since he had just finished Jump School, but nothing is easy when you find yourself sleeping while standing, and even nodding off for a second or two while running. It wasn't uncommon for a Ranger instructor to see a student running along a trail only to veer off into a ditch or a tree. There were candidates who thought they were putting coins in a vending machine when they were actually wedging quarters into the bark of a Georgia pine. Nobody slept while jumping out of airplanes, but they caught five minutes of shut-eye everywhere they could.

Instructors knew this and had their eyes peeled for napping. Land navigation drills, or "LanNav," as it was commonly called, was the easiest time to screw up. In the still, predawn hours with no sounds but the low melodic songs of the crickets and tree frogs, the candidates could simply nestle up to a tree to check their compasses and maps. For many, their next conscious memory was an instructor standing nose to nose with them asking them why they were asleep. It was the last thing they would hear before being shipped out of Ranger School.

Demolition training was another time when nobody nodded off. The adrenaline rush from blowing things up kept soldiers alert. But they all went through the training with a growing sense of dread. The final stage of RAP was a twelve-mile night march from Camp Rogers to Camp Darby (both located within Fort Benning's 182,000 acres) in full gear, carrying rucks, guns, ammo, and supplies.

"I had a 240 Bravo, the heavy machine gun," Chad said. "I was carrying that thing, and it was rough, but I was making it. But then guys started falling out. We had to bring everybody and everything, so we were taking their stuff and pulling them along. We started at midnight and didn't get there until first light. That, to me, was the most grueling part."

On May 19, 2003, just two weeks before Chad entered Ranger School, Brian graduated from the United States Naval Academy wearing his dress uniform, with his family watching from the stands of Navy–Marine Corps Memorial Stadium. Secretary of Defense Donald Rumsfeld spoke, and caps flew amid a chorus of cheers at the end. But the ceremony took on a more somber tone than normal. Two Naval Academy graduates had already been killed in Iraq. As

Brian accepted the gold bars indicative of his new status as a Marine Corps second lieutenant, he and his fellow classmates knew that those deaths would not be the last.

For Brian, the transition from Naval Academy firstie to Marine Corps officer was simple. He already fit the mold. As difficult as it is for some civilians to understand the culture, a marine is always easy to spot: the head shaved except for a flat strip of stubble on top, the lean muscle and erect stance as he props up the bar in a honky-tonk, fearing nothing except being asked out onto the dance floor. The marine has the loudest laugh at the party, but is also the most unfailingly polite; the one who never sees a woman walk by without checking out her backside, but never addresses her with anything but "ma'am." He can kill, skin, cook, and eat a rabbit in under an hour, but rarely hunts for sport. He will die for his country and for people he doesn't know, while his closest human connections, no matter how many years he's been married or how many children he has raised, are his fellow marines.

Just a couple weeks after graduation, Brian left for Quantico, Virginia, and The Basic School (TBS), the twenty-six-week course that turns newly commissioned Marine second lieutenants into combat-ready leaders. "To lead warriors, you have to be a warrior," is the unofficial motto at TBS. Enlisted marines went through basic at either the Recruit Training Depot in San Diego—"vacation basic," as some marines called it—or Parris Island, South Carolina, a place about which no one ever joked unless they were making comparisons to hell. No Marine basic course was easy. This was a group that prided themselves on working harder, withstanding more, and getting the job done with less than any other segment of the armed forces.

Just like Chad, Brian had been asked to stay on an extra year, as a graduate assistant on Coach Paul Johnson's staff at Annapolis. He turned the job down. "It was a great honor to be asked," he said. "But by my senior year the country was already at war. We had guys in the fight. There was no way I could stay stateside knowing that my classmates and my former teammates were in the thick of it."

The fate of timing can be a terrible thing in life, but especially in the military, as Brian would find out on more than one occasion. He didn't know it at the time, but he would have saved himself a great deal of heartache and anxiety if he had accepted Coach Johnson's offer and helped out with the football team for one more season.

As it was, he showed up at Quantico in June 2003 and the first thing he heard was one of the instructors barking, "You are going to war. Our job is to prepare you for that eventuality. Assuming you finish your basic school training and your MOS [military occupational specialty] training, nine months from now you will be leading men in combat. You will be responsible for the lives of the men under your command."

If they hadn't taken TBS seriously before, the marines in Brian's class did now. The instructors reminded them daily that failing to act as they were being instructed could get people killed.

"It wasn't just about being the best Marine officer anymore," Brian said. "It was about not being the guy who went over there and got people killed. Nobody wants to be that guy. If you didn't care or if you weren't taking it seriously enough, they rolled you back to another class, and if you really didn't care, they kicked you out. Every class had three or four guys that the instructors said, 'You're not good enough. You're going through again.'"

The first thing he had to accept was the lack of respect he'd get for being an academy grad. Instructors yelled that the Annapolis guys were soft and had gotten out of shape. Nothing could have been farther from the truth, especially for guys like Brian who had played football and remained in top physical condition. The real gripe, Brian learned later, was that they thought the academy grads were too comfortable and lackadaisical around officers. Marine captains at the Naval Academy were a dime a dozen. On any given day a midshipman would interact with five or six Marine captains or Navy JGs (lieutenants, junior grade). They might also see two or three Navy captains or Marine colonels and a general or admiral or two.

The place was always crawling with brass. In Brian's time at the academy the secretary of defense had visited numerous times, as had members of the Joint Chiefs of Staff. The vice president had taken a couple of tours and the president had spoken at commencement. So when a Marine captain walked by at TBS, the academy guys stood at attention and saluted, but they weren't doing backflips for him. The captains at TBS expected backflips, so Brian retooled his mind-set and gave them what they wanted.

Every Marine officer going through TBS, no matter whether he or she was going to be an aviator, a logistics specialist, infantry, or supply, learned to be a provisional rifle platoon commander and how to lead a platoon on a night raid or into an enemy house or compound. They learned how to handle being surrounded by hostiles and how to take a bridge or road and secure a perimeter. They learned how to use a bayonet attached to a rifle—a fighting tactic most civilians assumed went out with the doughboys of World War I—and they learned to pull themselves through a drainpipe full of water, combining the worst elements of fear and claustrophobia into one panic-inducing drill.

They were also taught hand-to-hand combat. In the middle of the night, Brian and his classmates were awakened by instructors barging into the barracks, firing weapons, and setting off blasts. They were herded outside, where they fell into formation and were led on a five-mile run through the darkness to an empty cinder-block house. There Brian was ordered to sit straight-legged on the floor in a room so dark he couldn't see an inch in front of his face. A second after being seated, Brian felt someone sit down behind him, pressing against him back-to-back. From the sound of things, he assumed the same scene was playing out throughout the room. Everyone in the class was paired off with a partner and each pair sat facing away from each other on the floor.

Once everyone was settled, the order came: "Fight!" Brian turned and fought the man behind him, just as every other marine in the room did. And just like every other person in the room, Brian didn't know if the guy behind him was fifty pounds heavier or lighter than him, whether he was a jujitsu master or a skinny kid from Manhattan who had never been in so much as a playground shoving match. It didn't matter. The second the order came, Brian turned and engaged his enemy for that night.

"They want you indoctrinated in violence so that you no longer become nervous about it," Brian said. "The physical pressure is tough, but the mental pressure is the greatest. They want to throw you a curveball, distract you, and take you out of your comfort level, and do everything they can to make sure you can lead through anything."

The Iraq War was just a few months old when Brian went to TBS, but the Afghanistan conflict would turn two years old while he was training. "Even at night when everybody was exhausted, guys would be reading publications and doing homework because they were getting the cutting-edge tactics from the front lines," Brian said.

Once Army Ranger candidates at Fort Benning left Camp Rogers and moved to Camp Darby, RAP was officially over, but you would have never known it from looking at the Darby Queen, a quiet, park-like area with wooden walls, a rope net, some other ropes hanging down from platforms, and logs and posts planted strategically around the soft dirt. It could have been mistaken for an adult playground until you watched the men work their way through the various obstacles. Almost immediately, Rangers were paired off into sets of "Ranger buddies." At Camp Darby, a Ranger buddy could occasionally be heard encouraging his partner, pulling him along, "Up and over, you got it. That's it. Dig deep, we've got this." Once paired in twos, Rangers were no longer looked upon as individuals. They were buddies, performing as one. Failure by one was failure for both, because a Ranger buddy's job was to make sure his partner succeeded.

Nobody wanted to get this far only to be shipped out because his buddy couldn't get through one more obstacle course.

After Chad passed the Darby Queen, a stressful test but one he flew through without any hiccups, he started on the tactical, or Squad Combat Operations, phase of the school. That included reconnaissance and assault missions, responding to ambushes, and working in rapid infils and exfils (shorthand for getting in and out of an area: infiltration and exfiltration). This was the nuts and bolts of what Chad would experience in the field: assaulting an enemy position, holding a strategic asset like a bridge or a building, reacting to enemy contact, breaking enemy contact, maintaining communication, and analyzing and assessing a combat situation. These were all the basics taught in a rapid-fire setting at Camp Darby.

"That was the part where I felt like I started making progress toward becoming a platoon leader," Chad said. "That was when the fundamentals of leadership began to apply.

He passed all the proficiencies, which meant that he would bus out of Fort Benning and head north for Phase II, the Mountain Phase.

"It can't get worse," he told himself. He couldn't have been more wrong.

Mountain Phase took place in the middle of nowhere, a place called Camp Merrill, in Dahlonega, Georgia, near the southern starting point of the Appalachian Trail. It was a part of the country that had always been no-man's-land, filled with bootleggers and hillbillies and, in recent years, meth labs. The movie *Deliverance* had been filmed a few miles away, and there were parts of the wilderness where little had changed in a century. The Celtic immigrants who settled the region were marauding looters who killed each other for sport and made their livings distilling whiskey from corn, the only crop that would grow on their inhospitable hillsides. They came over in clans from Scotland

and Ireland and in clans they remained, ever suspicious of newcomers and doing everything in their power to keep them away. During Prohibition, a third of all the bootleg whiskey crafted south of Tennessee came from the hills and hollows of Dahlonega.

It was the perfect spot to train for combat in the mountainous, tribal nation of Afghanistan.

A couple of days on the hillsides and Chad felt hungry, sleepy, and more fatigued than he ever thought possible, but he wasn't alone. All of his Ranger buddies had to dig deep within themselves to keep going. With all their spare body fat burned off during the Benning phase, the candidates who made it to Mountain Phase were burning muscle with every run and climb. For Chad the smell was the worst of it. When an athlete burns fat, it gives off a distinct but common odor, a thick, musty air like a gym locker room, but when he burns muscle, it smells like a mixture of ammonia and bleach, a putrid stench that Chad found nauseating. He had to get used to it, though. Whether it was rappelling off a fifty-foot cliff or climbing a thousand feet up a mountainside to carry out a search-and-destroy mission, he had no one else around him but men who were suffering just like he was.

It was funny to him now. Coaches talked about football breeding toughness, but the game was comic-book reading compared to this. Chad had long ago pushed through what he thought was his breaking point. Now it was just a matter of passing the tests to earn his Ranger tab, an insignia he had seen more times than he could count at West Point, but one he only now appreciated.

There were mundane drills: knot-tying, cliffside anchoring, and rope management, but it was during upper mountaineering, where he had to ascend and descend the 1,400 feet of Mount Yonah, a bald-topped rock in the Chattahoochee National Forest known for its black bears, poison ivy, and vertical face, when Chad said to himself, "What am I doing here?" Carrying zero percent body fat and stuck on Mount Yonah during one of the exercises, Chad and his Ranger buddy were caught in one of North Georgia's pop-up summer thunderstorms. It was a dangerous setting in the best of circumstances, but huddling under rocks and trees made them especially vulnerable. During the downpour, soaked and listless, Chad couldn't stop shivering. That is when he had the strangest thought: "Oh my God, I'm going to freeze to death in Georgia in July." He spent the rest of the day trying to elevate his body temperature, but the shivers never left.

Assault and ambush drills on mountainsides were more physically taxing than he expected. Carrying a ruck and cache of weapons for a quarter of a mile up a thirty-degree incline was twice as hard as lugging it on a twelve-mile march along the relative flatlands of Fort Benning. The field exercises included ambushing a mortar site that Chad and his squad had to climb a cliff to reach. As he was making that climb, he thought about the boys of Pointe du Hoc scaling the cliffs with hell raining down around them. For that brief instant, a surge ran though him, and he wasn't the least bit tired.

In Quantico, Brian called the Marine Corps "a meat-eater's world." Nowhere was that more evident than at TBS, where officers engaged in live-fire field exercises with mortars and .50-caliber machine guns as well as a series of progressive field exercises that tested every conceivable ambush or assault a leader might face.

"It was extremely dangerous," Brian said.

The final field exercise was the Eight-Day War, which included a long forced march and combat training exercises that combined all the strategic and tactical elements learned during every other part of training. No one admitted it, but marines claimed that the Eight-Day War was patterned after the Spartans, who used to go on something they called the *oktonyktia*, an eight-day (literally, "eight nights") drill in which they would march for four days eating only half rations, and then spend the next four days fighting with no food, little water, and less sleep. Many Spartan warriors died during *oktonyktia* training, but the ones who survived could take on any army in the ancient world. The marines who made it through TBS felt the same way.

The biggest day for the marines at The Basic School came toward the end of training when they found out if they had gotten their preferred MOS. Unlike in the Army, Marine officers had no guarantees of getting the jobs they wanted. A second lieutenant might have his heart set on Light Armored Reconnaissance, but if those jobs are filled and he falls somewhere down the list of guys in his class, he could very well end up in Field Artillery or as an Aerial Delivery Officer instead.

Classes in TBS are ranked in thirds, so with a class of 150, the breakout was top 50, middle 50, and bottom 50. Faceless people in headquarters run each officer's job choices through a computer, and the top people in each grouping, based on academic grades, leadership, and physical conditioning, get their first choice. It often defies logic, especially since the structure means that the person ranked fiftieth in the class might not get his first pick, but the guy ranked 101st most likely will.

"It fights the hand, and it seems unfair, but it's a way of spread-loading the leadership," Brian said. "You want to make sure all the best officers don't end up with the same MOS."

That was all well and good as long as Brian got Infantry. Just like Chad, Brian believed the infantry was the Marine Corps, the men leading the charge. Logistics and communications and intelligence officers were all critical to the effort, but they weren't the first contact, the guys who would engage the enemy up close and personal. Even artillery officers had some separation. Infantry officers were the whites-of-the-eyes guys.

On a Friday afternoon in November, with the fall air just crisp enough to make the twelve-mile hike they had just taken in "full battle rattle" seem almost pleasant, Brian and his classmates returned to their company to find the MOS assignments posted on a bulletin board like college grades in the age before the Internet. Brian and his old pal and teammate J. P. Blecksmith stood next to each other, searching the board for their names. When Brian saw that he had gotten Infantry, his first instinct was to shout "Fuck yeah!" but he held his tongue until he found J.P.'s name as well. When he did, they both gave loud whoops. Both had gotten Infantry. They would be leading the fight.

That night, Brian and his buddies and some friends from another Basic School piled into their cars and drove up to the Maryland line. He had rented a town house in Annapolis for just such weekend get-aways. Over time it had become a crash pad for TBS second lieutenants as well as some underclassmen from the academy. On any given Sunday morning, there might be eight, nine, ten, sometimes as many as a dozen people snoozing on futons, couches, or on the carpet near the television. Brian didn't mind. That's why he'd kept the place.

This time he and a group of buddies went pub-crawling through Annapolis to celebrate their MOS assignments. Brian didn't cut loose. Somebody had to make sure these marines made it home, and it was his name on the town house lease. He had four drinks over several hours, a number he would recall with absolute clarity later when asked about it numerous times.

It was one of those gatherings where not everyone knew everyone, but everyone knew someone. Brian knew the girl, but only a little, a friend of a friend who, it turned out, didn't know her that well, either. She will be referred to here as Carolyn James, although that is not her real name. She was cute and funny and a marine: a meat-eater like the rest of them. She and Brian hit it off and spent much of the night chatting and telling stories. It was flirty in a "let's all celebrate" sort of way, nothing overt or unprofessional on either side.

Brian had been a steady-relationship kind of guy his whole life. He hadn't broken up with his high school sweetheart until his sophomore year at the academy, and after that he had dated an older woman who was already a college graduate and schoolteacher in Annapolis. They had gone out until his First Class year. That was when she had gotten very serious, wanting to quit her job, marry Brian, and move to whatever encampment the Marines assigned them: a classic townie tale in the area. Brian felt for that woman, but he had gotten cold feet. He had way too much on his plate. He was going to war. He couldn't get married.

It had been eight months since that breakup, and with the adrenaline rush from the training and getting the good news about the infantry, it felt great to have some female company, if for nothing more than a drink and a laugh.

The gang took taxis back to the town house. Even though Brian wasn't drunk, he had been drinking. A DUI could ruin an officer's career before it got started, so he left his car in town and rode back with his buddies. Carolyn went back as well, riding just close enough to Brian for him to feel as though this might go farther. Once back at the town house, the party fizzled and everyone found a corner to crash in. It was a scrum of a dozen people piled throughout. Brian went to his room, closed the door, and got ready for bed, thinking nothing more about Carolyn or the night. It was a fun time, but it was over.

A few minutes later came a knock. He opened the door to find Carolyn, who looked him square in the eye and said, "Can I sleep in here?"

He said, "Sure," and invited her inside with every intention of taking the floor and giving her the futon, the only piece of furniture he had in his bedroom. Nothing happened. They both kept their clothes on, and Brian behaved like a gentleman, even though he was a marine who had consumed too much alcohol. It was weird having a woman and fellow officer in his room, but not strange enough to raise any alarms. Perhaps if he had been older or just a little more sober he would have seen the potential danger, but in the quiet confines of his own town house, with a fellow marine who had been one of the gang all night, he thought nothing about Carolyn crashing in his room.

Then, abruptly, Carolyn jumped up and said, "I can't do this."

"What?" Brian said. "What's wrong?"

"I can't do this," she said again, waving her hands as if shooing away a bad odor.

"Okay," Brian said. He walked her to the door, and she went to sleep in another room. Brian went to his futon and was asleep within minutes.

The next morning, they all ate breakfast together and watched football. Carolyn was friendly. She chatted as she'd done at the bars as if nothing had happened, and they all laughed about what a great time they'd had the night before.

Brian was barely in the door at Camp Barrett the following Monday morning in the summer of 2003 when his SPC (specialist), Major Cook, cornered him in his barracks along with another SPC, the one who was training Carolyn.

"Stann, drop your gear and meet me in five," Major Cook said.

Brian did as ordered without any hint of what the major might want. He had grown very fond of Major Cook during TBS, crediting his guidance for the fact that Brian ranked first in his platoon and second in the entire class.

When he walked into the major's office, he could sense that something wasn't right. Cook and the other SPC looked at him as if he were on the way to the brig. Racking his brain to figure out what he had done, he stood at ease and Major Cook said, "Lieutenant Stann, did you get into any trouble this weekend?"

"No, sir," Brian responded.

"Are you certain?"

"Yes, sir."

In a dead flat voice, Cook said, "That's not what we heard."

"What have you heard, sir?" Brian asked, his eyes widening in a "what the hell?" sort of way.

"There has been an accusation that you sexually assaulted a fellow officer," Cook said.

The words hit him like a club to the head. At first he thought it was a sick practical joke. The major's face told him that this was real, and it was serious.

"What, sir!" Brian exploded.

"Calm down, Lieutenant," Cook said. "Tell us what happened.

"There has to be some kind of mistake," Brian said. Then he recounted every second of Friday night in agonizing detail: the bars they visited, who was there, what was said, how many drinks he had, how long they stayed, where he left his car, what cab he took, what time he got home, what time Carolyn knocked on his door, what he said, what she said, and when she left. He left nothing out.

A few minutes later he was recounting the story again, this time for the company commander, Major Nicewarmer. That is when he learned that Carolyn was claiming something wildly different.

"You will need to visit with JAG," Nicewarmer told him. Then came the hardest blow. Nicewarmer said, "You're out of the company. We're moving you to Mike Company until this is resolved." Mike Company was the Marine equivalent of the rubber room, the place where injured officers or those in legal trouble hung out until the Corps figured out what to do with them.

The JAG prosecutors showed up at his room and talked to him, but the JAG defense attorney he had been provided told him to keep his mouth shut. That was tough, because he wanted to scream from the rooftops that this was wrong; he was innocent; nothing had happened! Why would Carolyn say such a thing? What could have possibly prompted this sort of accusation?

Then the prosecutors said, "You can't talk to any of the other officers who were there that night."

Those ten people, the other officers, were Brian's lifeline, and now they were being cut away from him. He felt isolated, alone. He had done nothing wrong. Nothing. This was not a case where he claimed certain activities were consensual and she claimed they were forced. There were no activities to consent to one way or the other. Nothing had happened. But his life, his career, his reputation, his world were suddenly in limbo. He understood the Marine Corps position on sexual misconduct. It was serious and severe, as it should have been, in Brian's opinion. Any man who would hurt a woman or force any sort of sex on anyone should not only never wear the uniform, Brian thought, he should be put behind bars for years. He also knew that after the Tailhook scandal in 1991, when eighty-three women accused Navy and Marine Corps aviators of sexual misconduct in a Las Vegas hotel room during the annual Tailhook convention, JAG officers would go after any sexual misconduct allegation with all they had.

By the time he reported to Mike Company that afternoon, the story had filtered throughout the camp. "I sat in the barracks and stared at the ceiling," Brian said. "It was the deepest despair I'd ever known. Getting accused of sexual misconduct in the Corps is like being a teacher accused of child abuse. It doesn't matter whether you're innocent: the allegations alone are like a scarlet letter. There's no escaping that and the destruction it does to a man's reputation."

Before the end of the day, he made the toughest call of all: the one to his mother. As he had done numerous times throughout the day, he recounted every detail to her: sparing nothing, embellishing nothing, just laying out the facts. It broke his heart to hear her soft sobs through the phone.

When he finished there was a slight pause, and he wondered if his mother believed him or if she, like everyone else, it seemed, would assume him guilty until proven innocent. When she spoke, it was in a firm voice, one he had heard many times growing up— *Brian, I need this room cleaned; Brian, wash up and get down here on the double; Brian, hurry up, you're going to be late for school.* This time she simply said, "Brian, fight this."

"I am, Mom. I am."

"No," she said with a voice full of resolve. "No matter how long it takes, no matter what it takes, you fight this."

He would do just that. But the last time he had felt this way was that lonely afternoon when the white van stopped in South Scranton and the two eighteen-year-olds jumped out and beat him.

That day, he had feared for his life. This time, the fears were much worse.

* * *

Fewer guys fell out at Mountain Phase of Ranger School, but the numbers still dwindled. The instructors threatened to recycle all of them after the entire platoon was caught with Copenhagen chewing tobacco in their gear, but in the end the instructors let that violation slide, not because they weren't upset, but because recycling an entire platoon would have raised some questions.

By the time they came down from the hills of Dahlonega, Chad felt like he was one of the hardest of hard-core soldiers, part of an elite group. They still weren't through, though. He and the rest of his classmates staggered onto another bus and rode to a nearby airfield, where they boarded a Lockheed Martin C-130. All of them caught some rack once the engines began to hum. The flight was only a couple of hours, but every minute of sleep was precious.

Phase III in Florida was next.

After jumping out of the plane and parachuting into the swamp, Chad's squad met up with some recycled candidates from the previous class and they were reorganized and assigned new Ranger buddies before being sent into the backwater areas of Florida that don't make any of the tourist brochures.

"Jenkins," Chad heard one of the instructors say. "Your Ranger buddy for this stage is Zickefoose."

"No way," Chad said as he looked through a crowd of sunken eyes and exhausted faces in search of his best friend and Army teammate.

"Hey, bud," 'Foose said from behind him.

Chad and Zickefoose were together once more, two of the four amigos gutting it out for one last stretch run.

Having a friend by his side saved Chad in some of the bleakest days of Florida Phase. His body never adjusted to the lack of sleep, but he did learn to fall into a virtual coma anywhere he had an opportunity to catch a few minutes of shut-eye. Their first night in the field, five minutes after settling in, Zickefoose heard something that sounded like a grizzly bear growling just a few feet away. Florida still had bears, and there were rumors of a panther or two, but there had been no recent sightings. Once he opened his eyes, he realized that the noise was coming from Chad.

"He wasn't a Heisman-winning quarterback, but he was a world-champion snorer," 'Foose said.

Florida Phase trained Rangers for potential actions in Central or South America, the Caribbean or the Pacific, any tropical or rain forest setting where swamps, bugs, reptiles, and murky tributaries were part of the theater. Soldiers learned how to insert squads on Zodiacs (small rubber crafts) and how to rapidly cross moving streams; how to use water as cover and how to transport equipment through swamps without bogging down.

They executed assaults and raids in urban and jungle settings, culminating in the raid of a fortified island using boats and small-unit tactics. Chad navigated the Zodiac better than his buddy expected, especially on that final mission. They got to their demarcation spot and quietly slipped into the black water. It was up to their chest and Zickefoose had to carry the M240 Bravo over his shoulder. Chad led the way past the water oaks, their roots fanning out into the swamp like tentacles, Spanish moss hanging lazily from their yawning branches. Suddenly Chad stopped and began swatting the air. He had walked into a spiderweb and had an arachnid the size of his fist crawling on his head.

"Would you cut it out? I'm too fucking tired to laugh," Zickefoose said.

If any two people could push each other across the finish line it was Chad and 'Foose. There was only one night when they each thought the other might mail it in. They were the lead machine gun team in a night patrol base: a triangle of men with gunners at the apex. Chad and 'Foose were the tip of the triangle. Chad found a decent tree for concealment and Zickefoose set up the tripod for the gun. A couple of seconds in, they both heard something that sounded like a maraca or a tambourine. They looked at each other and 'Foose whispered, "Chad, did you hear that?"

Chad said, "It's just locusts."

"That's not locusts, dude," 'Foose said. "That's a rattlesnake."

One more chime and Chad agreed that it might, indeed, be something other than bugs.

"Sergeant," 'Foose said to their instructor, breaking noise discipline, since the Army's "dangerous wildlife" rule allowed them to violate tactical silence. A rough, lean man in his forties with weathered skin and an ever-present dip of Copenhagen got in 'Foose's face and said, "What the hell are you doing?"

"Sergeant, there's a rattlesnake," he said.

The instructor looked no more than six feet from them and found the snake coiled and ready. He lifted it with his walking stick and said, "Yeah, good thing you didn't lie down on that." Three paces, no more than ten feet, later, the instructor tossed the rattler back into the brush.

"Are you shitting me?" Zickefoose said.

"Shut up, you'll be fine," the Ranger instructor ordered. "Back to tactical."

Their only other close call with wildlife came on a night raid when Zickefoose was stung by a scorpion.

"What color was it?" the sergeant said.

"Green," 'Foose said. Through night-vision goggles, everything was green.

That earned a hint of a grin from the sergeant. "Watch your hand for a few days and see what happens," he said. Nothing did, and they both made it out of Florida and Ranger School alive.

Chad got through Phase III in August 2003, in part by knowing that he had a thirty-day vacation coming. His leave request had been approved while he was still at Benning. He had decided to take Emily to Wrightsville Beach in North Carolina to propose, the same beach where his parents had taken him and his sisters when they were kids.

The ring purchase wasn't final, but his speech was ready. He was even planning to get down on one knee.

Then, right before he was to leave, he got a call from Major Chuck Schretzman, a former linebacker at West Point who had been the Army football liaison officer during Chad's junior year. Schretzman was now the battalion executive officer in 1st Battalion, 32nd Infantry Regiment, 10th Mountain Division.

"Jenkins, I saw you put in for thirty days," Schretzman said. "Sorry, but the entire battalion is about to deploy to Iraq. I need you. I'll give you seven days. Then you need to get your ass up here and take over for your platoon."

Five months into the Iraq War, every available officer was needed.

"Reality set in real quick after that phone call," Chad said. "I went back to Dublin for seven days and spent time with my family. Then Emily and I drove up to Fort Drum [New York] together."

That was August 28, 2003. On the morning of September 3, Lieutenant Chad Jenkins left American airspace en route to Shannon, Ireland, where he would change planes and fly to Cyprus, and then Kuwait.

He didn't propose to Emily. That would have to come later.

CHAPTER 8

Welcome to Dreamland
—U.S. ARMY'S HAND-PAINTED PLYWOOD SIGN AT THE
MAIN GATE OF UDAY HUSSEIN'S PLEASURE PALACE IN
FALLUJAH, IRAQ

When the jet door opened at the Ahmed Al Jaber Air Base, Chad stepped onto the top stair of the ramp for his first glimpse of the place and said, "Man, I wish that pilot would turn off the engines. That jet fuel burns hot." But the engines were off. It was 1945 (7:45 P.M.) on a beautiful September evening in Kuwait, with the sun a bright orange ball deep in the western sky and the temperature hovering around 117 degrees.

"No way," Chad said to no one as he walked down the stairs and onto the tarmac, realizing that he was experiencing a normal, even pleasant desert evening. The searing heat of Florida in August had been a cold shower compared to this.

Chad was in charge of Third Platoon, Attack Company, 1st Battalion, 32nd Infantry, 10th Mountain Division, a stream of identifiers every soldier could recite in his sleep. It was a light infantry unit that had only two guys with combat experience. One of them was Chad's platoon sergeant, Vern Pollard, a steely-eyed roughneck who spoke in short machine gun bursts as if he were on a daily word budget. Questions got answered, but there was no idle chitchat.

When Pollard had first heard about Chad before they met at Fort Drum, he had gone home and told his wife, "It's bad, honey: I'm getting a West Point grad." The next night, after learning a little more, he came home and said, "It's even worse than I thought: he's a football player." The third night, and the day before Chad and Emily arrived at Fort Drum, Pollard told his bride, "It's even worse: he's a quarterback."

Once Chad got to Drum, however, he and Pollard hit it off instantly. With little time to prep before they departed for Kuwait, Chad tried to get as much info about the men, the mission, and the conditions as he could. But as he was walking from the barracks to the headquarters, he kept turning around to find Pollard a step behind him.

"What are you doing, Sergeant? I can't talk to you back there."

Pollard shook his head and said, "Sir, am I going to have to teach you everything? You're an officer: you're supposed to walk ahead of me."

Chad said, "Look, Sergeant"—pronounced "Sarnt" in the quick and slurred vernacular of the Rangers—"you need to know something about me right off. I don't care about that shit. I need to get up to speed before we get over there, so we don't get anybody killed. So, walk beside me and brief me up. Got it?"

"Roger that, sir," Pollard said, and from that moment forward the two were as close as any platoon leader and platoon sergeant in the Army.

Now, in their staging area seventy-five miles south of the Iraq border, they had a rather unique problem: the war had come on so fast that they hadn't had any Humvees to practice driving at Fort Drum. No one in the unit had ever piloted the wide-bodied vehicles in convoy formation, and no one had ever driven anything in the desert. They had to learn on the fly in Kuwait.

The problem wasn't so much the driving; it was the darkness.

Convoys traveled under total blackout with drivers wearing night-vision goggles. Chad and others had trained with night vision at Fort Benning and at Phase III of Ranger School in Florida, so the green hue from the magnified ambient light wasn't a problem. They were all used to that. What threw them off was the lack of depth perception in an unfamiliar setting. The world looked two-dimensional through NVGs, much like a video game.

That was fine as long as you had trees or rocks or hills or some other visual reference the brain recognized and could process to add distance and depth to what you were seeing. But in the desert, there was nothing but flat earth and sand for hundreds of miles in every direction. That made getting from point A (Kuwait) to point B (Iraq) a lot trickier.

On Chad's orders, the platoon drove around in large circles, making as many practice runs as possible during their time in Kuwait. When it was time for the convoy to roll, they weren't ready, but they moved out like everyone else. It was a six-hundred-mile journey with seven hundred vehicles. The plan was for about half the force to split off and head to Iskandariya and the other half, including Chad, to veer toward Fallujah, the most dangerous city on earth. They weren't a hundred miles inside Iraq when the first snafu occurred. (Though not a formally recognized military acronym, the original term, *SNAFU*, was created during World War II by a couple of radio operators with the 160th Infantry Regiment. It stands for "Situation Normal All Fucked Up"). This one was a doozy, even though none of Chad's novice drivers was involved.

They were Humvee rookies, so the Third Platoon Attack brought up the rear of the convoy with the fuel trucks. As they were plodding along through the desert, one of the tanker trucks veered off the road and crashed, rolling and spilling fuel into the sand, creating a highly flammable and ever-growing sinkhole. Chad saw the accident. He got on the radio and called it in before moving his Humvees into a defensive position. Then he sent two of his men to retrieve the driver and passenger from the wreck.

Those men weren't out of their vehicles for ten seconds before they started taking small-arms fire from somewhere in the distant buildings. It wasn't a major firefight, but it only takes one lucky or well-placed round to kill a soldier, so the convoy stopped. Fire was returned and a medevac chopper flew in to cart out the wounded driver of the truck.

Welcome to Iraq.

It wasn't long before Chad's company was detached from their regular battalion and assigned to the legendary 82nd Airborne Division, known in Army circles as the "All-Americans." During World War II, they were the men who parachuted behind enemy lines before the D-Day invasion and fought the Germans for thirty-three days without relief or reinforcements. More than five thousand All-Americans were killed in France, but as Major General Matthew Ridgway wrote in his report, "Every mission accomplished. No ground gained was ever relinquished."

Baghdad had fallen within a month of the initial invasion, but unlike World War II, when the fall of Berlin and the surrender by the Japanese on the USS *Missouri* marked the end of all but scattered and isolated hostilities, the fall of Baghdad did not bring the war to a close. In fact, the heaviest fighting came after Saddam Hussein's regime fell. By September 2003, roadside bombs and insurgent ambushes were on the rise and American commanders were scrambling to develop a strategy to deal with this new type of warfare. Fallujah was the center point of most of the insurgent activity, the vipers' nest for the fighters who seemed to be flowing into Iraq from all corners of the terrorist world. The ground operations base for Chad's company was a place known as "Dreamland," a name given to it by its previous owner. It had been the pleasure palace of Uday Hussein, Saddam's eldest and most brutal son, located about six miles east of Fallujah.

"The main house of the palace had been demolished in the initial bombings," Chad explained. "But Uday had these man-made lakes throughout the compound with hundreds of little three-room bungalows all around the water. That was where his concubines stayed."

It was the best little whorehouse in Fallujah, a place where U.S. forces had cots and a roof, a luxury not usually found in a battlefield environment, ready-made walls that were easy to secure, and a garden where daily missions could be prepared and trained for.

The missions, unfortunately, were a problem. During daylight hours, Chad's platoon went out on IED route clearances and atmospheric patrols, going out to be seen by the locals as a show of strength. They were, in essence, driving around town until somebody either shot at them or tried to blow them up. "This was before we had the up-armored Humvees," he said. "I can't tell you how many times I was riding around with my feet hanging out where the door had been. In our infinite wisdom, we took the doors off, figuring it would cause less shrapnel. If we'd been hit by an IED, it would have been all over."

In addition to finding explosives and calling in the engineers to dispose of them, they talked to the locals and tried to show them that the Americans were not a conquering force. This was not Alexander the Great slaughtering innocents and naming cities after himself (Iskandariya is roughly translated to Alexandria, one of the many cities in the Middle East bearing that name). Lieutenant Colonel Brian Drinkwine, commander of the 1st Battalion of the 505th Regiment, 82nd Airborne, met with town elders and did a lot of community relations, explaining to anyone who would listen that the goal was not to hang around and rule Iraq as others had done throughout the centuries. The Americans wanted to help Iraqis stabilize the place, and then to get out. But it was easy to understand why the elders were suspicious. By night Chad and his men were conducting target raids where they killed or captured insurgents inside Fallujah.

"If someone tells you they have no fear here, they're lying," Chad said at the time.

Conditions inside Fallujah appalled him. Sewage ran through

the streets, not because of the bombing but because there was no modern waste disposal. Even the high-rise buildings had "shit pits," as the soldiers began calling them: open chutes that fed into large holes. It was the urban equivalent of an outhouse. Several squads had to stop patrols for vomit breaks because of the acidic stench of urine and the fecal dust that swirled with the sand on breezy afternoons. Trash was dumped in the streets out of doors and windows, not in bags or receptacles but unfettered and raw. Unidentifiable animal carcasses rotted beside groups of kids playing outside their homes.

In a letter to his parents several weeks into his first tour, Chad wrote, "I understand why I'm over here. The children do not deserve to live the way they are now, or, even worse, the way they did before. They are so innocent and the only ones to wave and smile and cheer as we go through Fallujah on patrols. You can see the cutoff and when they pretty much get brainwashed, because any child older than, I'd say, nine or ten will no longer wave or smile. But the children eight and younger have no idea. They absolutely love us."

The first stint at Dreamland wasn't a long one. In October, Chad and his unit temporarily transferred down to a place called Rock ASP (Ammunitions Supply Point), an area south of Fallujah with munitions bunkers that Chad and his platoon had been ordered to secure. Ammo was everywhere: in a hurry the Iraqis had abandoned most of it. All of it, whether it belonged to coalition forces or Saddam, had to be guarded.

They left Dreamland at night, but rather than take Route Michigan, the direct east–west route through the city that U.S. forces patrolled regularly, they swung south to try to avoid an ambush. It didn't work. Perhaps it was their lack of experience driving the Humvees, or maybe it was the isolated dirt roads, or maybe they were just unlucky, but Chad's company was lit up by insurgent gunfire the second they turned south.

"I remember tracer fire hitting vehicles right in front of us," he said. "We had a .50-caliber and were returning fire, but at night you don't have any idea where all the fire's coming from. You're just so amped up, the instant you hear that first crack everything kicks in and you're on your A-game. That's why everybody says things slow down, because once all your senses and the adrenaline kick in, everything seems to move slower."

Sergeant Blain Stevens was the driver, Chris Teffer his machine gunner, and Justin Black his radio control operator, names and faces Chad would never forget. You always remember those around you the first time you get lit up—really lit up—by enemy fire. And you remember the orders you gave: "Distance and direction, Teffer," and then, "Call out, Justin," to get a status from the radiotelephone operator. Details of the second firefight become a little fuzzier, and the third blurrier still: after the fourth or fifth time, they all blend together.

Living conditions were tough at Rock ASP, especially after the relatively lavish comforts of Uday's Dreamland cottages. With only a couple of small outbuildings housing one hundred soldiers, the body odor became almost unbearable. Showering consisted of hanging a bag of water on a hook above a vehicle, letting the sun heat it, and then opening a nozzle and trying to get as clean as possible before it ran dry.

Bottled water, a Leatherman knife, and the mirror of a Humvee were ideal for shaving, and rack was wherever you could catch a nap, often on the hood of whatever vehicle happened to be around. Every meal was an MRE (the military abbreviation for Meals, Ready to Eat): gelatinous blocks of protein mixed with whatever chemicals kept the things from spoiling as they sat in the 130-degree desert for days on end. The only good thing about the place was that everyone knew it was temporary.

The patrols were routine. Intel would identify a group of bad guys or a cache of guns in a house or a barn or just buried in a field.

Chad and his team would root them out, capture them, or at the very least find and confiscate the weapons.

He also spent time talking with reporters, something he hadn't expected, but which had become an integral part of this war-fighting effort. The "embedded reporter" concept was taken to extremes in the Iraq War, with camera crews and big-shot talent tagging along on some dangerous missions. It was an annoyance. Even though the brass made sure everyone understood that these people were not to get in the way or disrupt the conduct of an operation, there was always a slight hesitation when you knew a camera was around. And in a firefight, hesitation was the enemy.

Within four weeks of arriving in Iraq, Chad was tapped for a major Associated Press feature as well as an ABC *Nightline* special. CBS News was also putting together a package that the network planned to repurpose as part of their halftime show for the Army-Navy Game.

Stateside, the network asked Lee and Dave Jenkins to participate. They agreed on the condition that CBS give them copies of the raw footage. Not only did Dave understand the power of the edit suite, he wanted as much footage of Chad as he could get. Conversations with their son had been relegated to ten-minute Internet phone calls filled with long pauses and not much information.

"He couldn't really tell us anything," Dave said. "He couldn't tell us where he was or what he was doing. All he could say was that he was fine and he'd see us when he got home. As desperately as we wanted more, that was enough, really."

CBS even asked Emily to be involved. "I was only his girlfriend at the time, so I didn't get much information from the Tenth Mountain Division. Only wives get the full info," she said. "He would call me, but it was usually short and awkward. Most of the information I got came from his parents. Still, I did the segment and talked about what it was like to go to Fort Drum and watch all those soldiers board that plane. I was twenty-five years old at the time and some of those boys were just eighteen. It broke my heart to watch those boys—they were just boys—loading up to go fight for our freedom. I mean, what is that? What kind of person does that? At the time, I didn't understand. Sometimes I still don't."

A young producer gathered the footage from Chad, so he never got to see any of the network's on-air stars behind the piece. She had done her homework. She asked him about Zickefoose, who was a combat engineer, and Omari Thompson, the receiver who ran back the second-half kickoff for a touchdown in Chad's last game. Omari was a tank commander somewhere in Fallujah. It wasn't likely that they would run into each other.

"Colonel Adamczyk says hello," the producer told him.

"What?"

"Yeah, he said to let you know how much he thinks about you guys and how he is honored to have been your brigade tactical officer. He even welled up a little when I mentioned your name."

"Skeletor? Don't put that in there," Chad said.

The producer chuckled at Adamczyk's nickname, which let Chad know they were talking about the same guy. The last memory Chad had of Adamczyk was when he told Huck Finn to forget about the NFL. There would be no New York Giants camp.

"He's a dick," Chad said. "If he cried for the cameras I know two hundred men who'll laugh out loud if you show it."

The colonel didn't make the final cut.

Eight weeks in, things were going pretty well. The IED sweeps had been successful; nobody in Chad's unit had triggered any of the devices. The night raids had yielded some good captures. Then, on November 2, with a group about to rotate home for Thanksgiving and the temperatures dipping to a relatively brisk 101, Chad and his platoon went out on nighttime security patrol of Rock ASP. He and "Sarnt" Pollard drove a Humvee around the perimeter of the compound to check on everyone. It was a quiet night, made even quieter by the fact that Vern's idea of compelling conversation was "yes, sir," "no, sir," and "what the fuck, sir."

It was an easy night, just the kind Chad liked. He came off at 0730, just as another platoon was heading out. Because this was the last meal a number of guys would have before heading home for some R&R, the cooks had brought in a special Thanksgiving breakfast from a forward operating base (FOB) about twenty miles away. Chad stood in line to get eggs and toast. Bacon was out of the question in a Muslim country, but other meat products often found their way onto the buffet. It looked like a great spread, especially by Rock ASP standards.

Chad shuffled forward, letting his mind wander to the Army football team and their new coach, John Mumford, who had coached the defensive line when Chad was there. The cadets hadn't won a game so far. Things were not looking great.

He looked to his north and saw two Chinook helicopters flying west to east, apparently heading to one of the FOBs near the city, their metal skin glowing in the morning sun. He turned back to grab another scoop of eggs. That's when he heard the explosion. Chad swung his head around. Now there was only one Chinook and a plume of black smoke.

He dropped his plate and sprinted to his Humvee, his men in close tow. Since his platoon had just come off their shift, they were the most prepared to go. Everyone was on high alert. Ambushes were always expected after explosions. But taking down a Chinook, one of the largest transport helicopters in service, was such a huge deal that the entire world would be there soon.

Chad led the convoy, which wasn't as easy as driving straight from the Rock ASP to the crash site. That area of Iraq was farmland, irrigated by a network of man-made canals. With no maps or GPS at his disposal, he eyeballed the waterways to make sure he didn't lead them to a dead end.

Once they arrived at the scene, it was like running headlong through the front gates of hell. Smoldering black metal lay scattered everywhere, while twisted rotor blades stuck out of the sandy soil like gnarled, broken limbs. There were survivors. Injured soldiers moved around the scene, most in the limp-armed shuffle of shock. But there were also many dead.

By now, the second Chinook had landed, and the men onboard, close to thirty of them, piled out to help. Unfortunately, they only added to the chaos. The men from the second chopper knew the victims. They were friends with many of them, so they ran to the scene yelling and full of distress. Emotions mixed with adrenaline and confusion made for a toxic stew. Chad had to calm things down— and do so quickly.

"You can train for everything, including mass-casualty situations, but until it's real and you get there in person and see the bodies . . . nothing can prepare you for that," he said. "Gunfights and IEDs and reactions to contact: you can effectively train for those things. But the mass-casualty scenario is not something a human being can prepare for until you're there, until you see it and feel it."

Chad and Sergeant Corey Dole, one of the team leaders from Third Platoon, searched the wreckage for survivors. They found one man trapped beneath a large section of the Chinook that had been ripped away by the explosion. Chad corralled three others to help lift the sheet metal off the soldier, who kept saying, "Thank you guys, I'm just stuck. Thanks for getting me out. How many made it okay?" But Chad realized too late that the weight of the wreckage had pinned the soldier's organs in place. The moment they heaved the thousand pounds of metal off, the man started to bleed out, closing his eyes and breathing a final sigh in front of them within seconds. He was gone.

They stood silent for a second, but only for a second. Chad had to put that away. The men, his and the ones from the other chopper, were looking to him as an example. If he panicked or got emotional or appeared to lose control, the situation could fall apart. He had to hold it together and be the calm, firm voice of authority.

On Chad's orders, "Doc" Martin Mendez from Corpus Christi, Texas, along with Sergeant Larry North, set up the casualty collection point, establishing three areas: a killed in action (KIA) body collection area, a triage area for those in need of immediate medical assistance, and a walking-wounded area. After the initial pandemonium, Chad had troops working to get people into those three spots. Checking perimeter security was another crucial component. A classic tactic was to lure forces into a rescue and then launch another attack, pinning them down. With air support and medevac on the way, he needed to make sure that nobody was hiding in a window with a surface-to-air missile.

Casualty collection was under way, and with his guys reporting that the perimeter was secure, Chad prepared to jump back into the triage, helping whomever he could until medical personnel arrived.

Then he saw the trucks pulling up from the west, two of them, civilian. He rushed forward to be there when they were stopped. The last thing he needed was for innocents to get shot. It might be sightseers or Good Samaritans coming out to help. Of course, the trucks could also be insurgents on a suicide mission. Either way, Chad had to assess and neutralize the situation.

As he got closer he thought he saw a woman, a civilian with red hair and makeup. *What the hell?*

The back doors of the trucks opened and two men got out with a shoulder-held camera and a microphone. Out of the other truck piled what appeared to be contract security guards from Blackwater USA or one of the other outfits that did such things, and an Iraqi guide and translator.

"Hey, you can't be here! Get out of here! Get those cameras out of here!" Chad yelled.

"I'm Kelly O'Donnell with NBC," the woman said. "What can you tell me about the crash? How many casualties?"

"I don't care who you are!" Chad didn't think he could shout any louder, but he was wrong. His decibel level rose with each breath. This could not be happening. "You are not filming this! Now get back! That is a direct order! Acknowledge that you understand this command!"

O'Donnell stared at him for a second in stunned disbelief. She looked as though she wanted to say, "Don't you know who I am?" Instead she just came out with a weak "But this is my job."

Chad said, "And this is mine, lady. Now get your shit and get out of here. You will not put that footage out."

Of course footage of the crash made it out, as did Chad screaming at Kelly O'Donnell. One of Dave Jenkins's friends called him the morning of November 3 and said, "Dave, have you heard from Chad?"

The crash was all over the news, but they hadn't heard, so the entire Jenkins family was worried sick. "No," he said. "We're hoping to hear something soon."

"Well, don't worry, I just heard him on TV chewing out one of the reporters for getting too close. He's fine. He's there, but he's fine."

Years later it still amazed him. "I don't know how they got out there," Chad said. "There was no military escort, no military personnel around her at all. It was crazy. They could have been blown up or shot at any moment. Fallujah was the most dangerous place in the world at that time. To this day, I can't imagine what they were thinking."

Once the NBC crew was gone, Chad checked on the progress at the site. The wounded were being treated and more helicopters were headed in to assist. By now it was 2:00 P.M. The Chinook had been shot down at 7:30 A.M., probably by a lucky shot from somebody in the back of a truck with a shoulder-mounted rocket-propelled grenade (RPG). The randomness of it wouldn't hit him for another few hours. At that moment, he just needed to catch his breath.

Then he looked down in the oil-soaked sand and saw a mangled bundle. He moved closer to have a look. It was a teddy bear, about two feet tall, one arm and one leg stuck in tar from the seeping wreckage. An eye was missing and the nose was charred. The other eye stared back at Chad.

The Chinooks had been transporting men home for Thanksgiving. At least one was taking a gift home to a child.

Sixteen were killed, twenty-six wounded. Chad and his platoon spent the next five days and nights guarding the wreckage from looters and propagandists. The nights were the worst, with the smell from the fuel, and the desert, and the death. And the hot wind howled like an angry ghost.

Helplessness was a sickening feeling, one Brian Stann was not accustomed to feeling. Brian recognized his personal flaws. His intensity was legendary among his family and classmates. Even his closest friends said things to him like "Dude, chill," even though they knew that would never happen. He was the kind of man who thrived on order and control. Now he had neither. Staring into the black abyss of a court-martial for a sexual assault he didn't commit, Brian realized that this, too, was a test of leadership and character, but most of all patience.

Thanksgiving came and went. He saw the Chinook crash on television like the rest of the country, and he read the names of those killed. Each one was like a prick to his soul. Then Christmas rolled by, and Brian realized that "swift justice" was a laughable fantasy. In the cold New Year prosecutors offered him a plea deal to cop to a lesser charge, badgering him to take it. They made it sound like he'd get a slap on the wrist and be on his way, but Brian was having none of it. He had done nothing except let the wrong woman into his room. He wanted the accusation proved false so that everyone would know he was not a sexual predator. His character was on the line. Nothing was more important.

His lawyer understood his position, but he also understood that if this went to trial, the JAG prosecutor would go after him. The Corps needed to prove they didn't coddle sex offenders. Leniency would be out the window once the deal went away, but Brian was adamant. They had painted him with a red brush. He would either clear his name completely or spend the next decade proclaiming his innocence from the brig.

His court-martial was set for August 2004, another eight months of nothing but depositions and building a defense while his friends and classmates went to war without him. It was hard to watch as one TBS class after another graduated and headed out to MOS training and then off to the front lines. He could do nothing but plod and plan and work with his lawyers on a defense.

His lawyers suspected that Carolyn might have a history of this sort of thing. Women who falsely accuse men of a sexual assault don't do it just once. Like shoplifting, it is a compulsion. Sure enough, Brian's legal team found out that Carolyn had made similar accusations in the past. And those claims had been proven false. They also learned that prosecutors had been hesitant to bring this case, but Carolyn had threatened to call her congressman if action wasn't taken against Brian.

Then came a bombshell: a friend from Annapolis called and said, "Brian, you're not going to believe this. She's engaged to another marine. He's overseas."

Now it all made sense. Tipsy from a drink or two, she had found a nice companion in Brian, and before she could think clearly she was alone with him in the bedroom of his town house. Guilt and a sense of obligation overcame her, and she made her abrupt exit. But the Marine community is small and close. With ten other marines in the town house, word was bound to trickle out about what she'd done, even if she hadn't really done anything. So she invented the story that Brian had forced himself on her.

It didn't make it better or easier—her actions were still deplorable and an affront to every woman who has ever been the legitimate victim of sexual misconduct—but it did make sense. Now it was just a matter of convincing a jury.

The silver linings of life aren't always bright, especially in the beginning. Brian might have gone mad from boredom sitting in the rubber room of Mike Company were it not for a light that came in the form of a gruff lieutenant colonel named Joseph Shusko, who was the commander of the Marine Corps Martial Arts Center for Excellence (MACE). Shusko was as Corps as they came. He had flown the Marine One helicopter for President Reagan, and he'd flown combat missions in the Persian Gulf War.

Even now, in his fifties, he could run three miles in under eighteen minutes and rip off more chin-ups than most of the men serving under him. He was also a good judge of character, and in Brian, Shusko saw a hard-nosed officer who had plenty of time on his hands. So, in the winter of 2004 he pulled Brian into the newly built MACE museum in Quantico and ordered Brian to help decorate the place.

"Walk with me and let me show you what I want done," Shusko said.

They toured the $1.8 million facility, which would open in August, and talked about the MACE program. It began in 2001 as a way to further immerse marines in hand-to-hand combat. The Corps wanted marines in the field who were better rounded in mixed martial arts, the fusion of wrestling, kickboxing, and Brazilian jujitsu. "I want this place to be dedicated to the Raiders," Shusko said. The Marine Raiders were one of the most decorated units in the Corps. They lost almost a thousand men in the Pacific in World War II, a sixth of their total strength. The fact that Shusko wanted Brian to decorate the walls with memorabilia from that group was an honor, even though interior design was not his forte.

Then the colonel got around to the elephant in the room. "Lieutenant, why are you in Mike Company?" he asked.

Brian knew that Shusko was not the kind of guy you could soft-shoe. "Sir, I've been charged with sexual misconduct, and I'm awaiting my court-martial," he said.

Shusko stopped midstride and stared a hole through the back of Brian's eyes. "Did you do it, Lieutenant Stann?"

Again, Brian didn't hesitate. "No, sir," he said. "Absolutely not."

Shusko nodded and said, "Okay then," and continued with the tour.

After all those weeks of wearing the scarlet letter, Brian had finally found an officer who believed him.

It infuriated Brian that his career had devolved into picking out pictures and plaques, but when he thought about Colonel Shusko, he realized he would shovel sewers or drive through walls for that man. Still, it hurt when friends like J. P. Blecksmith got assigned to the 3rd Battalion, 5th Marines and were in the rotation to go to Iraq. Brian channeled his frustration into physical activity. "I became a gym rat, and MACE became my escape," he said.

He worked out every hour he wasn't hanging pictures. "All that time in the MACE drew the attention of several instructors," he said. One of them, a Gunnery Sergeant Marlow, took a special interest in Brian. They talked about workout techniques and Brian's football career at the academy. Marlow told him that he could attend any class at MACE he wanted. With nothing better to do, Brian attended them all.

"In the mornings, I'd work on the Raider memorial," he said. "I spent the afternoons and evenings attending classes at MACE or doing more training. I returned to the Siberia of my barracks only when I absolutely had to in order to get a few hours of sleep."

He became the lone commissioned officer in an unofficial club of noncommissioned officers around the gym. Starting at 0500, Brian would show up at MACE and work out with Gunny Marlow as well as other gunnery sergeants, Richmond, Wargo, and Collette (last names only, as even their wives called them "Gunny"). Brian not only learned a lot about mixed martial arts from those NCOs; he also learned a lot about commanding a platoon from the top-enlisted perspective.

He moved slowly from tan belt to gray belt to green belt. The MACE motto was "One Mind, Any Weapon." Brian took those words to heart, just as he followed the character-building lessons of martial arts.

Because he wanted to stay away from the barracks as much as possible, he also joined Gunny Marlow at weekly Bible study. Brian had long pushed spiritual matters aside, solving problems with his mind or his fists. Now he could do neither, so he turned where most men eventually turn in times of crisis: the Almighty. Psalm 30 was one of his favorites: "I will extol thee, O Lord; for thou hast lifted me up, and hast not made my foes to rejoice over me."

At MACE, he learned fighting techniques using bayonets and clubs and his bare hands. He also learned to maintain composure under extreme conditions. In one drill, the instructors divided a windowless room into four stations. One area had stationary bikes, another weights, a third had grappling mats, and a fourth was where M16s were to be held horizontal to the ground at arm's length while standing at attention. No one could move from one station to the next until the unit leader had perfected each drill. Then, just to spice things up, the instructors turned off the lights and blared combat sounds through concert-sized speakers. When that wasn't enough, they filled the room with smoke and turned on strobe lights.

Brian plowed through the drills unfazed by the distractions. Colonel Shusko noticed. He also saw a passion and enthusiasm in Brian that was rare, even among marines. So the colonel transferred him over to MACE, chewing out anyone (but especially the TBS instructors) who dared question why an officer awaiting court-martial would be given such a plum assignment.

It was a dream come true. Even though technically Brian was still in the rubber room, practically he was a full-time MACE instructor.

"The marine with the scarlet letter was now giving lectures to officers and NCOs from around the Corps on values and character," Brian said. "It was extremely redemptive, and I put everything I had into it."

Occasionally he put too much into it. During one of his grappling sessions with his first class, he broke a general's rib. He couldn't have been more apologetic, but those things happened in training.

Brian had all the tools for martial arts: strength, speed, smarts, a fighter's instincts, and a naturally powerful punch. After one of his classes late in the winter, Gunny Marlow said, "Sir, would you consider entering some amateur MMA fights? There are a lot of them in the area."

Brian was thrilled. Given where he had been, the thought of competing again made his heart race. A passage from the book of Matthew crossed his mind: "Ask and it will be given to you; seek and you will find; knock and the door will be opened to you. For everyone who asks, receives; he who seeks finds; and to him who knocks, the door will be opened."

He had been as down as a man could be. Now, even though a trial still loomed, he felt whole, at peace with the world and confident that the door would be opened for greater things.

A pal named Travis Manion, who was a wrestler, drove down from Annapolis on the weekends to help Brian improve his ground game (MMA-speak for the moves employed on the mat). Brian's only wrestling moves were based on the tackling drills he'd learned in football. He and Travis worked long and hard to break those habits, although they continued to flare up at times. Brian's default was always to punch his way out of a jam. He was what MMA folks called a "stand-up striker," someone who knew enough kickboxing moves to take down an opponent but was vulnerable to a fast wrestler who could get to his legs. More than once Brian ended up on his back.

His first fight was an event called the Combat Sports Challenge, only a half step above a bare-knuckle parking lot brawl. It was held in a ratty warehouse in Fredericksburg, Virginia. There were about eighty spectators, most of them drunk, with heavy-metal music playing from speakers ill-designed for the task. The floor was concrete with a smattering of sawdust. Blood splatters were fresh, and no one was in any hurry to clean them up.

Brian's opponent was a townie with a shaved head, a mustache, a soul patch, a couple tattoos, and a bad scowl, a poor attempt to look like Chuck Liddell, the famous UFC light heavyweight champion. The bell sounded and Brian moved in. The kid was fast and slipped behind Brian, getting him in a guillotine choke hold. Had the kid been a more seasoned fighter or a better-trained athlete, he probably would have won. Brian was sucking air and getting lightheaded from the choke, knowing he had made a tactical error by allowing the fight to go to the ground in the first few seconds.

Then the guy's arm began to tire, and the choke hold loosened. Brian escaped, but not before the kid poked him in the eye. Blood dripped down Brian's cheek, and the fury of the previous months surged through him. The kid threw a wild punch that missed, and Brian moved in, hitting him first with a right cross that staggered him back. Then Brian charged, pummeling the kid with a series of blows that split his forehead.

Doctors examined him and said it was the kid's call whether or not to continue, but he threw in the towel. The fight lasted two minutes and forty-five seconds. Stann by TKO.

The crowd, filled with veterans, went wild. Two of the NCOs he had trained with, Master Gunny Sanders and Gunny Collette, worked Brian's corner and came rushing into the ring to hug him and hold his hands aloft. Beer flew in like liquid confetti, dousing everyone.

For the first time in months, Brian allowed himself a cathartic yell and a genuine smile. To paraphrase his old coach Charlie Weatherbie, it was a great day to fight by the bay.

CHAPTER 9

*Be convinced that to be happy means to be free and
that to be free means to be brave. Therefore do not take
lightly the perils of war.*
—Thucydides

The Chinook crash changed Chad—not in dramatic, outward ways, but
in subtle ways that only those who knew him best picked up on. He
was probably a better leader afterward, more demanding of perfection from the men around him and more urgent in his attention to
detail. But his wit was not quite so quick, and his voice was a little
softer and more serious than before. For the first time, his ten-minute
conversations with Emily included what she termed "the M-word."

At first she didn't want to hear about marriage and found it hard
to believe he was bringing it up. "I wrote it off to the fact that they
didn't have beer in Iraq," she would later say. Her parents had stayed
married for twenty-five years before finally getting divorced, so she
wasn't thinking about marriage. After the crash, Chad took each day
of his own life more seriously, and marrying Emily was something
he felt he needed to do.

Around this time, word came down that Chad's tour would be
extended. Instead of a six-month rotation, he and his unit would be

there for a year. This kind of news can sink morale, especially among guys who think they are close to going home. Chad did his best to keep spirits high.

"Your job as a leader is to keep your men up and focused, and that means not letting them sense that you're upset about something, even if you are," he said. "I made sure that they never saw me bitch about anything. If I had to bitch, I bitched up the chain of command, not down."

Low morale moved like the wind and could turn quickly and inexplicably while spreading like an airborne virus. There was no one sure way of turning it around, or even stopping its spread. Work helped. As with everything else in the Army, the busier a soldier was today, the easier it was for him to forget the bad news from yesterday. But the men needed a victory. A small one would suffice, but whatever it was, they needed some nugget that would make them feel they had accomplished something lasting and good.

So while they were still at Rock ASP, mere days after the Chinook crash, several of the officers put together a plan to deal with a trouble spot once and for all.

Two of the main bridges in Fallujah had been renamed the George Washington and the Brooklyn by U.S. commanders. They connected the city to the Fallujah peninsula, so they were a hotbed of activity and a constant thorn in the side of U.S. forces. They would later be spots for major action, but now they were just a nuisance, especially on the Rock ASP side. A traffic roundabout on the road running east to west between the two bridges had become the most dangerous circle in the world. During one daytime run, Chad's team had found twenty-six IEDs in the one circle.

Sick of all those explosives reappearing in one area, the men decided to set up bases near the circle and send out roving night patrols to kill or capture whoever was booby-trapping the road. This was a precursor to General Petraeus's surge strategy. But during the surge, the size of the force made it all but impossible for AQI (Al Qaeda in Iraq) to move; here, two platoons on some temporary patrol runs were not enough to win over the hearts and minds of the locals.

Chad didn't know much about Iraqi history or culture when he arrived, just the basics: Sunni, Shia, Babylon, Ottoman Turks, British, and Saddam. He knew nothing of Wahhabism and the ruthless tribal feuds in the region. He believed that offering protection to the residents near the Fallujah roundabout made perfect sense. Americans would root out the bad guys, and the locals would no longer have to worry about their streets being rigged with explosives. Unfortunately, things didn't work out that way. The evening after the patrol base went operational, they were attacked. Locals had tipped off the insurgents, and a firefight ensued. When squads went out on night patrol, the bad guys slipped into the shadows like rats down a hole.

"We were all like, 'Gee, that worked well,'" Chad said. "'Glad we were here to protect your neighborhoods.'"

On the third night of the five-night experiment, Chad was in the patrol base, a walled compound near the traffic circle, catching a little rack on the hood of a Humvee. By this time in his career, sleep came like an on-off switch: no eyelid flutters or deep, transitional yawns. Like a lullaby doll, eyes flew open or closed, awake or asleep, no in-between. Chad was motionless when his subconscious heard the distinct whistle of an incoming rocket-propelled grenade. He rolled off the hood just as the wall behind him exploded. The Humvee took the brunt of the shrapnel and stone, but Chad still felt the concussion before being showered with residue from the blast.

"Nobody took our presence seriously," he said. "Nobody came over to our side or provided us with information, because they knew we were leaving."

Chad had no idea at the time, but that five-day patrol run along the Euphrates River would be a microcosm of the problems U.S. forces would have for the rest of the decade. No matter how noble the intentions were, winning hearts and minds was tough when the residents knew you were eventually going to leave and the insurgents were there to stay.

* * *

By the end of November, Chad and the rest of Third Platoon, Alpha Company were back in Dreamland, where they stayed through Christmas. Morale wavered between fair and poor during that time because the holidays reminded everyone what they were missing at home. During one of his calls to Emily, Chad said, "I'd rather not think about Christmas. It's a hundred degrees here, and we're going out on patrol, so I'd rather just let it go: pretend it's just another day."

It worried her that he sounded so down, but his conversations with her were some of the only times when he felt like he could vent his true feelings. Even Vern Pollard was under Chad's command, so Chad couldn't confide everything in him. Pollard and Chad had become perfect tag-team managers for the platoon, with the six-foot-three, 180-pound platoon sergeant playing the hard-ass, and Chad coming in as the calm, soothing voice the men sometimes needed.

But he could keep his game face on for only so long. Chad would often slip over to an adjacent Dreamland bungalow where the guys from Two Alpha were living. There he would dip Copenhagen with their platoon sergeant, Larry North, an older NCO. It was one of the few times he could let his guard down and relax. North had Avril Lavigne on his iPod, and he and Chad shared an affinity for off-key renditions of female pop songs. More than a few evenings, their voices caused involuntary cringes from the men walking patrol outside: *"Why you have to go and make things so complicated . . ."*

IED clearance sweeps were the most frustrating of all, especially because the platoon rarely caught the guys who planted the devices. During one IED route clearance mission near the Rock ASP, Chad's unit found thirty-three 155 mm artillery rounds daisy-chained together. The bombs covered a full kilometer. The engineers detonated them all at the same time, and the noise sent a chill up Chad's spine. Had they been accidentally triggered, the damage could have been unspeakable.

Chad's mission did get better after the New Year, especially as the direct action raids started showing results. AQI had made Fallujah its central command. The group's main goal was to kill Americans, and they traveled from far and wide to that city to earn the chance. On that front, the strategy of deploying so many troops in the so-called Sunni Triangle had worked: it attracted the worst of the worst to one spot. It was always easier to trap and kill an enemy in one location than chase him around the globe. But in the process, that one location became hell on earth, which was exactly how those who were there described Fallujah in the early months of 2004.

Chad had four squads he used when planning and executing an assault. The first, a weapons squad, was composed of drivers and top gunners, the guys responsible for the most dangerous part of the missions: ingress and egress. The time of the actual assault was when you were in your most aggressive offensive posture, so, technically, that was when you were safest, especially since you had the element of surprise and all the angles covered. Getting in and out was the trick. The enemy knew the Americans were the most vulnerable during ingress and egress, and that was why so many casualties in Iraq were IED-related.

The second, third, and fourth squads Chad had were all part of the assault. One squad was made up of dedicated breachers, the guys who would take axes, circular saws, battering rams, and occasionally explosives to break through a gate or a door or a wall. Another squad would secure a foothold inside the area, while a third would float and help in whatever areas heated up. Chad had to plan it all out the day before. Then he would head to battalion HQ inside Dreamland and present his action plan along with every other platoon leader.

"Lieutenant Jenkins, call sign Attack-three-six: the mission is to conduct a direct-action raid to kill or capture target at Lima Bravo [grid location] on or about 2300 IOT [in order to] disrupt the insurgent network," he would say. Then he would go through his action plan: what routes they would take, what the rallying points were, and where other platoons were in the area. The last thing they needed was to be bumping into each other out there.

Once everything was approved, Chad would go back and brief

his men, letting them in on every detail and coaching everyone up. "It was like pregame before kickoff," he said, describing the feelings of anticipation he had before those missions. "You joke a little with your guys, but everybody is in the zone. You know that the second you go outside that wire, the game is on."

Five vehicles would pull out into the night and head into the streets of Fallujah. Chad was always in the number-one vehicle, his NVGs casting a haunting green glow over every block. Zero dark thirty (0030) was a typical start time. They wanted the darkest part of the night when the only creatures stirring were the wild dogs that roamed Iraq like coyotes.

Every house was walled. Sometimes two houses would sit back-to-back, taking up one block with an eight- to ten-foot wall surrounding both of them. That made it tough if you were hitting one house but not the other. Civilians were bound to be in the line of fire, and even though the rules of engagement at that time were as liberal as at any point in the war, every soldier worked tirelessly to avoid collateral casualties.

Once the assault started, it was like a choreographed dance. One squad would fan out to provide 360-degree security, with some guys looking in and others looking out. Occasionally a target would try to escape by scurrying along a rooftop—Rangers called them "squirters"—but they never got far. Every escape route was covered from every angle. Then the breachers would either cut through a gate with a saw or batter their way inside with a battering ram. Blasting breaches were rare in early 2004 for conventional Army units like the 10th Mountain. Later in the war, the doors got stronger, and more sophisticated explosive breaching came into play.

With the opening created, the assault squad flooded in, covering every corner and reaching what they called their "points of domination" to eliminate any immediate threat. Sometimes that meant engaging the enemy, but more often than not the insurgents were cowards when confronted by overwhelming force. Even if weapons were within reach, they usually threw up their hands and surrendered.

Once everyone was flex-cuffed, Chad and his translator would go through battlefield interrogations. Kids were usually the best. A kind word and a Snickers bar could buy quality intel from the youngsters, including the identities of all the adults in the house and the location of any weapons or bomb-making equipment.

Successful raids like that boosted morale and gave every soldier a sense of accomplishment. But as spring rolled around a new offensive tested their resolve.

On March 31, 2004, four private security agents working for Blackwater were guarding a food convoy when they were attacked by insurgents in downtown Fallujah. Wesley Batalona, Scott Helvenston, Michael Teague, and Jerko Zovko were killed by machine gun fire and grenade blasts in their vehicle. Their bodies were burned and then dragged through the streets by a mob. The corpses were then hung from the Brooklyn Bridge, the northernmost of the two main bridges crossing the Euphrates. Photographs hit the wire services by nightfall and made it into every major publication back in the States the next day.

No one on the ground had a sense of the outrage the pictures generated at home. Chad and his men were incensed, but they weren't shocked. They knew what kind of animals they were dealing with in Fallujah. Officially the enemy included Ba'athists, AQI, the Islamic Army of Iraq, and Chechens, the same bunch that had been giving the Russians fits for years. But on the ground they were all referred to as *Muj*, shorthand for *mujahideen*, which is itself a catchall for most factions of jihadists. The biggest question Chad and his guys had was not who did it, but what the hell were those Blackwater guys doing out there by themselves?

Within forty-eight hours of the pictures going to press, the orders started flying and it was obvious a response would be swift and massive. The Marines took the lead, encircling the city with a plan to root out the terrorists. Chad's platoon was assigned the George Washington Bridge. Nobody was to enter or leave.

"We relieved an armored unit on the bridge, and they had put up a couple of HESCOs [barriers made of four-by-four-by-four-foot wire-and-mesh bags filled with dirt or sand], but that was it," Chad said. "It was the worst defensive position I'd ever seen."

Chad reinforced the bridge with a .50-caliber machine gun he and his men sandbagged and barricaded into the bridge, along with two M240 machine guns and a cache of AT4 antitank rockets—not that they expected the bad guys to roll up in tanks, but the Muj had been known to charge fortified positions in sedans or trucks rigged with explosives. You take extra precautions when the enemy doesn't mind committing suicide. They also brought up more sandbags and concertina wire, and they set up claymore mines on the bridge just in case a suicide driver got lucky.

The first night, around 0200, Chad took a small squad three-quarters of the way across the bridge to lay more concertina wire. The sky was black as ink and without NVGs you couldn't see your hand in front of your face, so he felt confident making the run. He didn't count on the dogs. When he'd first arrived in Fallujah, he'd wondered why the poverty-stricken residents didn't eat the large canines that seemed to roam everywhere. Then he realized they were the best alarm system in the land. Nothing moved day or night that the dogs didn't hear. He figured he might at least be safe from them on a bridge, but no such luck. The howling and barking began in earnest as they unspooled the wire.

Then came the cracks of weapons and bright streaks of incoming tracer rounds.

Chad and his squad sprinted back toward the covered position with tracer rounds whizzing overhead. There is no sound like the whistle of a bullet as it passes your ear, close enough that you know how lucky you were to have heard it. Because they were between the fortifications and the incoming fire, the .50-cal gunner couldn't open up until the entire squad was back behind the HESCOs. Chad was yelling, "Move, move, move!" as they ran for cover. After a quick head count, the gunners opened up with everything they had.

The original plan was to secure the bridge for two, maybe three days. But four days came and went, and then five, then six, then seven, with no relief in sight. They ran low on food, and they couldn't shave, so everyone grew a week's worth of beard. Chad ran out of Copenhagen, which almost drove him over the edge. Still, they were happy to be there. The light show alone was worth it. Every night AC-130 gunships bombarded the city, lighting the sky and rocking the George Washington Bridge like a baby's cradle. They loved every minute of it.

"You put guys in shitty situations, but if they're doing their jobs and it's life-or-death, morale actually goes up," Chad said. "It's the boredom of not doing much, not accomplishing much, or riding around looking for IEDs, that's the morale killer. When you give guys a sense of purpose and there's a clear mission—don't let anybody leave Fallujah across this bridge and if somebody shoots at you, kill them—that's what pumps guys up."

Their last day on the bridge, somebody decided to launch mortar rounds at their position from the city. One round hit the water on Chad's left, and the next hit the water on his right. Before they could launch a third, he called in air support from a squadron of A-10s in the area. Then he sat back and watched as the insurgents got a taste of the Warthog. He couldn't help smiling when the black smoke rose from the mortar site.

"Hell yeah," said one of the men behind him. That summed it up perfectly.

Back home, Emily wasn't handling the stress as well as she would have liked. While Chad was going through tobacco withdrawal on the George Washington Bridge during the First Battle of Fallujah, Emily was traveling the Ohio countryside selling Levitra, the GlaxoSmith-Kline alternative to Viagra. Gray-haired doctors throughout the Midwest got a kick out of this perky college girl and her erectile dysfunction pitch. But few knew the anxiety she was going through.

"I kept telling myself, 'Don't watch the news. Don't read the papers,'" she said. "But then I wouldn't hear from him for a week, and I would almost freak out."

One morning she did more than freak out. After stopping for her standard scone and cup of coffee, she hit the road in rural Ohio for a day filled with appointments. It was 8:45 A.M. Her next conscious memory was of hanging upside down by the seat belt of her car, the airbags deployed, a woman lying beside her asking her if she knew her own name.

According to the accident report, the company Taurus hit black ice at approximately forty-five miles per hour. It slid head-on into a telephone pole and flipped three times before coming to rest on its hood. By fate, or chance, or, in Emily's opinion, divine intervention, the first person to come upon the accident was a nurse who knew enough to keep her talking and not to move her until emergency personnel arrived.

There were no broken bones, but a lot of cuts and bruises, tremendous swelling and headaches. She would be out of work for three months. "It was embarrassing and depressing," she said.

Chad didn't find out until four days later, when he came down off the bridge.

"He called, and I was at my dad's house," she said. "I tried to soft-sell it so as not to freak him out. But when I said, 'Well, I sort of flipped my car a little bit,' he immediately turned into Lieutenant Jenkins wanting the full debrief. It hurt him that he was over there and helpless at that moment."

Being unable to work or move in any way that didn't hurt, Emily spent a lot of time reflecting. And for the first time in years, she spent serious time in prayer. She began Bible study in the home of the pastor at the New Life Assembly of God, and she became more engrossed in scripture.

The worry remained. It would never go away. But faith and friends helped make it manageable. Chad had changed, she could sense it. But when he finally got home, he would find a changed woman as well. Of that she was sure.

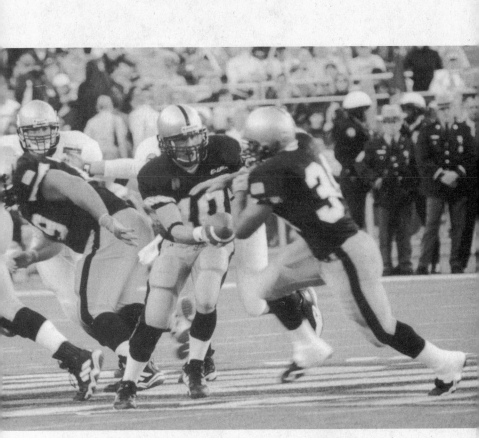

Chad Jenkins (center) had played quarterback since childhood and became a Division I starter at Army in 2000. *(Getty Images)*

The classic quarterback pose: Chad looks downfield for an open receiver in 2001. Play-action quarterbacks are always susceptible to knee injuries. Chad was lucky until his senior year.

Brian Stann came to Navy in the hopes of playing quarterback. But the triple-option offense did not suit his style, so he transitioned to linebacker, where he fit in perfectly.

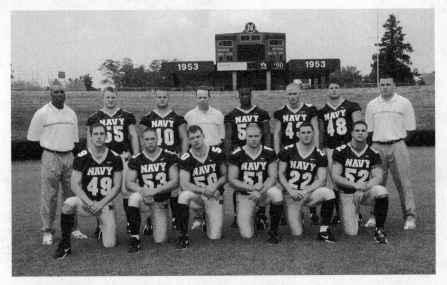

The Naval Academy linebacker corps, including Brian Stann (No. 48, back row, second from right).

What Brian lacked in size he made up for in tenacity and will, often fighting off blockers and tackling bigger and faster backs.

Brian Stann moving in to make a tackle, his eyes never leaving the ball.

Before the 2001 Army-Navy Game, President Bush visited the teams in their locker rooms. Then the President went to midfield and shook hands with the captains before the coin toss.

The Brigade of Midshipmen, 4,400 strong, salute the colors before the start of the 2001 Army-Navy Game. *(AP Images)*

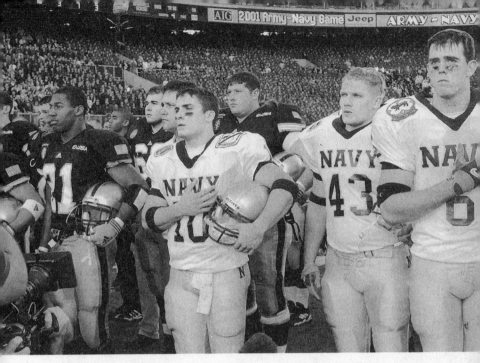

As is tradition, both teams stood before each other's student bodies and sang the alma maters. Navy players were visibly dejected after the 2001 game. It was a defeat they would not suffer again for more than a dozen years. *(AP Images)*

The 2002 Navy Midshipmen football team, including No. 48, linebacker Brian Stann, and new head coach Paul Johnson.

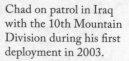

Chad on patrol in Iraq with the 10th Mountain Division during his first deployment in 2003.

Brian with his Navy football teammate J. P. Blecksmith at The Basic School, Marine Corps officer basic training, Quantico, Virginia, 2003. Blecksmith would be killed by insurgent gunfire in Fallujah, Iraq, on November 11, 2004.

Lieutenant and Mrs. Chad Jenkins, December 2004.

It took longer than he wanted, but when Brian (right) finally joined the fight, Fallujah, Iraq, was the most dangerous place on earth.

Chad (right) with part of his platoon, 2nd Ranger Battalion, 75th Ranger Regiment, ready to own the night.

Brian's platoon, 3rd Battalion, 2nd Marine Regiment, before heading into battle during Operation Matador, Al Qa'im, Iraq, May 2005.

For gallantry in action during Operation Matador, Lieutenant Brian Stann received the Silver Star, the nation's third-highest military honor.

Chad (bottom) and Army Sergeant First Class Kristoffer B. Domeij, who would be killed in action on October 22, 2011, during his fourteenth combat deployment.

There were few light moments in Iraq, but there were always friends, brothers, and fellow marines.

Between deployments, Brian proposed to Teressa at a Philadelphia Eagles game, where she worked weekends as a cheerleader.

Brian (center) and fellow marines in solemn prayer for lost friends and the loved ones they left behind.

One of the lighter moments: Brian, Teressa, and Brian's mom, Beth.

Remembering the fallen: 3rd Battalion, 2nd Marine Division, the Betio Bastards; Camp Lejeune, North Carolina.

Chad brought every soldier under his command back inside the wire, but by the fourth deployment, the stress was beginning to show on his face.

A welcome homecoming as Emily greets Chad upon his return from his final deployment in 2006.

Portrait of a hero who recoils at the word.

Men who experienced the intense combat Chad encountered on a nightly basis have trouble transitioning to normal life. That was why the FBI's counterterrorism unit was the perfect fit.

Brian traded one form of combat for another. He won the light heavyweight title in the WEC before moving into the UFC in the middleweight division. When he knocked out Jorge Santiago on Memorial Day weekend 2011, he became one of the leading middleweight title contenders. *(AP Images)*

Fighting, either in uniform or for sport, is for young men. Brian has established himself as one of the best color commentators in the UFC.

Finally able to relax, Chad and Emily Jenkins are raising a family and enjoying life in South Florida.

* * *

After Fallujah, in May 2004, Chad's division reconnected with the 10th Mountain in Iskandariya, but the attitudes were different. The rookies who had been such novices that they had to practice driving Humvees in circles in Kuwait were now the grizzled veterans, the guys who had been at the heart of the fight for the past seven months. "We felt like we were tougher than they were because we had been in Fallujah," Chad recalled.

There was a Russian power plant on the Euphrates that had been converted into living quarters for the men. The group that had been with the 82nd blew in with some swagger that they would soon need. Chad waltzed in and met his battalion commander for the 1st Battalion, 32nd Infantry Regiment, a Lieutenant Colonel Douglas Mulberry, who began his briefing with a series of statements based on single-source intelligence that Chad believed, based on his experience, to be blarney. "I immediately started sharpshooting him with questions," he said. "It was bullshit because it's our guys' lives that were on the line. If he couldn't answer tough questions, then something was wrong."

Chad's company commander was not pleased by the John Wayne antics, but several NCOs came to his defense. "I had only been there seven months, but I understood what command presence and warrior ethos was all about," Chad said. "You can't fake the funk and make out like you're a warrior when you're not. Mulberry wasn't a bad person, but he wasn't a warrior, either."

A few weeks later, with Chad's unit out on patrol, the FOB began taking mortar fire, lots of mortar fire. Artillery had the position of the incoming mortars pinpointed and requested permission to take them out, but Mulberry denied the request. He said he needed verification that no civilians were in the area. Forty-two mortar rounds hit the FOB, killing three soldiers and burning thirty tents and all their contents to the ground.

* * *

Fallujah had taught Chad the importance of taking an offensive posture whenever possible. Unfortunately, those times were rare.

"That was the problem with those early years in Iraq," he said. "You took fire and returned fire, and you put up with IEDs going off all the time, but it was like you were fighting ghosts."

A particular sore spot was the tiny village of Momadia, south of Iskandariya on the way to Ramadi, where the Euphrates took a serpentine bend. Once you crossed the bridge west into Momadia, it was, as Chad called it, "Indian country." Every time a squad went through there they took potshots. Fire was returned but nothing ever came of it.

At 2:00 P.M. one hot summer afternoon in 2004, Chad's platoon got a call that an MP unit had been ambushed on the road to Momadia. They were the quick reaction force (QRF) for the day, so Chad's platoon scrambled to their vehicles and headed south. Because the QRFs were, by definition, moving on the fly without much of a plan, they were prime targets for ambush. A lot of times the Muj would pick a fight they knew they couldn't win just to get the QRF rolling. Then they would hit the response force harder than the initial attack.

Chad's platoon crossed the bridge and turned west toward the village. They were in the middle of nowhere, and he remembered looking at an ancient relic wall on the left side of the road that stretched at least a hundred yards and thinking, "What on earth was that wall built for?" There was also a palm grove oasis on their right. It all looked peaceful enough. Then, just as Chad's vehicle passed the wall—BOOM, BOOM, BOOM—the ground quaked beneath them.

He looked in the rearview and saw black smoke. IEDs. Then, as the vehicles slowed, he heard machine gun fire. The Muj had knocked out bricks from the ancient wall and were using the small holes as their firing ports.

Specialist Michael Riley from Third Squad turned his attention toward the wall and opened up with his 240 Bravo from the cargo

Humvee. But when he turned his back on the palm grove, RPG fire came screaming out of the trees.

Riley took a round to the leg. He went down, but quickly patched himself up and returned to his 240B. He killed the Muj machine gunner by shooting him right through his firing port, a hole no bigger than a standard cinder block, from a hundred yards away.

Chad grabbed his M4 and fired at the palm grove. Over his radio he heard that Specialist Corey McGee was down and then that First Sergeant Ernie Thrush was down, and then that the first sergeant's driver was down. As he was firing, Chad calculated the men he had left. Four down was more than four down. Men were helping the wounded, so they weren't manning guns. Any more casualties and they might reach the point of being "mission ineffective."

When the assault slowed down, everyone broke for their vehicles and raced north for a kilometer, where Chad ordered the Humvees into a 360-degree perimeter. Then they assessed the damage.

First Sergeant Thrush had two of his fingers blown off. His driver, Specialist Hernandez, lost one finger. They all thought Riley was the worst. A leg shot can bleed out in minutes or hours if it isn't treated quickly, plus he had shrapnel from the IED.

Corey McGee, the top gunner on one of the trailing Humvees, had shrapnel in his throat that nicked his spinal cord, an injury suffered when a bullet hit the front sight post on his machine gun. He had also been shot in the shoulder. But he had never stopped firing his weapon. When everyone broke for their vehicles, McGee jumped down into the driver's seat of his Humvee and drove others out of the kill zone.

Once the perimeter was secure and the wounded were being treated, McGee was embarrassed to tell anyone he'd been hit.

Chad called in medevac for Riley and McGee. Hernandez and Thrush patched up their mangled hands and rode back with the men. On the way back to Iskandariya after nightfall, Chad replayed the events over and over in his mind. It was as sophisticated a two-sided ambush as he'd seen from the Muj, starting with three 155 mm IEDs and including machine guns and RPGs. They had coordinated and timed it perfectly. It didn't stop him from being pissed about it, but he swore from that moment forward he would never underestimate this enemy again.

A couple of days after the ambush, Chad was on another routine run through Momadia to make sure no one was setting up mortars when he got into another firefight. At a Y intersection, his convoy took fire from two RPGs. They returned fire, but with no more incoming grenades, they assumed this was the same bullshit as always: some one-shot wonders fired their RPGs, dropped the launcher, and walked away as if they were innocent bystanders on the way to the market to pick up bread.

"I've had enough of this shit," Chad said.

Rather than move out after returning fire, he and his platoon stuck around to see what would happen next. Within five minutes, two young Iraqi men walked down the street with their hands in their pockets as if they were unaware there was a war going on. Chad had them flex-cuffed. Then he went to the roof of the building where the RPGs had been fired to see what else might transpire that night. His squad set up the M240 Bravos, and they waited.

Sure enough, when Charlie Company rolled through an hour or so later on their way to an assault mission, an IED went off at the Y intersection. Charlie Company took fire from a rooftop on the opposite side of the village, but they were able to return fire and move out of the kill zone and on with their mission.

Immediately Chad could sense that something good was about to happen. For the first time, he and his platoon were the ones waiting for the post-ambush ambush, the "second wave," as reporters liked to call it when writing about such things.

Within minutes a group of Muj came out to the intersection to inspect the damage from their IED. They all carried AK-47s, but no one seemed at all concerned that they were being watched.

"Ready," Chad said, trying to keep the excitement out of his voice. "Three . . . two . . . one . . . execute."

Everyone on the rooftop fired, and the insurgents went down in a heap.

"That was the greatest feeling in the world," Chad said. "It wasn't often that we got to do to them what they did to us."

It was a sense of accomplishment he wanted more often. The worst feeling for a warrior is the wait, letting the battle come to you rather than taking it to the enemy. Chad had always been an offense-minded person. His objective in football had always been to strike early and often and put enough points on the board that the opposition could never catch up. Defense wasn't in his DNA. He needed to be in a position to apply that mind-set to the battlefield.

The chance came when he ran into a former West Point linebacker named Pat Work at an FOB between Fallujah and Ramadi. Even though they had never played on the same team (Work had graduated from West Point when Chad was a sophomore in high school), they knew each other well enough. Work was the only cadet ever to register twenty or more tackles in three games, and he was still heralded as the hero of the 1993 Army-Navy Game for the game-saving shoestring tackle he made to give Army the win. Chad was the last Army quarterback to beat Navy, and his one-legged performance that afternoon in Philadelphia was becoming more epic with each retelling.

Work had just arrived in the region after spending two years in Afghanistan establishing foothold bases on the Pakistan border. After he and Chad exchanged a few pleasantries, Work said, "Hey, you're going into the Ranger Regiment, aren't you?"

The 75th Ranger Regiment was the Army's elite, special operations, light infantry unit used in rapid-deployment direct-action raids. They were the guys taking the fight to the enemy. When that knock on the door came at zero dark thirty, if it was the Army, it was the 75th Ranger Regiment.

"I don't know," Chad said. "I want to, but I haven't gotten the paperwork in."

Work pointed his finger at Chad's chest and said, "Get it in. Let's get going. We need you."

That was all it took. If Chad was going to be in this war, he wanted to be the aggressor. That meant joining the Ranger Regiment. When he returned home after 372 days, Chad was ready for the next phase of his life as one of the Army's very best.

Brian's court-martial started exactly nine months after the allegations made against him threw his life and career into limbo. The resolution of the trial took one day, and if the JAG prosecutor hadn't felt compelled to go through the motions of continuing the case, it could have wrapped in an hour.

Brian still hadn't been allowed to speak to any of his friends who were in his town house that night, but in the end, it didn't matter. The case was so weak, and the charges so obviously false, that the court seemed embarrassed that it had come to this.

Carolyn was the prosecution's first witness, and she was a disaster. A court-martial differs from a civilian trial in that all the jurors are Marine or Navy officers, and they are allowed to question the witnesses. If jurors in civilian trials want to ask questions, the process becomes an ordeal. Proceedings have to stop, the other jurors have to shuffle out, and the question has to be submitted in writing so the judge and attorneys can examine and argue over its relevance. Military jurors are bound by no such restraints. They are officers, and they ask officer questions.

Two of the jurors in Brian's case were Marine women, and they had some pointed questions for Carolyn. With ten fellow marines in the house less than fifty feet away, why didn't you yell? Wouldn't one call for help have been enough? If he pinned you down, as you claim, why didn't you say anything to the other marines immediately? Did you have any marks or bruises? Did you show them to anyone? Why did you stay in the town house the next day? Why did you have breakfast? And is it your assertion that you found a burst of energy and threw this two-hundred-pound marine off of you? Really?

Her answers varied between a weak "I don't know, ma'am" and "That's just the way it happened, ma'am."

Sensing they were being lied to—an offense that will draw the ire of any marine—the jurors amped up the questioning while Brian's lawyer tried not to gloat. Why had she waited two days to report the incident? Why not call the police and give a full accounting immediately? Did none of her Marine training kick in? Did none of the leadership and decision-making skills the U.S. government had spent countless dollars training her to perfect take hold?

It was obvious Carolyn hadn't thought the matter through, especially the part about following her Marine instincts.

The prosecution attempted to salvage their case by calling several of the witnesses who had been in the town house that night. They all testified that Carolyn had been out with the group, that she'd had a few drinks, and that she had ridden back home with Brian. Some claimed to have heard her conversing with Brian through the thin walls. All acknowledged that she had hung around the next day.

That was it. They offered no testimony to support Carolyn's claims other than to say she was there—which Brian had said from the beginning. On cross-examination, they bolstered Brian's case by telling the jury they hadn't heard cries for help, or anything that sounded like a scuffle. Some said they were still awake when the incident allegedly occurred, and they felt certain they would have heard a tussle between a man of Brian's size and woman of Carolyn's.

It would have been easy for Brian's lawyer to move for summary judgment, but his client would have none of it. Brian had waited nine months for this moment, and he was going to profess his innocence for the record. When he took the stand, Brian looked every juror in the eye and went through every moment of that night, step by step, minute by minute, in agonizing detail, leaving out nothing.

They had a few questions for him, but nothing like the grilling they had given Carolyn. He answered firmly and honestly, telling them that taking a fellow officer back to his town house was foolish, a mistake he would certainly never make again, but nothing criminal or even modestly inappropriate had occurred. Even though the defense had information about Carolyn's prior false accusations, and that she was engaged to a marine who was deployed overseas but had not told this to anyone in the town house that night, they chose not to use it.

There was no need. The jury acquitted Brian in less than three hours.

When handing down the verdict of "Not guilty on all charges," the judge took a deep breath and said, "Good luck to you, Lieutenant Stann." That and the righteous looks he got from the jurors on the way out of the courtroom were the closest thing to an apology Brian would ever receive from the Marine Corps. He could have pursued Carolyn in civil court, but he didn't want to spend another second thinking about her. Her career was forever tarnished, and if she ever tried anything like that again, the JAG Corps would throw the book at her. That was all Brian needed to move on.

He never got over it, though. The effects lingered for years. For the rest of his military career, Brian kept a professional distance from female officers. He would attend meetings with female marines only if other people were in the room, or if a door was open so that he could be seen and heard. Even casual conversations with new female acquaintances were stilted and reserved.

While home on a break several months before the trial, Brian had been introduced to Teressa Ruspi, a student at Scranton's Marywood University, a small college of about 3,500 students on one of the most beautiful wooded campuses in the Northeast. Teressa was smart and engaging, stunning and athletic. Brian stayed as far away as he could without being rude. They met a few more times in the following weeks and months, always in group settings. He made sure there were others around. Once he finally worked up the nerve to ask her out on a date, he talked with her and did all the right things, but he avoided physical contact and would not kiss her good night.

It wasn't until they had been out several times that he finally opened up about what had happened. When he explained it all, it was like a switch had been flipped. Teressa understood why he had been so distant. They agreed to continue dating, but take things slowly. She had another year before graduating from Marywood anyway, and Brian had a lot of catching up to do.

He would move on with his professional career without any blemishes on his record. But he would never truly move on from the scars the court-martial left behind.

Brian also suffered from something he called "benchwarmer guilt." While he had been in Mike Company and then in MACE (the grand opening of the museum with all of Brian's Marine Raider memorabilia received rave reviews), his classmates and former teammates were doing their MOS training and deploying overseas. It didn't make sense that he would harbor guilt, given his circumstances, but he couldn't shake the feeling that he had let everyone down by not being there.

He immediately got back into TBS to finish his final days and graduate, and he enrolled in IOBC as well as a martial arts class to keep his skills sharp. With the help of his NCO buddies, he had won two more amateur fights, which earned him a bout in mid-November for the Virginia amateur light heavyweight title. But he had a lot of work to do beforehand.

Once he finished TBS, he took a couple weeks off to head home before starting his nine weeks of IOBC training, a course the marines call "the man school," for its rigorous tactical field work. Brian couldn't wait. He was in the gym in Scranton on September 4, punching a bag, when his cell phone rang. He would normally ignore a call in the middle of a workout, but something made him answer it this time.

"Brian," one of his former classmates said, "bad news, man. Ronnie Winchester was killed today in Iraq."

He found a chair and took a few deep breaths. Ronnie had been two years ahead of Brian, a big offensive lineman who made up for his lack of speed with a scrappy determination to win every down. Brian would never forget their last game together, the 2000 Army-Navy Game, when Ronnie, a senior, had stood up in the locker room and said, "Hey, I might not be that good at football, but I know I'm good at one thing, and that's fighting!"

Ronnie fought one of his best friends that afternoon. Army's defensive tackle Doug Larsen was a high school classmate of Ronnie's. They had grown up together, so they jawed and picked at each other the entire game like they had throughout high school. Both team captains warned the officiating crew not to take them too seriously or to penalize them for unsportsmanlike conduct. "They've been best friends forever," one of the players told the line judge.

After Navy's win, Ronnie found Larsen, and they hugged at midfield. It was a memory that flashed in Brian's mind as if it were happening right in front of him. The joy Ronnie felt while at the same time expressing love and empathy for his friend: those were the things Brian wanted to remember forever.

The details of Ronnie's death were all too familiar. He was starting his second tour in Iraq, already a first lieutenant, and he was a platoon commander taking his guys out on patrol. He had written his family e-mails about his growing concerns. The insurgency in Anbar Province was out of control, or so he thought. Things were going to get worse before they got better. Not long after he got back, he was out front leading his company on their first combat patrol. That was when Ronnie's vehicle hit an IED.

Four were killed, including Ronnie, who was still giving orders, getting his men out of the kill zone, when he lost consciousness.

Ronnie Winchester was the first Navy football player killed in action after 2001. Now Brian felt sick, not just for having lost a friend and teammate, but for not having been there in the fight when it happened.

He had no idea how much worse his guilt would get.

Another classmate of Brian's was killed the same day as Ronnie, although not in combat. Brett Harman had been a wrestler at Annapolis and was now a Marine second lieutenant temporarily stationed at Camp Lejeune awaiting deployment. That day, he and a buddy from his high school drove an hour up to Raleigh to see an NC State game. They were shot to death at a tailgate party.

As Brian tried to digest the deaths of two marines he had known so well, he remembered a running joke they all had with Brett about his car, an economy-size Saturn that looked like it wasn't going to make it out of the parking lot. One time when another midshipman was giving Brett grief about it, Brian yelled, "Screw that, Brett! That's a manly Saturn!"

"Why thank you, Brian," Brett had said with great affect. "It is a manly Saturn."

That joke ran for weeks, with Brian and Brett replaying their routine at least a dozen times. Now he was gone, and there was nothing Brian could do about it.

He poured his grief and guilt into IOBC, attacking the field exercises as if each day were his last day on earth. He learned later that his buddy Brett had been killed after a truck had driven too fast and too close to a little girl outside the stadium. Brett's buddies had confronted the drivers, and Brett went over to calm things down. But an hour later, the driver, Timothy Wayne Johnson, and his brother, Tony, returned and shot Brett and Kevin McCann in the chest at point-blank range. Brett died in the arms of another man at the game, the whole time saying, "I'm good. Don't worry, I'm good."

It was hard to put those thoughts aside, but Brian had no choice during training. Live-fire exercises at twilight, climbing uphill through trenches with .50-caliber rounds flying off over your head, close-range M16 exercises under NVGs: IOBC was as tough and dangerous as any training in the world. At one point, instructors sent the class out on a nine-day field exercise, and each marine was given only three MREs. Resupply didn't come until day four. Brian lost a total of twelve pounds.

The final day of the exercise was a live-fire shoot followed by an eight-mile fast-paced hike with all their weapons and gear. Finally the trucks showed up and the weapons and gear were loaded. Brian and his classmates looked around for the buses. After a couple of minutes, they realized that no one was coming to get them.

The captain walked up and said, "Gentlemen, it is seven miles back to the armory to clean your weapons. You're going to run it in fifty minutes. For every minute you are over, you will give me one round of grappling."

They made it in fifty-two, which meant everyone had to go to the ground for two rounds of grappling before finally being dismissed.

"It was incredibly hard," Brian remembered. "But when I got to Iraq, I was so well prepared. I felt immediately comfortable when I got to Iraq, because of everything I'd been through."

Brian had to endure one more blow before deployment, though. On November 11, 2004, he and his buddy Travis Manion, who had been training him to wrestle, drove to Virginia Beach to fight for the Virginia amateur light heavyweight mixed martial arts title. Gunny Marlow and Gunny Collette were to meet them there to work his corner. They had been at his side for every fight, and they had gone to great lengths to improve his striking technique, making him more than just a bruising puncher.

They arrived early the day of the fight and checked into the hotel.

Brian wanted to rest a little and get a small bite to eat before head-ing out. Then Travis's phone rang, and a sledgehammer dropped on Brian's world.

Earlier that very day, as the Second Battle of Fallujah (known officially as Operation Phantom Fury) raged on, India Company, 3rd Battalion, 2nd Marine Regiment entered the Jolan District of the city and began house-to-house clearance, rooting out insurgents and squeezing the noose that would finally bring Fallujah under control. The process was going well, until a sniper opened up, pin-ning down Third Platoon behind a cluster of buildings. The platoon leader, Second Lieutenant J. P. Blecksmith, scrambled to the roof to pinpoint the location of the sniper.

Once there, Blecksmith called in. Within seconds, he was hit in the shoulder by a single round. The bullet deflected off his body armor and went through his chest, piercing his heart. A quarter inch in any other direction and he would have been fine.

His last words were "I'm hit."

The smoothest-throwing quarterback Brian had ever seen, the California kid, big and strong and always happy, the receiver who caught a late pass in the 2001 Army-Navy Game to set up the Mids' final touchdown, and one of Brian's closest friends, was gone.

In the ring later that night, Brian exploded on his opponent the second the bell rang, letting loose with a long and furious combination of punches, each more cathartic than the one before. His opponent stag-gered back, and Brian charged. But the emotion in his punches was not enough. His opponent crouched low and made a wrestling move for Brian's legs that drove him into the mat. Brian tried to counter, but it was too late. The fight was over almost before it began.

Brian lost his first title fight that night, which meant nothing. He had lost one of his best friends, a classmate, and a great marine, while Brian was still away from it all. It was time to put the bullshit behind him and get into the real fight. It was time to be a marine at war.

CHAPTER 10

Once we have a war there is only one thing to do. It
must be won. For defeat brings worse things than any
that can ever happen in war.

—ERNEST HEMINGWAY

Chad missed the Second Battle of Fallujah at the end of 2004. He had arrived back at Fort Drum in September, eight weeks before the operation launched, and remained stateside through its end. He was busy, though. Within an hour of hitting U.S. soil, he proposed to Emily. When he got down on one knee, she assumed he had stolen a trinket out of one of Saddam's palaces. Actually, he had gotten his sister to buy the ring for him, and she had slipped it to him in a sweatshirt the second he hit the ground.

That night, their first together in more than a year, Chad fell into the kind of deep slumber soldiers can only find at home, while Emily stared at the ceiling. She had known he snored, but time softens memories. She'd remembered the sound as a gentle hum. But now, in the darkness of a borrowed apartment in Sackets Harbor, New York, he sounded like a John Deere tractor pulling a Bush Hog. She tried nudging him. That didn't work. Then she rearranged the covers, thinking a change in temperature might do it, but he still rumbled on.

"Finally, I thought, maybe if I whistle, he'll turn over and stop," she said. So she pursed her lips and blew a soft, steady whistle, not realizing that she sounded just like an incoming mortar round. "He bolted up and grabbed me," she said. "It scared the daylights out of both of us."

That was her introduction to the new Chad. During the day he spent most of his hours as happy as he was on the day he left. But he was also a guy who bolted upright in his sleep to fight an enemy that was not there, and who slipped occasionally into silent reflection, still and deadly serious.

He would soon head to Fort Benning and Ranger Regiment training, called ROPE (Ranger Officer Program of Excellence), but before he left, he and Emily began planning a military wedding that would take place when he returned in December. It would be in Dublin, Ohio, complete with dress uniforms and swords. "It was not what I had dreamed about at all," Emily said. "But then, I never thought I would meet somebody like Chad."

During this time, when Chad was at home, Emily realized that the things she found most attractive about him, his inherent goodness and his compulsory need to lead, had grown stronger and more polished during his time away. But there were things he pushed inside, parts of himself he could not share. Just a few days before he left for Benning, as they were having dinner, she asked him about the Chinook crash. It had been all over the television, and in the papers. She wanted to hear it from him.

His face fell into a cold mask. "I can't talk about it," he said. "I'll never talk about it. Please don't ask again."

For seven years he kept his word, never once discussing a single detail or feeling from that day.

Most civilians confuse Rangers (the soldiers with the Ranger tab on their uniform below their Airborne patch) with the 75th Ranger

Regiment, which was created after the Vietnam War as a light, quick, mobile special operations force. The confusion is understandable, and while the Army does its best to complicate the matter, the clearest analogy is the simplest: Imagine the Rangers as the NFL, an elite group of athletes who have reached the pinnacle of their sport. Now imagine the Ranger Regiment as the Pro Bowl, an even more elite subset trained in specific skills: mostly direct-action raids. These were the men who took the Panamanian airfields and Manuel Noriega's house in a matter of minutes during Operation Just Cause in 1989, capturing more than a thousand combatants in a day. They were also the guys who fought their way out of overwhelming odds in Somalia during the episode commonly known by the title of Mark Bowden's book *Black Hawk Down*.

It is less well known that they spearheaded the first airborne operations against the Taliban in Afghanistan and led the first airborne assaults in Iraq in March 2003. During a single deployment in Afghanistan, 1st Ranger Battalion, 75th Ranger Regiment conducted almost a thousand missions, killing more than four hundred Taliban and Al Qaeda fighters and capturing almost four hundred high-value targets, many of them part of the famous deck of cards President Bush kept in his desk. These guys operate with lightning speed and are as proficient as any military unit in the history of warfare. In Army-speak, they work at a "high operational tempo."

"I loved the Ranger Regiment more than anything else I've ever done in my life," Chad said. "It was the most humbling and rewarding experience I could have ever had."

The training at Benning included more running and jumping and maneuvering over obstacles as well as getting through the Ranger First Responder program, where he learned enough medicine to save a life in the field. Chad became proficient at fast-roping out of all the different helicopters at the Rangers' disposal, and he mastered the nuances of explosive breaching, learning to blast his way into a building in ways that didn't kill any innocent bystanders.

Mainly, he learned how to raid and dominate buildings, airfields, compounds, and any other area where the enemy might set up shop. The drills were relentless: single-team raids on a single room; single-team raids on two rooms; two-team raids on two rooms; two-team raids on three rooms, and so on. Speed was always the key. Rangers achieved their objectives—capturing or killing bad guys—because they got on target before the target had time to sit up in bed and rub his eyes.

When Chad completed ROPE—a program he found to be tougher than Ranger School, even though every man who went through it was already a proven warrior—he hustled back to Dublin, where he and Emily were married on December 10, 2004. After a brief honeymoon, they loaded up the truck the day after Christmas and drove to Fort Lewis, Washington, halfway between Tacoma and Olympia and as far away from normal as Mrs. Jenkins had ever been.

She knew no one. Emily had never been to Washington, never lived on or even near an Army post, and never been part of the distinct culture that defines Army officers' wives. She couldn't even speak the language. "Chad would come home from work and start speaking in all these acronyms, and it might as well have been Japanese," she said.

Even the look of the place threw her. Like most Army posts, Fort Lewis was an odd mix of Spartan buildings with no discernible architectural theme: no ornate trim, no quaint or quirky fixtures, nothing that would catch an average passerby's eye. Yet every part of it was manicured like a country club lawn: spotless, weedless, and pristine. Every structure was freshly painted and every curb immaculately edged. All the trees were limbed up to a uniform height, and all the shrubs were squared off at perfect ninety-degree angles. No one aspect of this stood out to Emily, but the combination had a jarring subliminal effect. Like stop signs or Coca-Cola bottles in a foreign language, she knew what she was seeing, but she also knew it was a little off. Then there were all the tanks and Humvees and helicopters, as ubiquitous as sedans in a mall parking lot.

"I had never seen any of that before," she said. "It was intimidating. Plus, the place where we stayed smelled like old dead people."

She had also never shopped at a post exchange, or PX, never flashed a military ID, and never been called "ma'am" more than a dozen times in her life, and it was easy to see why Emily wasn't immediately comfortable in her new life.

On their one-month anniversary, she walked to the store to buy food for a celebration dinner. Then she did her best to cook it in their little apartment. Chad had the flu, but that didn't stop him from working to earn his Expert Infantry Badge by disassembling and reassembling an M2 machine gun and running a function check on it between sneezes. When he got home that night, he looked like hell but squared up to the table and heaped all the praise he could muster on his new wife's first big meal.

"Oh, honey, this is the best peanut butter chicken I've ever had," he said.

She burst into tears and yelled, "It's not peanut butter chicken; it's my grandma's nutmeg chicken! I walked to the store to get it, and you"—sob—"should"—sniffle—"know"—sob—"the"—sniffle— "difference!"

Emily didn't think she was the perfect Army wife in those first few weeks, but there was a light moment or two, like the first time Chad showed her his PT clothes, a nondescript cotton shirt with "Ranger Regiment" in script along the side, and matching gym shorts, the short hip-hugging kind seen only in Richard Simmons's workout videos. The soldiers called them Ranger panties, and being one of the few who could wear them was a big deal in the community. The minute you qualified for the regiment you ran out to Ranger Joe's, a supply store outside the gates of Fort Benning, and bought a pair.

The first time Chad showed them to Emily she doubled over in laughter. "You tough Ranger guys don't really wear those, do you?" she said between chortles.

"Yeah, these are a big deal," he said. "It's tradition."

It was one of many strange Ranger traditions she had to learn on the fly.

Others weren't quite so funny, like when she learned her husband could not tell her anything about his job. He couldn't tell her how many men he worked with, what they did, how they got to and from their job sites, or what the job entailed once they got there. Everything was cloaked in "operational security," even among family members.

"You mean you can't tell me anything," she said to him one day as she was driving him in to the HQ.

"Not really," he said. "It's all classified."

"Everything?"

"Pretty much, yeah. Sorry."

As they pulled into the parking lot, she noticed a four-wheel-drive truck with knobby tires and a large sticker in the back window that read, RANGER: I JUMP OUT OF AIRPLANES AND KILL PEOPLE FOR A LIVING.

"Well, that settles it," she said. "From now on I'll just tell everyone my husband jumps out of planes and kills people. That'll be a great conversation starter."

Life became more manageable when Emily went back to work. GlaxoSmithKline loved her and wanted her back, even if it meant shifting her territory from Findlay, Ohio, to Tacoma, Washington. After the initial culture shock, she also realized the Ranger Regiment went out of its way to include families as much as possible. Even though almost all work-related information was classified, the community outreach through meetings and newsletters and social functions far exceeded that of the typical Army unit. The Ranger 2/75 Wives Club would meet every other week, and the Rear Detachment (or Rear D) regularly sent out e-mails to let the families know they were not forgotten.

She found a Bible study group of other military wives in the area and a church where she felt comfortable. By the time the next deployment drew near, Emily had embraced her new life and put away what she termed "selfish things." Chad hadn't turned her around. Not even her church friends had made the difference. It was the young boys standing on the line with their rucks and M4s that brought reality home for her. Every morning she saw a new batch of kids barely out of high school ramping up for war.

The looks on their faces, fighting back fear with clenched jaws and snappy salutes: it made her angry at herself that she had ever been so woeful. "I looked at their young faces and at their guns, and I realized that they were going to defend themselves and probably have to kill people with those very weapons," she said. "I wanted to give every one of them a hug."

The day Chad left for Iraq, Emily stood with other wives and girlfriends and watched the plane's lumbering ascent. Young kids grabbed tight to their mother's legs, and a baby wailed near the end of the line.

She swore she wouldn't cry, but when the tears came, she couldn't stop them. After a while, she no longer tried.

Second Ranger Battalion operated under what soldiers liked to refer to as "big-boy rules," meaning that much of the bureaucracy and red tape was swept aside for them. If, for example, Chad needed different gloves or some new NVGs for a particular mission, he no longer had to bounce the request around two or three different chains of command. He simply went to supply and got what he needed. On a much larger scale, if he was planning a single platoon mission in a densely populated area, he might decide he needed two Black Hawks instead of one Chinook. That request would also sail through without a problem.

The relationships between the men in his unit were different as well. There was less interest in rank and who had the tightest haircut and more emphasis on who could get the job done. In many respects, it was more like his days as a quarterback than any of his previous Army experiences. Rather than an eleven-man offense, Chad was now responsible for between five guys (a fire team) and forty-five (a platoon), but he was still calling the plays and coaching them up, relying on them to execute so that every mission was a success.

They were based out of a ten-thousand-square-foot house in one of the nicer areas of Baghdad, a walled estate with separate servants' quarters that U.S. Rangers quickly converted into a gym. There was also a pool and a volleyball court in the back, and a yard large enough to build a mock shoot house. They couldn't practice live-fire drills there, but they could go through dry runs and work on any techniques that needed perfecting if something didn't go smoothly the night before. The place had probably belonged to one of Saddam's ministers, although Chad never asked. He was surprised by how civilized Baghdad looked compared to Fallujah. There were freeways and exits and commercial areas that looked like a lot of Western cities. "Parts of Baghdad looked like West Palm Beach, Florida," he said.

Those were not the parts he saw at night. The Ranger Regiment was proud that when they were called upon, they could be in action anywhere in the world within eighteen hours. They could be anywhere in Iraq in a single period of darkness. "Not all of our objectives were in Baghdad, but we based out of there because it was a good spot, and we could get to where we needed to go," Chad said. "We would work out, tan, and swim every day and get the job done every night."

During that time frame, Chad's unit was assigned to take on the network of Abu Musab al-Zarqawi, who held the absurd title of "Emir of Al Qaeda in the City of Two Rivers," and who was responsible for most of the roadside bombs and beheadings in Iraq during that time. Chad's job was to disrupt the emir's activities by killing his leadership, and if the opportunity presented itself, also killing Zarqawi.

To Chad, they were always after a Mahmud or an Ahmed or a Muhammad, most with an *al* somewhere in their names. Other than that, he didn't know that much about his targets. The intelligence guys would get very excited at the briefings, talking about the value of this one or that, but Chad would invariably interrupt the discussions with a series of tough questions that set the intelligence officers back on their heels. He didn't need to know the target's biography. All he needed to know was where the guy was, and what sort of situation Chad and his men were about to walk into.

Once the word came down that a mission was a go, the Rangers headed out. The platoons broke down into squads and the squads broke down into five-man fire teams, so by the time they rolled outside the wire, they were divided into five-man groups that all worked together as a seamless unit. One of Chad's team leaders was First Sergeant Zac Dean, the kind of guy you would shepherd your kids away from if you saw him in a restaurant wearing a tank top, but a man you always wanted by your side in a fight.

He was also a voice of authority and experience during the AARs, the after-action reviews. Every night, the Rangers headed out into the blackness with another compound to raid, another combatant to capture or kill. Sometimes it went flawlessly (not often) and sometimes it was a mess. Every time they returned to their Baghdad home, they would gather and review the action. No mistake was ever covered up and nobody tried to soft-sell screw-ups. Dean was like a coach in a film room after a game, analyzing each motion, each action, and each second of the raid. Then he critiqued and offered suggestions on how to get better. That was one of the advantages of the makeshift shoot house in the backyard. If the third man through the door was a fraction of a second off in securing his zone of responsibility, he could work it out through practice the next day.

"If you don't pay attention to the minutiae, to the little details, something big is eventually going to bite you in the ass," Chad said. "You have to be a finely oiled machine so that you can anticipate everything that's coming. You have to know how long it takes to get on a target, how long it takes to identify an objective, and how long it takes to get in and get out. You have to have surgical precision, and that only happens when you make sure every detail is done correctly. You can't let little things slide."

On good nights, nobody got shot and the bad guys were brought back in flex-cuffs and Army-issue flip-flops—"we had to walk them out of there in something," Chad said. "Flip-flops were quick, so it helped reduce our time on target, which cut down on opportunities for the enemy to attack Rangers on exfils." On bad nights, rounds were exchanged. He didn't know what he would feel the first time he or his team had to shoot a woman. They had trained for it and knew it would probably come. Women were not immune from jihadist influence, and many of them would go for weapons even as the men were putting their hands in the air. One night during a single-house raid, it happened. A woman hesitated at first, obviously realizing that raising the AK-47 was suicide, but she did it anyway, even after seeing her husband shot for raising the very same weapon just moments earlier.

Afterward, Chad checked every member of his team to make sure they were okay. They all claimed that they were fine, although there wasn't a lot of chatter that night during the AAR.

The men learned quickly which areas were going to be easy and which had the potential to go wrong in a hurry. Raids in the countryside were almost always better. Teams could usually fast-rope in from a helicopter and be on the target in a matter of seconds. Then, depending on how isolated the area was, they could take their time gathering battlefield intelligence, let the target get dressed (assuming he was taken alive), and lead him out for pickup and departure.

Urban areas were tougher. Sadr City was the worst. The Shia section of Baghdad, filled with high-rise slums, Sadr City was a gangland shooting gallery with tribes of residents taking potshots at everything that moved, including their neighbors. Violence erupted there so frequently that nobody kept stats of the killings. In May 2005, thirteen bound and blindfolded bodies were found in a shallow and hastily dug grave. A week later, a car bomb went off outside of a restaurant, killing eight and wounding eighty-nine.

This was not all AQI violence. Most of it was a sectarian gang war between Shia and Sunni factions. But any time Chad and his teams had to go into the area, they took gunfire. It was a hard area to get into and an even harder one to get out of. Once you conducted a raid and "went loud" with an explosive breach, whether the target was captured or killed, his neighbors knew you were there. The longer you stayed there the more apt the neighbors were to try to surround the house or set up a sniper nest or plant a roadside bomb on your exit route. Many nights, Chad would see locals who weren't a part of any organized unit running through the streets of Sadr City with AK-47s. Unless they were part of the specific mission that night, or on the kill-and-capture list, most times the Rangers would let them go. The last thing you wanted was to jeopardize your objective and mission by engaging some gangbangers.

During one of Chad's missions in early 2005, the vagaries of modern Iraq came home for him and his team. The objective was an insurgent holing up in a small shack in a dense palm tree grove on the outskirts of Baghdad. As always, Chad's unit prepped with the intelligence people and then mapped out their insertion and extraction plans as well as going through all the "what-if" contingencies. When night fell, the team headed out to the tarmac, where two MH-47 Chinooks were waiting.

The insertion went without a hitch from the Rangers' perspective, but after that things got a little weird. First the ISR (intelligence, surveillance, and reconnaissance—the airborne assets that include everything from drones to satellites to cameras on planes that look like tiny, remote-controlled models) identified multiple people scrambling around the shack, which wasn't supposed to be the case. Then, as the team was walking toward the shack after being dropped off, they encountered a couple of "hot spots," one to the north and the other to the south. This seemed strange, but not so unusual that Chad thought it jeopardized the mission. But things only got more complicated from there. As the team got closer, they saw a couple of squirters exit the shack itself with weapons. Thankfully, Chad had an AC-130 gunship overhead for air support. The plane engaged and eliminated one of the squirters on a nearby riverbank.

Then Chad heard some explosions. The AC-130 had taken fire from the hot spots and set off several secondary blasts in the process of taking out the bad guys. That must have startled the other squirters around the house—a house the Rangers had thought would be relatively empty except for the target. Five men ran out toward Chad's team. On the fly, Chad coordinated a quick ambush to kill the guys charging their way. Only then did the Rangers enter the shack.

When they got there, Chad and his Rangers encountered two men holding weapons. They killed them immediately. But the men had not been aiming their weapons at the Rangers. They had been pointing their AK-47s at a third man, who was naked and tied to a chair with a hood over his head. When the shooting started, the man in the chair started yelling, "Don't shoot, don't shoot!" in Arabic.

"What the hell?" Zac Dean said.

A translator was called, and after some aggressive questioning by Chad, they determined that the man was from a rival sect and had been kidnapped, a common occurrence at the time given all the civil unrest in that area. No one had known or expected the Rangers to break up a kidnapping ring, but as Sergeant Dean said that night, "Hey, two birds with one stone."

Sometimes the actions were larger and far more detailed, especially as the insurgency continued to rain death and mayhem on innocents. One night in the early summer of 2005, Chad's entire platoon and two others flew west to a desert village in Iraq with the objective of doing a complete sweep. The three platoons would go through the entire village wiping out any and all insurgents residing there.

They were surprised to discover that there weren't as many insurgents as originally expected, which was great, but a firefight did erupt early, and three insurgents were killed. The problem with this was that it took too long. Even with Chad's platoon leapfrogging the other two as they cleared and swept the village, going through a hundred houses took longer than one period of darkness.

It looked like they might have to wait a full day and fly out the next night, which was a pain but not uncommon. When that happened, it often gave the Rangers a chance to conduct more thorough battlefield interrogations, which often yielded the best intelligence. But then an Air Force pilot broke the landing gear of a Sikorsky CH-53 Sea Stallion (a big, gray helicopter) when he came in for the exfiltration landing. Another CH-53 was in the area, so the crew of the first loaded onto the second and left the Rangers on the ground to guard the downed bird.

"Now a one-night operation turned into a ninety-six-hour operation all because somebody flew his CH-53 into the ground," Chad said.

No one planned for three platoons to be on the ground that long. The village was secure, but they had no water and no food and no way to get the bird out of the dirt. Then they started taking mortar fire from the next village. When Americans were vulnerable, word spread quickly.

One well-placed JDAM (Joint Direct Attack Munition, a thousand-pound bomb) put an end to the mortar fire, and air support dropped bottled water and MREs, but there was nothing anyone could do about the sun. Wearing nighttime gear in the daylight was like wearing a parka in a sauna. Chad put his watch on a nearby pickup truck to measure the temperature. It came back: 154 degrees.

"Hey, Lieutenant Jenkins, I can blow the thing," the platoon's master breacher, Mike Burke, said, pointing to the chopper. "Just let the CO know that it's an option if they need me to do it."

Chad said, "Thanks, Mike, but they're not going to blow a helicopter because the front landing gear broke off."

A day later the order came over, "Prepare the helicopter to be blown in place."

"You have got to be kidding me," Chad said. But he did as ordered, pulling the radios and other vital components out of the bird and letting Burke have a field day. The master breacher looked like a kid at Disney World as he was rigging it to blow. But thirty minutes prior to the "fire-in-the-hole" order, or "going loud," another order came through. Cooler heads had prevailed. Another helicopter was being dispatched to haul the CH-53 out of the soft soil.

Crestfallen, Burke pulled his explosives out, and they all stood and watched as a crew took off the rotors and assembled a cradle beneath the big Sikorsky. It took several hours, but the feat of engineering worked, and the CH-53 was sling-loaded out. When Chad and his men were extracted, they had been in the village for the better part of four days, a record snafu in his book.

Chad never lost a single man, never even had any life-threatening injuries to himself or anyone in his unit. It was a blessing he thanked God for every day, especially because at one point he and his team were in firefights seventeen consecutive nights. Being the aggressor helped. The Ranger Regiment was never out walking the streets waiting to see who shot first. They struck, secured an objective, and moved out. It was all they did, and they were masters at it.

After one capture operation that had gone nearly flawlessly, Chad and Zac Dean loaded their prisoner onto a Black Hawk and then hooked their D-ring clips to the O-rings on the floor. That way they could sit in the open doorway for the trip back.

Flying over Baghdad in the middle of the night with their feet hanging out into the blackness, Dean turned to Chad and said, "Did you ever in a million years think you'd be flying here like this?"

"No way," Chad said.

Then Dean looked out at the city lights and said, "This is the best adrenaline rush ever. Nothing else comes close."

CHAPTER 11

I come in peace, I didn't bring artillery. But I am
pleading with you with tears in my eyes: if you fuck
with me, I'll kill you all.

—MARINE GENERAL JAMES MATTIS TO
IRAQI TRIBAL LEADERS

May 2005 was a beautiful time to be in Maryland and Virginia, where Brian had spent the majority of his military career, with cherry blossoms blooming virgin white and the water of the Chesapeake glimmering blue in the warm spring sun. But in Iraq, where he was now, Al Qa'im was hotter than three hundred hells, even in the pitch-black hours before dawn.

Brian was as accustomed to the heat as a human could be while living in a slow-roasting Crock-Pot, covered from head to toe in one hundred pounds of body armor and gear. After being sidelined for so long, he never complained about the heat in Anbar Province, even though there were times when he thought the biggest enemy they were fighting was the relentless, unblinking sun. The wry joke going around was "Yeah, but it's a dry heat." That was true. It was also true that you cooked Thanksgiving turkey in a dry heat.

As the minutes ticked away before the launch of Operation Matador, a major offensive in Anbar, Brian felt a chill and a tingle in the tips of his fingers. It was the body's reflexive cry to flee from impending danger, a feeling he recognized and had come to embrace. As a platoon leader in Weapons Company, 3rd Battalion, 2nd Marines (or Weapons 3/2, in Marine shorthand), Brian was prepping to lead his men to meet the enemy. The sensation he felt had stopped being fear—he had long since pushed that away—but was rather the instinctive response to what he knew was coming. Gunfire in the distance sounded like popcorn. Firefights had been sporadic throughout the night. Brian shook his hands to ward off the shivers and worked through his checklist.

Al Qa'im was a midsize town at the westernmost tip of Anbar, where the Euphrates makes its first serpentine bend east of the Syrian border. The train depot had been converted into an FOB for about a thousand marines and the staging area for one of the largest offensives in the region.

The mission was tough but simple: After the invasion in 2003, Anbar Province and the villages on both sides of the Euphrates River had become gateways for foreign fighters flowing in from Syria like water from the river. Al Qa'im was a particularly nasty area, as it had morphed into a safe haven for the fighters of Musab al-Zarqawi. Some of the Zarqawi loyalists were Iraqis, but most were Jordanians, Yemeni, and even some Afghanis who had slipped across the border during the chaos. These free-range killers terrorized villagers and slaughtered entire families to ensure they had a place to stage their strike-and-retreat ambushes. Operation Matador was designed to clean out the viper nest with a methodical east-to-west, village-to-village, house-to-house surge. Marines would either push the bad guys back across the border or kill them where they stood.

Brian was to lead his company, code-named War Pig Two, into an area where no U.S. force had ever been and take the Ramana Bridge near the village of New Ubaydi, the only place Zarqawi could send reinforcements across the Euphrates to counter the U.S. attack on the north shore of the river. It was a divide-and-conquer strategy:

take the bridge to the west to split the forces in half, and then wipe them out on both sides of the river. War Pig One, a company of ten Humvees and twenty-one men, had gone ahead, but they had gotten bogged down in the sandy terrain, so Brian's group was ordered on point for the operation.

The battalion operations officer, Major Day, glanced at Brian and said, "Stann, we ready to go?"

"Ready now, sir," Brian said.

At 0530 Major Day said, "Okay, Stannley, get to the bridge ASAP."

"Roger that, sir," Brian said.

War Pig Two lit out on an untraveled dirt road that took them through several villages until they hit a pavement north to the bridge. There were other ways of getting there, but if the enemy was waiting, they'd probably be on the more frequently traveled routes.

"We're going!" Brian shouted to his group as he climbed into the second Humvee in the column. They also had two M1 Abrams tanks waiting to hit the trail. His gunner, Corporal Rene DeLatorre, gave him a thumbs-up as they rolled outside the wire and into the Iraq night.

It surprised and concerned Brian that none of the houses they passed as they turned west had the lights on. Shopkeepers were normally up before dawn preparing for business to start at first light. Brian's training had taught him not to believe in coincidences. The lack of activity meant something, and his senses went on high alert.

The moment they entered the town of Saddah, someone with a machine gun opened fire on them.

"We're taking small-arms fire, sir," said a Corporal Culver in a bland but direct drawl, the kind of tone he might have used to point out a McDonald's on the side of the road. It was Culver's second tour.

"Return fire," Brian ordered in an equally level voice. Calmness mattered in combat. Men on both sides were looking for the first whiff of panic or frustration. They weren't going to get it from Lieutenant Stann.

"It doesn't matter if you're panicking on the inside," Brian said. "You have to remain in control and in charge. Your men will feed off of you. If you're calm, cool, and collected, they will be calm as well. If you're flipping out, they will be flipping out. The ultimate goal is that when your voice comes over the radio or when you reach that point of friction, everyone else takes a deep breath and said, 'Whew, thank God he's here.'"

On Brian's orders, Culver opened up a couple of bursts from an M240 Golf machine gun, not the lightest gun nor the biggest, but certainly the most reliable. It was impossible to tell if he had hit the insurgents, but the firing stopped for a moment. All was quiet except for the hum of the engines as the convoy rolled through town. Then, like a Roman candle lighting the night, a rocket-propelled grenade whizzed past the column of Humvees and exploded on the south wall of one of the shops. It was like a "go" signal to the insurgents. Another RPG shot past within seconds of the first.

Gunners on the convoy's lead vehicles opened up and took out two insurgents in a yard on the north side of the trail.

A minute later, just as the column turned north onto the paved road they had named Route Diamond, the one that would take them to the Ramana Bridge, a black sedan sped in front of them, windows down, muzzle flashes erupting from the front and back seats. Without hesitation, Corporal DeLatorre unleashed with his big .50-caliber machine gun, a weapon that could blow through concrete walls.

The bullets blew fist-sized holes through the sedan. It wobbled and rolled to a stop. As Brian rolled past it, he saw three men, all dead. Did they really think they could launch a drive-by attack and get away? Was it a suicide mission? Either way, what sort of person took on an armored Marine infantry platoon with an ordinary car and a couple of machine guns?

"Keep moving," Brian radioed to the column, and the tanks and Humvees rolled north. Now gunfire erupted, muzzle flashes and machine gun rounds coming from both sides of the road. The river lay just ahead, the creaky steel latticework of the Ramana Bridge glowing in the first rays of sunlight. They had made it, but not without alerting every enemy fighter in the area to their presence.

Brian ordered the vehicles into position behind a couple grassy knolls at the south entrance of the bridge. Realizing that War Pig was attempting to take the bridge and that such a move would effectively cut them off from escape, the Muj hammered Brian's group with everything they had, including mortars and rocket-propelled grenades. It was impossible to gauge the size or strength of the enemy, but one thing was certain: this was not a ragtag bunch. They attacked quickly and in a coordinated fashion. Small groups of insurgents began to maneuver on the northwest corner while others streamed into buildings to the south and east. They were swarming, surrounding the platoon.

As the sun poked over the ledge of the bridge, machine gun fire erupted all around. Nobody crossed the river at the Ramana, which was the objective, but now War Pig Two was surrounded and outnumbered.

Brian couldn't let the tanks unleash their big guns because of potential collateral damage. The Muj didn't care how many civilian casualties occurred during their attacks so they launched their assaults with innocents in the area, especially children, as a way of keeping the Marines, who were more sensitive to seeing civilians killed, from blowing everything around them to smithereens. One or two well-placed bombs would have ended the whole thing, but the casualty count would have been astronomical. And that would have defeated the purpose.

"It's so hard to ensure that you're not going to kill innocents or blow up their houses," Brian said later. "The key to counterinsurgency isn't killing the insurgents. The key isn't the enemy, and the key isn't us. The key is the people. Whoever wins the people wins the fight. If you're blowing up their houses or killing their neighbors, you aren't winning. They are going to hate you, and raise their kids to hate you. And they're going to happily accept money from Al Qaeda to plant an IED on the road to try to kill you."

Target discrimination in a large firefight is one of the hardest things a leader has to do. But when a resupply truck pulled up to bring ammunition to the enemy, the task became a lot easier. That was clearly a high-value enemy target, so the M1 crew whirled the turret and disintegrated the truck and all the insurgents around it.

They saw another good target when two Muj sprinted behind a dump truck and used it as a firing position. The tank again wheeled the big gun around the blasted the truck and everyone behind it.

Brian kept his vehicles moving so the enemy's mortars couldn't lock in on their position. Several mortars exploded on the riverbank immediately behind him, and he realized that insurgents were firing RPGs and machine guns from dugout positions on the other side of the river. They were caught in a 180-degree firefight. From the window of his Humvee, Brian could see DeLatorre dip down below his .50-caliber's turret. In a second Brian saw the corporal's hand come up. He was holding a video camera, capturing some footage of the firefight, maybe for the brass back at the depot, but probably for his home collection: something to show his grandkids one day.

That is one cool customer, Brian thought.

At 0645, after an hour of taking fire, Brian realized that there were too many insurgents shooting from too many places for War Pig Two to establish fire superiority. The first order of business in a firefight was to outgun the enemy and either force them to retreat or hunker down. Brian needed help if he was going to get control of this battle. He called in air support and within minutes a couple of Huey Cobras delivered Hellfire missiles on the targets Brian identified. Incoming fire from those locations ceased.

The rest of the operation was moving slower than expected, though. Lima 3/25 Marines were stuck on the wrong side of the river as the Army engineers, who were building a makeshift bridge to get them over at a strategically advantageous location, began taking mortar fire. What had been planned out as a twelve-hour operation was now going to be at least a full day.

Brian kept fighting the Muj and maneuvering his vehicles so

nobody could get a clean shot, but there were too many insurgents firing from windows and doorways for him to gain total control. It would have frustrated most leaders. The simple answer would have been to unleash the big guns every time some numbskull with an AK fired off a potshot, but Al Jazeera couldn't wait to broadcast video of dead women and children with mourners wailing and some indignant elder describing Americans as indiscriminate killing machines. The BBC and CNN were all too quick to pick up those stories as well. There was no doubt that U.S. forces could have blown every insurgent within a hundred miles of Al Qa'im to smithereens, but the collateral price was far too high.

They fought a jab-and-move battle for five hours. Finally at 1030, War Pig One made it to the action, their ten Humvees rolling in like cowboys on horseback. They were a welcome sight. Still fighting every second, Brian and the platoon leader of War Pig One executed something called a "relief in place," where one group replaced another while fighting continued. War Pig One was fresh and ready, so they assumed the knolls War Pig Two had occupied since sunup.

Brian ordered his convey to a hill on the east side of the road.

Then came the explosion, an earth-rattling blast. The concussion hit Brian like a fist, and dirt and sand showered the area as smoke bellowed skyward. A radio call came over. "One of the tanks was hit by a mortar." But Brian knew the blast was far too large for a mortar. The M1 had hit an IED, a big one. The tank was on fire.

Sensing a momentary advantage, the insurgents peppered the area with gunfire. Brian radioed for a medical evacuation helicopter but was told that another unit had taken heavy casualties and all the med choppers were tied up. Another Huey pilot heard the call and said he would be right there. The gunship wasn't large enough to get everybody out, but they would make do with that they had.

"Lay down fire to protect the bird!" Brian ordered, and gunfire rattled like one long pulsing explosion.

The driver and gunner leaped from the burning tank just as the Huey landed. One of them had a badly injured leg, but both were able to crawl aboard the chopper. Within seconds, the pilot lifted off for Al Qa'im.

"Anchorman, this is War Pig Two Actual!" Brian shouted into the radio. "We need another medevac!"

"Negative, War Pig Two, all medevac engaged," a voice replied.

The heroic pilot of the first chopper heard the conversation and radioed back to Brian, telling him he would be back to pick up the rest of the tank crew. The problem was, nobody had heard from them. Were they dead? Were they unconscious and burning inside the tank?

Ignoring the noise and the smoke, the bullets and explosions coming in from all sides, Brian and his platoon sergeant, Staff Sergeant James Robertson, jumped from the Humvee and ran toward the burning tank. This was the moment that all the training, the drills, the discipline, the lectures on leadership and what it meant to serve a calling higher than yourself, and all sacrifices going back to his plebe year at the academy kicked in and took over. This was what it meant to be a marine.

Robertson got there first and used the turret of the tank as cover to lay down as much suppression fire as possible.

Brian sprinted like he had on Navy kickoffs, hard and fast, his legs churning despite the burn. He was a few steps behind Robertson. The insurgents, sensing a potential kill, intensified and focused their fire.

Robertson waved Brian back just as a hail of machine gun bullets hit the dirt in front of him. Brian called for another round of cover fire and then ran forward to the tank.

Once secure behind the turret, Robertson laid down more cover fire as Brian climbed headfirst into the open hatch. There he found Lance Corporal Jonathan Lowe, barely conscious, but covered in blood and paralyzed from the waist down. Brian tried to pull him out, but Lowe was stuck.

Bullets rattled the hull of the tank. Another member of Brian's platoon, Corporal Richard Mcelhinny, had run to the tank as well.

Both he and Robertson were laying down serious suppression fire.

Finally, Brian realized that the radio cord was entangled around Lowe's leg. With bullets whizzing overhead and fire intensifying on both sides, he unsheathed his knife and cut the cord, freeing his injured man. But Lowe couldn't move. It was impossible to gauge the extent of his injuries, but he was alive, so Brian wrapped his arms beneath Lowe's shoulders and, using every ounce of core strength he could muster, hoisted the paralyzed man out of the tank.

Corporal Mcelhinny laid down more fire as Sergeant Robertson grabbed Lowe and pulled him clear.

As promised, the Huey returned. The pilot circled once and sat the bird down next to the tank, as cool as if he were returning from a sightseeing tour. Brian joined Mcelhinny in laying down suppression fire as Lowe was carried to the chopper.

Brian and Robertson laid down more cover fire while the Huey took off again for Al Qa'im. NCOs swarmed the tank and got the rest of the crew out, while Brian called in another air strike. Gunships launched more Hellfire missiles, and the insurgent fire backed off, at least temporarily.

But the battle wasn't over. Battalion called and ordered Brian back to Al Qa'im, which meant he had to drive back the same way he'd come, right through a gauntlet of gunmen.

His men loaded up and the column—down one tank—headed south. To their shock, they drove in peace. The insurgents had slithered out of sight.

The pops of gunfire grew dimmer, and the Humvees' engines provided an eerily quiet sound track after the cacophony of a firefight. Then, as they turned east, Brian saw the roadblock: two sedans parked end to end. It was a classic Muj maneuver, one they had learned from the Battle of Mogadishu in 1993. Back then, the Rangers had been sent to rescue a downed Black Hawk crew, but they were cut off by a series of roadblocks. What was intended to be an operation of a couple of hours stretched into an overnight urban battle that resulted in eighteen American soldiers dead and eighty wounded.

There was a parallel road a few yards to the south, so Brian ordered the column to turn toward it. That's when the thought hit him: we're being funneled this way for a reason.

No sooner had the thought formed than rockets exploded around them on all sides. Tracers raced across the Humvees like bottle rockets, and bullets rattled off the reinforced steel plates with a sickening clang.

Gunners yelled out targets and returned fire. Then Brian saw a horde of insurgents wearing black Kevlar vests and full black ski masks coming out ahead of them. He knew this was no ordinary attack. A Syrian or Yemeni jihadist was lucky to own shoes. None of them had Kevlar. These guys opened up with AK-47s in a coordinated attack. These were pros.

Brian didn't have time to analyze the motivations of the men firing at him. "Blow through it!" he yelled.

The column barreled ahead, cutting down as many of the gunmen as possible. They also had to kill another sedan driver who tried to ram them. Brian would never know if the lone passenger in that car was a suicide bomber or just a scared Iraqi who'd panicked in the mayhem and hit the accelerator instead of the brake. Shooting the car and driver was the only thing they could do. It was one of hundreds of decisions Brian would roll over in his mind for years to come.

When they pulled into the depot at Al Qa'im, the Humvees looked like they had been parked on a firing range for months. There were too many bullet holes to count. Brian raced to the combat operations center to brief everyone on the battle and the insurgents' strength and coordination. When he got to the part about the hooded, Kevlar-wearing assault squad on the road back, several of the intelligence guys sat up a little straighter. When Brian thought the briefing was complete, an intelligence team from the regiment came in and asked him more questions about the masked assailants. The intelligence guys believed that the assailants were Zarqawi's personal security detail. Rumors had swirled for months that the Emir of AQI had been hiding in the region, jumping back and forth across the Syrian border like a desert jackrabbit and blowing up markets, banks, and even mosques.

Months after this operation and Brian's briefing, it would be reported that Zarqawi had been wounded during Operation Matador. His bodyguards reportedly threw him in the trunk of a car and drove him to a hospital. Doctors recognized him, but Zarqawi threatened to kill the entire medical staff if they said anything. Brian would never know whether War Pig Two shot Zarqawi that morning, but those insurgents fought awfully hard in a battle they knew they couldn't win. No matter what, Brian's team killed a lot of bad guys on the road back to Al Qa'im.

That night, Brian received his next batch of orders. War Pig One had been fighting since 1030. They were low on fuel and supplies. After a brief discussion about sending in helicopters, operational command decided that Brian's team would head back and resupply the marines on the ground.

They had two hours to get in, drop the fuel and supplies, and get back to Al Qa'im. It was a quick turnaround, but Brian wasn't worried about his marines. His concern was the fuel truck and ammo delivery guys. They acted like they were making a resupply run to Walmart. Brian grew downright worried when he realized those guys didn't even have their own NVGs. Without fuel and ammo, War Pig One was in deep trouble. Those guys weren't going to beat the Muj with rocks and harsh language.

War Pig Two made it back to the bridge without incident, driving fast in total darkness using NVGs. If they had encountered trouble they would have blown through it with guns blazing. But the streets were quiet. Even the roadblock they had encountered earlier was gone. Insurgents needed their cars, or so Brian assumed.

After unloading the fuel and ammo, they turned back for Al Qa'im. This time they weren't so lucky. Seconds after swinging the convoy onto Route Jade, one of the roads used to get in and out of the fight, they were ambushed, tracer fire and RPGs flying at them.

When two more RPGs flew over the tops of the vehicles and exploded on the buildings behind, Corporal Forrest, who was manning a Mark 19 automatic grenade launcher, spotted the insurgent who fired the RPGs, and with one swift shot took him out with a grenade. Few of Brian's marines had ever seen a grenade explode inside a man's chest. It was one of many sights they would never forget.

The loss of one of their RPG gunners must have upset the Muj because the incoming RPG fire intensified. One grenade bounced off the skin of a Humvee and exploded perilously close to the tanker truck, which still had enough fuel and residue to cause quite the explosion.

That was close, Brian said to himself.

Then the trouble became self-inflicted. The tanker driver panicked and turned down a side street away from the convoy and right into the enemy strength.

"I got those guys," Staff Sergeant Robertson radioed to Brian.

Brian called to Sergeant Pete, who was in charge of another Humvee, and said, "Cut through the desert. We'll wait for Robertson here."

Unfortunately, Sergeant Pete's driver took the order way too seriously. He made an immediate right, drove down an embankment, and got the Humvee stuck in the sand. Brian had to revamp the strategy on the fly. He had the rest of the convoy follow Robertson and the rogue tanker truck, and he and his Humvee drove down the bank, arriving just in time to see Sergeant Pete finish a colorful asschewing of his driver.

Brian's team pulled Pete's Humvee out of the muck, and soon they reconvened with the rest of the unit and headed back to Al Qa'im.

By the time they checked and cleaned the vehicles, they had

been up for twenty-four hours, fighting for a good portion of that time. When they hit the rack, sleep found them all like a warm ocean wave.

The next night Brian took a new group out to relieve War Pig One. His .50-cal machine gunner for this run was a big South Carolinian named Corporal Robert Gass, a strong guy with a strong personality who had challenged Brian to more than a few grappling matches. It was like an amateur boxer climbing into the ring for a couple of rounds with Evander Holyfield. Brian beat him easily, but Gass never gave up.

Corporal Jeff Lamson was also new. He drove the lead vehicle and had been one of Brian's problem children, a guy who sometimes tested the bounds of military discipline. That night, before they rode out into the darkness, Lamson had worn his helmet too far back on his head, looking more like a movie star version of a marine than the real deal.

"Goddamnit, Lamson!" Brian yelled. Then he got in the corporal's face and said, "If I see this again I'm going to stick it up your ass. Are we clear?"

"Yes, sir," the corporal said.

Brian warned his team that they were going to get hit between Al Qa'im and the bridge, either on the way out, on the way back, or both. He'd been there twice, and it had happened both times. The Muj weren't stupid. They knew supplies and replacements were coming, and there were only so many ways to get from point A to point B. Every marine had his game face on as they lit out at 2300. It would be another long night.

Once again the buildings were empty and shuttered. It was like they were driving through a ghost town, no lights or movement. He wasn't sure if this was the Iraqis being early to bed and early to rise, or if the residents were bunkered in to avoid the crossfire.

Within minutes he had his answer. The attack this time was

more coordinated than ever, with machine gunners peppering them from rooftops and windows. One group would leapfrog another so that the fire was perpetual. As soon as Brian's gunners turned their attention to one area, incoming fire would erupt from another. This time concerns about civilian casualties took a backseat to getting in and out alive. The lead Abrams tank unloaded a round into one of the buildings and the place erupted. Debris, dust, and ash shot up and out like a sandstorm. Suddenly the NVGs were worthless. All anyone could see was a green cloud.

Fire continued. The gunner on Brian's vehicle, Lance Corporal Jacobs, unleashed a stream of profanity as he fired. "Fuck you, motherfuckers! Get some now, bitches!"

Then Brian saw an explosion up ahead. One of the Humvee leaders, Staff Sergeant Francis, came on and said, "We took an RPG to our rear." In the confusion, Corporal Lamson, who was driving the vehicle, gunned it and missed a turn. Brian radioed ahead and directed Lamson to stay put. The rest of the vehicles would drive down the new route to get them and then double back. Nobody could be left alone in this sort of firefight.

They crept down the route, slower than Brian had ever thought possible, acquiring targets and eliminating them. Finally he saw the vehicle about fifty yards ahead. Corporal Gass, the gunner on the lost Humvee, was on the .50-cal laying down fire. Everybody was getting peppered with machine guns from every angle.

"Okay, Alpha One, turn around and take it slow," Brian said. "We'll follow. I don't want to lose anyone else."

"Roger that, sir."

They made the tedious turn. Another of the Abrams tanks blasted a second building, filling the sky with more dust and debris. Lamson pointed the Humvee eastward, and it appeared as though they would be back on track. Then a vehicle appeared like an apparition out of the haze. It sped between two buildings toward Alpha One.

Brian doesn't remember if he heard the blast first or felt it. Both sensations were the most jarring he could ever remember. It was as if God had reached down and slapped the earth right next to them. Every vehicle shook and the ground trembled beneath them. A towering cloud of black smoke poured skyward.

"Alpha One," Brian heard himself call over the radio. "Alpha One, what happened?"

There was no response.

Lieutenant Leahy, the platoon leader of War Pig One, the group they were on the way to relieve, radioed in and said, "What the hell happened? That was the biggest blast I've ever heard."

Leahy was three kilometers away.

Brian radioed Bravo Section back at Al Qa'im, the guys who had been out with him in similar circumstances just eighteen hours before. "Get a medevac out here," he said.

He heard Sergeant Robertson's voice say, "Roger that, sir."

Then Brian threw open the door of the Humvee and ran toward the horror, assuming with every step that he had just gotten five marines killed.

Rounds continued to crackle all around him. His lungs burned and his legs ached as he sprinted toward the blast site. Behind him, his marines continued to pour fire at the insurgents, and a tank blasted another building, rocking the ground and staggering Brian's stride.

When he got there, he saw the charred remains of what had once been a Humvee. "No, no!" Brian yelled as he got close.

Then he saw the passenger door open. Staff Sergeant Francis pulled himself and Corporal Goldsmith, a professional masseur back home who went by Old Goldie, from the wreckage. Both were badly burned but alive. Goldsmith was convulsing as if he was going into shock or bleeding internally. They needed the medevac now.

Brian looked inside the vehicle to find the others. Corporal Hauslyak was bleeding but appeared to be okay. Then Brian saw Lamson, but it took a second for what had happened to register. Lamson had climbed from the driver's side, through the fire, and into the turret to get Corporal Gass. When Brian arrived Lamson was heaving Gass out. Brian climbed up to help, but what he saw didn't look right. Something was wrong with Gass's helmet. Then he realized that a seven-inch triangular hunk of shrapnel was protruding from Gass's skull. It had gone right through the Kevlar helmet, the tip embedding in his brain.

Lamson ignored the gunfire and the growing flames coming from what used to be the engine area. He pushed Gass up and out. Brian grabbed on and helped. Together they got the big man out of the turret and onto the ground. While Brian was doing a battle-field medical assessment, Lamson grabbed the fire extinguisher and suppressed the flames, rounds of incoming fire still pinging off the charred skin of the wreckage.

Brian called to the tank commander, "Kill anything that comes near us," he said. "Nothing gets close."

The Abramses set up positions front and rear and secured them from incoming vehicles. One suicide car bomb a night was enough. When another vehicle raced in their direction, the lead tank blew it to bits.

"We need to get these wounded to the Mike 88," Brian said, indicating the M88 transport, an ox of a vehicle that looked like a tank without the guns.

Lamson carried Gass, a much bigger man, to the M88 amid a hail of incoming machine gun and RPG fire. Then he ran back to help Goldsmith, who did not look good. As he and Sergeant Francis, who had second- and third-degree burns and was covered in his own blood, carried Goldsmith to the M88, Brian noticed that Lamson was hobbling on an injured leg. After loading the patients into the vehicle, Lamson wove his way through the incoming fire, limping and dodging back to the wreckage, where he took up a defensive position beside Brian.

"Lamson, you're injured, get back to the Mike 88," Brian said.

"I just bruised my leg, sir. I'm fine," he said and began firing at enemy positions.

According to the corpsman who examined them, Staff Sergeant Francis and Corporals Goldsmith and Gass would need surgery quickly. Gass and Francis had lost a lot of blood.

Brian called another of his staff sergeants to meet them at Alpha One. Standing orders were very simple: You never, ever left a vehicle for the enemy. Intelligence could be gathered, and propaganda photos taken. You could sometimes blow one up, but you never left one out there.

"Sergeant Cherry, prepare to tow Alpha One," Brian said.

"On my way, sir," the sergeant radioed back.

At that moment Brian decided to split up War Pig Two. He would take Alpha Three and escort the Mike 88 with the wounded three kilometers to the bridge. War Pig One could provide cover for them until the medevac got his men out of there. The rest of the column would stay behind to cover Sergeant Cherry as he hauled Alpha One out.

Alpha Three was led by Lance Corporal Miller. Brian got close to his face and said, "Miller, listen up, stud. I gotta lead the wounded outta here. I need you to take me."

"Fuck yeah, let's go, sir," Miller said.

They crept along at ten miles per hour, the gunners chewing through ammo. When they made a left toward the bridge, RPGs flew in from two sides. The Muj were throwing everything they had at them. Brian felt himself rocking forward, trying to will everything to move quicker. The M88 lumbered along with Alpha Three. The driver, Corporal Hernandez, did his best to maneuver through as hot a zone as anyone had seen, while the gunner, Corporal Jacobs, laid down as much cover fire as possible.

"We're hit!" came a call from the M88. RPGs were banging the side of the big vehicle. It was a large, slow target and this group of Muj was as determined as any Brian had ever seen.

Behind them another sedan broke through the line and made

a charge toward Alpha One. The Abrams blasted it, and another explosion rocked the area. It was yet another suicide bomber. They were coming out of the woodwork that night. The concussion from the blast lifted the rear of the Alpha Three Humvee and shook it, but Hernandez did a great job of keeping them on the road, and Jacobs continued to fire.

"Keep moving!" Miller shouted.

Then another blast, this one larger than the last: "IED, we're hit!" came another voice from the Mike 88.

"Status," Brian said.

"Track's blown. Hull's warped. We're down, sir."

Now they were trapped in the kill zone with no way to evacuate the wounded. The Humvee couldn't hold anyone else, and it wouldn't be safe even if it could. They needed help.

Brian radioed ahead, "War Pig One, the Mike 88's down. We need vehicle support to get the wounded out. Can you assist?"

"We're on the way, Lieutenant," Gunnery Sergeant Harmon replied.

It was time to put collateral concerns aside for good. Screw them. This was not a civilian district anymore; every inch was a battlefield. Brian radioed in for air support. Within a couple of minutes, Cobra helicopters swooped in and unleashed their Hellfire missiles and 20 mm cannons on the buildings. The Muj were still running on the rooftops with their RPGs when the missiles obliterated the neighborhood.

Gunny Harmon raced toward them in a 998 Humvee, a variation on the standard vehicle that had high-backed armor and would hold and protect the wounded. He leaped out and helped load Sergeant Francis and Corporals Gass and Goldsmith. Then he sped north to the landing zone, one hero among many in a battle few remember except for those who were there—all of whom made it out alive.

As War Pig Two gathered behind War Pig One, Brian watched as the Cobras strafed the neighborhood again. The firing quieted after that.

Later that summer, Brian would find out why there were no locals in the area. When the Muj had moved in, they had angered the local smugglers who ran things and a gang war broke out. The residents lost. Many had been brutalized in torture chambers that the Marines would find in the coming months. Anyone who thought this enemy didn't need killing should have walked through those rooms and seen the carnage. This was pure evil.

War Pig Two had lost too many men and too much firepower to execute a relief in place. Brian took what remained of his forces and provided support alongside Lieutenant Leahy and War Pig One. None of them doubted that the attacks would resume. This would be the Muj's last stand, and they would take out as many Americans as they could.

As the first rays of sunlight broke, the mortar fire resumed. Fortunately, War Pig One had a fantastic joint tactical attack controller (JTAC). He was the guy with the antennas sticking up: the guy who called in coordinates and orchestrated multiple platform responses. Once he identified a mortar position, he would call in the location and air support would blast the site.

Later in the morning, they saw a group ducking into a local gas station. A few minutes later, armed insurgents fired from nearby areas. It didn't take a genius to figure out that the gas station had become an armory. Brian called in three hits, one with a tank, one with a 120 mm gun, and one with a Javelin, an incredible and devastating weapon that would soar toward a target, turn up for a hundred or so feet, and then come straight down on top of whatever it was trying to hit. It was great for wiping out rooftop fighters, and not bad for taking out gas stations full of weapons, but this building seemed to be the armory that couldn't be destroyed.

After evening prayers, the platoon was hit again and insurgents were seen scurrying in and out of the gas station with new rifles and RPGs. Brian was sick of it. They called in a Cobra strike, and after a couple of Hellfire missile explosions, the place looked like little more than a pile of rubble. Amazingly, there were still enough weapons in there, either underground or in some sort of vault, that the Muj were going in empty-handed and coming out armed.

Brian wanted to put an end to it once and for all. He went to the JTAC, a major, and said, "Sir, we've tried everything to destroy that cache. Nothing's worked. They're still using it as a resupply point and I'm fucking tired of getting shot at."

"What do you propose, Lieutenant?" he asked.

"Let's put a JDAM on it and end this thing for good." (A JDAM is a satellite-guided bomb launched from an aircraft.)

"Roger that," the major said. The coordinates were called in, and an F-18 dropped a five-hundred-pound bomb onto the gas station. Nobody would go in or out of it again, as all that was left was a large black hole.

The men were thrilled. It was one of the best morale boosters of the battle. Unfortunately for Brian, the politics of this war sometimes defied all logic or reason. He soon got a call from regimental command wanting to know what the hell he was thinking using that much firepower. Somebody somewhere was getting in a tizzy about potential overkill, using too much force and wounding the delicate sensibilities of the Iraqi people.

"You'd better be able to answer some very pointed questions about that five-hundred-pounder," one of the staff officers radioed in to Brian.

The JTAC heard it and came over to reassure Brian that he had nothing to worry about. It was the right call no matter what the officers sitting in chairs miles away from the battlefield thought.

That was the moment it dawned on Brian that this war could stretch on for a very long time. If it came down to killing the enemy, the marines could get the job done and do so quickly. They could take ground, hold it, and clean out an area of all the operators. But if action was being second-guessed, every weapon choice being scrutinized, every contact with an enemy taking place under tighter rules of engagement, then the marines weren't fighting to win: they were fighting to not hurt anybody's feelings. And in that scenario, good men were bound to get killed.

Lamson and Mcelhinny received Bronze Stars with V's for their bravery. And Brian received the Silver Star for his actions during Operation Matador, the nation's third-highest military citation behind the Medal of Honor and Navy Cross. It was not a medal he wanted or one he would talk about at any length. The price was far too high.

"Would I give that thing up to have guys walk again, or be able to talk right again, or not have to go through life with the scars of what happened? Are you kidding?" he said. "I think about what I did every day, and I always run through the scenarios: if I'd done this differently or that differently would this guy be walking today, or would this guy be living a normal life? I won't talk about it. I'm done talking about it. But I think about it. I think about it all the time."

The man who pinned the Silver Star on Brian was the general whose ribs he had broken during the training session at MACE. As large as the Marine Corps was, it could sometimes seem like a small fraternity: an order of the faithful. And no matter how much he questioned himself, Brian felt more connected to his marines than to any other humans on earth.

CHAPTER 12

*Honor to the Soldier, and Sailor everywhere, who
bravely bears his country's cause. Honor also to the
citizen who cares for his brother in the field, and
serves, as he best can, the same cause—honor to him,
only less than to him, who braves, for the common
good, the storms of heaven and the storms of battle.*
—PRESIDENT ABRAHAM LINCOLN, DECEMBER 2, 1863

Never losing anyone was nothing short of a miracle, considering the
danger of Chad's missions and how close he came to the enemy on
such a regular basis. Of all the successes—they were legend and, for
the most part, top secret—his proudest accomplishment was having
brought every Ranger under his command back inside the wire. His
happiest moments in Iraq came when he boarded a chopper for an
exfil and called on the radio, "LZ clear, all eagles up." But this record
also worried him. In Chad's eyes his team was the most effective
light tactical fighting force there had ever been, but their good fortune was bound to run out eventually.

Those thoughts and others made it hard for him to transition between tours. Combat could not be turned on and off. The adrenaline
and intensity and responsibility were far too great. It showed when

he was home. Just a few days after he returned from his second tour, for example, Emily went outside at 6:30 A.M. to find Chad weeding his front yard by hand.

"What are you doing?" she asked.

"Squaring away this yard," he said as he bent over to rip another offending weed up from the roots. "I can't believe the yard got this way."

Unsure of what to say, Emily shook her head and went inside to make coffee.

Then, right before heading back for his third tour, Chad took Emily snowboarding at the Summit at Snoqualmie, a resort not far from Fort Lewis. It was a new experience for Emily, and learning was difficult. During one run, she fell several times, despite Chad's instructions. Finally she sat down in the snow and cried.

He didn't know how to handle a woman crying on a ski slope, even the woman he loved. Still in a battlefield mind-set, he was not prepared for this kind of thing.

"Are you okay, ma'am?" a ski patrol officer asked.

Chad chimed in first, saying, "She's fine. She's just a little emotional."

Looking back years later, he realized what a jackass he was to his wife. "Not my finest hour, for sure," he said.

Like many veterans, when he was away from combat, he found himself missing it. Not that he loved combat—no one who has been at war longs for it, and all sane men want it to end—but no other experience heightens the senses so much or provides the same rush. Training helped, but it was simulated. Ranger training was always dangerous, and jumping out of airplanes or fast-roping out of heli-copters could never be considered routine, but imitating combat got you only so close to the real thing.

The routine of training also had its frustrations. Anytime some-one new joined a fire team, the training had to start afresh. The rest of the unit might be so well versed at complex insertions and tech-niques that they could anticipate what the person next to them was going to do in almost every circumstance, but when the new guy came in it was back to single-team, single-room training, followed by single-team, two rooms; two teams, two rooms; and so on: the same training Chad and the rest of the guys had been living for more than a year. They all understood it and embraced it. After all, they had been the new guys once, and they were all thrilled for the support they had gotten from the veterans, who in no way resented training the cheery. But it was hard to recapture the intensity when you were going back to the basics over and over again.

There was also the natural human tendency to ease up, to take a training session slightly less seriously, especially after being in combat and understanding that no training can prepare you for the total mind-and-body experience that comes with the real thing. But training has to come as close as possible to mirroring the intensity of the real thing; otherwise there is no point in doing it. Chad remembered that lesson during an airfield seizure training op, where the mission was to jump out of an airplane and secure the airfield below. From Grenada to Panama to Afghanistan, airfield seizure had always been the Ranger Regiment's buttered bread, the one action that got congressional attention. As important as the kill-and-capture missions were, they often got lost in the mix with similar missions executed by the Navy SEALs and Delta Force (a unit so secretive that Chad referred to them as "the guys that don't exist"). They all nabbed high-profile targets, so there was always a little professional jealousy when SEALs got credit for taking down Bad Guy X, even though Bad Guy Y, a Ranger kill, was a bigger immediate threat. Airfields, though: that was Ranger territory all the way. No one else could take credit for seizing an airport in the first phase of an invasion.

But like for every other discipline, training for this skill could get tedious, not because assaulting a terminal was easy or routine, but because you had to train on multiple platforms. You had to prepare to jump out of every kind of aircraft that could possibly take you to the fight. Sometimes the harnesses were different; sometimes the O-rings were in different places; interior configurations varied, so you had to figure out who was going to sit where: all important, but not the kind of things that amped you up.

On the second night of one three-night airfield seizure exercise, Chad and his fellow Rangers had been flying around for an hour and a half strapped into their chutes with rucks hanging from their waists. It was like having seventy pounds of free weights harnessed to your torso: even if you weren't moving around, it was still tiring and uncomfortable.

Finally, Battalion Commander David Haight, from the 2/75 Ranger Regiment, made the call. "All units, air land, air land."

That meant they were landing instead of jumping. It also meant the Rangers could get out of the chutes and take a leak if needed. A cheer went up throughout the aircraft. A few high-fives were shared and several said, "Yeah, awesome!" Only one sat stone-faced. Master Sergeant Bernie Folino, the kind of guy the Army would never put on a recruiting poster for fear of scaring away every potential prospect, but the kind of warrior every Ranger aspired to be, grabbed the microphone, even though he didn't need it. Everyone on the aircraft could hear him over the roar of the engines.

"You should not be fucking cheering!" he yelled, even though Chad and others onboard were his superior officers. "Look at yourselves! You have forgotten everything that it means to be a Ranger, everything that every Ranger who came before you worked for and sacrificed for. Those men gave it all. A lot of them made the ultimate sacrifice. You should be honored to follow in their footsteps. Instead you're cheering because you don't have to jump in a fucking training exercise."

More than a few "hooahs" went out, but other than that the plane was silent for the rest of the trip. Bernie had reminded them it was an honor and a privilege to jump out of airplanes and kill people. They all wanted to suit up and jump on the spot.

Once back in Iraq in 2006, Chad felt as though he'd never left. His platoon operated out of the same house, so it was easy for him to slip back into the same routine, sleeping a little in the morning, then working out in the afternoon; prepping for a mission in the evening and then slipping out at night to bring war to someone's doorstep. Building and training the Iraqi Army had become a major focus of U.S. ground forces, and the recruitment and training of the locals was a big part of the news of the day. But the Rangers were still doing what they always did: getting rid of bad guys. Insurgent attacks—car bombs, IEDs, the indiscriminate murder of civilians, and ambushes—were worse than ever when Chad arrived back a third time. The men who carried out those acts needed, in the words of President Bush, "to be brought to justice."

Chad and his men were justice.

Some of the politics had changed, though. On one mission to capture an insurgent out in the boondocks, a couple of guys from the FBI showed up to tag along. This was a new attachment and something that made a lot of guys nervous. A Ranger's operational superiority depended on speed and efficiency. Teams had gotten the job done without casualties because everyone knew when everyone else took a breath.

The FBI guys, named Mike and Dave, said they were there to be assets, not liabilities. Anytime Chad needed them to step aside, they would do just that.

The mission was a capture or kill of a single insurgent in a small village in the eastern desert. But because of added security concerns, the team was inserted some distance away and forced to walk in. The problem arose with the overhead imagery of the route Chad and his men were to take from the landing site to the village. Chad had seen better security camera footage from 7-Eleven. The imagery looked like grainy photos from the moon. There appeared to be a dry creek bed somewhere along the way, but other than that, Chad couldn't tell if he was looking at sand dunes or shadows.

Once they got there, Chad stayed in the rear with the JTAC. Platoon Sergeant Jake Denman led the way. A few minutes into their walk, Jake radioed in and said, "Sir, we've got a problem. That creek

bed we saw appears to be about a seventy-foot-deep ravine. We've
got some beams stretching about thirty yards across it. Looks like it
might have been from an old bridge or trestle."

"What do you think, Jake?" Chad asked.

"Screw it, sir. Let's do it," he said.

Chad hadn't seen the situation yet, but he trusted Jake's judgment. Their team had heavy machine guns, rucks, and sixty-pound
extension ladders with them, as well as a radioman and a dog. Sergeant Denman wouldn't lead them, literally, off a cliff.

When Chad finally got to the site, he said, "Holy shit!" The
beams were nothing more than one-foot rails stretching the length
of what appeared to be a cavern. He knew that an entire Ranger
platoon crossing a flimsy beam in full battle gear at night would
have no depth perception. Not only that, but the beams had large
spikes sticking out that everyone had to step around. The Ranger
with the dog almost fell as he was getting off the trestle, but his
buddies pulled him, and the dog, to safety.

One of the FBI guys looked like he might throw up. "Mike, you
guys going to be okay doing this?" Chad asked.

They swore they were, but Dave ended up crawling across the
beam. He was called "All Fours" from that point on.

Once everyone made it across, Rangers slapped each other on the
back and congratulated one another on navigating an obstacle that
looked like it was out of an Indiana Jones movie. Unfortunately, less
than one hundred yards away, they came to another canyon and another trestle they had to navigate. Fortunately, the second one wasn't
as long as the first, and the Rangers knew what they were doing the
second time around.

Still, Dave slid across on all fours.

That was just one of many instances when intel was far too sketchy for
Chad's liking. His men in the Ranger Regiment were solid with every
step, but he felt like they were being sent down a number of dry holes.

In 2006, Jill Carroll, a reporter with the *Christian Science Monitor*, was kidnapped in Iraq. There was great outrage at home, but once again, while the Rangers felt bad about what had happened, everyone was asking, "What the hell was she doing riding around Baghdad with just an interpreter and a driver?"

The woman's mother went on CNN and said, "I, her father, and her sister are appealing directly to her captors to release this young woman who has worked so hard to show the sufferings of Iraqis to the world." Their pleas went unanswered.

Chad and his team were part of the manhunt for Carroll. Every day intelligence officers brought new information about her whereabouts and the number of insurgents that the Rangers could expect to encounter when going in to get her. Hostage rescue was always tricky because they had to get on target quickly and quietly, surprising the kidnappers before they could get to their guns and harm the victim. The good news was that this was most likely a ransom situation or a group looking to grab some cheap headlines and attention. One thing Chad had learned from his time in Iraq: the Muj didn't hold hostages very long. Carroll's head hadn't been found in the street, so all signs pointed away from AQI.

The team went out on one hostage rescue mission after another, and each one turned out to be a dry hole. It was frustrating, especially given the risk of assaulting the wrong target. What if innocents grabbed guns, thinking they were being overrun by insurgents? Every false lead was a potential disaster waiting to happen.

One of the targets U.S. forces raided while looking for Carroll was a mosque in western Baghdad. That went over about as well as one would expect.

Chad became more aggressive in challenging intelligence, especially after the mosque fiasco and the other bad leads in the Carroll incident. His tone ruffled a few feathers. But if his guys were going out into the night, he wanted to know they were in the right spots and going after the right people.

Fortunately, there were still enough successes that morale remained high. During his second and third deployments Chad's teams nabbed a large number of high-value targets: captures and kills that brought tears to the eyes of some intelligence officers who had been working tirelessly, sometimes for years, to bring those guys down.

Carroll was eventually released unharmed. After three videos aired on Al Jazeera with demands for this and that, her captors drove her to the Sunni Party headquarters building and put her out at the curb. She walked in and introduced herself. Just like that, it was over.

Brian proposed to Teressa not long after returning from Al Qa'im. It was New Year's Day 2006 at a Philadelphia Eagles game (the Eagles lost to the Redskins 31–20). Teressa was a cheerleader for the home team, one of three jobs she held at the time.

She had no idea it was coming, which was exactly how Brian wanted it. In what would later become a standard emotional affair for many returning servicemen at many sporting events, Teressa was surrounded by the cheerleading squad immediately after the game. When they parted, Brian was there in uniform, on one knee with a ring in his hand. As she said yes, thousands of jaded and otherwise unhappy Eagles fans—a group famous for throwing snowballs at Santa Claus—erupted in applause, most wiping away tears.

From Philly it was back to Camp Lejeune in North Carolina, where the 3/2 was awaiting their next deployment orders. With the cool waters of the Atlantic just a few feet away and a mild winter breeze rustling though the pines, the Carolinas' main Marine base north of Parris Island should have been like a five-star vacation compared to Anbar Province.

But Brian had too many reminders for him to relax. Camp Lejeune was home of Wounded Warrior Battalion–East, a place where marines with devastating, life-altering injuries transitioned after being released from Walter Reed Army Medical Center. There was even a Wounded Warrior barracks under the command of Colonel Tim Maxwell, himself a Wounded Warrior, on Paradise Point, one of the main thoroughfares through the camp. Brian couldn't see any of those guys without thinking about Al Qa'im.

As he had always done when reflection moved into his room, Brian filled the hours before and after work with training at a ratty old gym he and a couple buddies found on base. It had some moldy grappling mats in the corner, and Brian joked that the area had probably been used to teach hand-to-hand to marines on their way to Vietnam. But after a little cleaning fluid and elbow grease, the place was perfect for working on his kicking techniques and ground game.

His old chum Travis Manion from Annapolis—the guy who had been his wrestling coach and had been in his corner during his first couple fights—had all but threatened to find Brian and put him in a choke hold if he didn't make the jump to the professional ranks. There were no rules against a marine turning pro (although Brian filtered it up the chain of command just to make sure), so after returning stateside Brian found a promoter, Ryan Schwartz, with an outfit called SportFight, who agreed to put him on the undercard of an MMA fight in Portland, Oregon. The pay was five hundred dollars, but Brian had to pay his own travel and lodging expenses, which made his professional debut a money loser no matter how the fight turned out.

No matter. This was an outlet, a respite from his real job, which was far more serious and deadly than beating on other men while wearing gloves. So, on an early January night, Brian climbed into the ring at Rose Garden Arena, the home of the NBA's Portland Trailblazers, and took on another two-hundred-pound fighter named Aaron Stark, a former Big 10 wrestler and a member of Mensa who also owned a California winery.

Travis was at Camp Pendleton, north of San Diego, ramping up to head to Iraq with the 1st Reconnaissance, 1st Marine, or One Recon, as the marines called it, so Teressa's father, Frank, flew out with Brian to work his corner. They were so unprepared they had to borrow tape from another fighter so Brian could get into his gloves. But his MACE skills and heart for the fight proved too much for

Aaron the Vintner. Brian knocked him out with a left-right combination three minutes and fifteen seconds into the first round.

His future father-in-law leaped into the ring and hoisted Brian
into the air. With fists raised high, it was one of the most cathartic
moments Brian had had since Al Qa'im. He was now a legitimate
MMA fighter, a professional with a 1-0 record.

Ryan Schwartz dropped Brian and Frank off at an all-night diner
near their cheap hotel, Brian with his duffle bag under the table and
Frank with a smile that he couldn't wipe away. As they were walking
back to the hotel in the rain, Brian carried his bag over his shoulder
and Frank threw his arms around him and said, "Everybody was
wondering, 'Who the hell is that guy?'"

"Sure looked that way," Brian said with a smile.

"I'll tell you one thing," Frank said. "They're gonna know who
you are from now on."

Brian's second fight was in California in June, mere weeks before he
would deploy back to Iraq. It was a larger event in World Extreme
Cagefighting (WEC). The WEC league was a big step up from some
of the shadier MMA outfits. Some of their fights were televised (although not live at the time), but the pay still stunk. The real money
in mixed martial arts didn't come until you got on pay-per-view with
the UFC, the major league of the sport.

After six weeks of advanced training in the desert with the 3/2
Marines, where he worked on urban warfare, Brian was showing
up for his second bout as a professional having worked very little on
his fighting. Plus he threw his back out a week before he and Frank
were to fly out for the event. Once they arrived at the San Manuel
Indian Casino outside San Bernardino, near Lake Arrowhead, Brian
trained for one day. He spent the rest of his time lying flat on his
back and hoping that his quadratus lumborum and iliocostalis would
ease enough for him to be able to move.

His opponent was Miguel Cosio. Again, Brian knew very little about him, but the feeling was mutual. Some MMA websites were buzzing about this marine with a wicked punch, but almost no one had seen him. Brian was like the yarns baseball scouts told on the road of the kid working at a car wash who could throw a 101 mph fastball, or the urban legends of the schoolyard basketballer who beat Michael Jordan one-on-one. No one had ever witnessed these feats, just as almost no one within the MMA world had seen Brian fight, but everyone seemed to know someone who had seen it with their own eyes.

His back didn't feel great when he climbed into the cage, but all that pain turned to anger when he saw Cosio take off his shirt. The guy was bouncing and rolling, trying to give Brian some badass stare, which was almost comical. But then Brian saw a large 666 tattoo on his back. When a man has seen pure evil—when he has watched another human being blow himself up in a car just to kill and maim others—seeing a halfwit wannabe celebrate evil is enough to push him over the edge. The tattoo made Cosio a pathetic poser in Brian's book. He couldn't wait for the opening bell.

When it rang, Brian charged with a fury that shocked everyone. Even the referee stepped back with a look of astonishment. Cosio stepped back as well, but not quickly enough. Brian hit him with two massive blows. Mr. 666 crumpled to the mat. Brian moved in and hit him twice more when he was down before the referee jumped in between them and waved his arms.

In a matter of fifteen seconds Brian was 2-0 as a professional fighter.

The respite of the ring came to an end with the dog days of summer. Brian returned to Iraq at the hottest time of the year, and the hardest time in the war. "If anything, Anbar had gotten worse in the year since we'd been gone," Brian said. "The battalion started taking casualties almost immediately."

He was officially a married man by then. Although they were

planning a larger, formal ceremony when he returned, he and Teressa were married by a justice of the peace right before he left. It was
important to him that they marry before he went back.

Snipers were the new menace in Anbar, and not just the rooftop
variety. The Muj had learned from watching cable news. Some of
them cut firing holes in the trunks of cars and took out the backseats
like the D.C. snipers John Muhammad and Lee Malvo, while others
would just shoot civilians walking down the street to create havoc
and terror and shut down the economy in a country just beginning
to pull itself up.

Adding to the frustration for U.S. forces, the rules of engagement had reached a point of absurdity. Not only did a marine have
to worry about returning fire when fired upon; he also had to worry
about the caliber of the round he used. If you were shot at with a
small-caliber weapon, returning fire with a large-caliber weapon
could be deemed an escalation.

"In my first tour we could return fire with a .50-caliber and a
Mark 19," Brian said. "My second tour, you were not allowed to do
that. The highest caliber you could use was a 240 Golf."

They also couldn't round up suspects and search residents and
businesses where bad guys were known to be hiding. It was better,
the thinking went, to allow a few insurgents to escape and win the
hearts and minds of the innocents than to capture or kill the insurgents at the risk of alienating the locals.

Brian was now executive officer (XO) of India Company 3/2 Marines, a move that happened so quickly he didn't get to know many
of his men before they were into the wild once more. The FOB was
in Habbaniyah, but they weren't there long before the company was
broken into four different patrol bases, with Brian traveling back and
forth among them. It was a problem for him, not from an operational
perspective but at a personal level. He wanted to know his men. He
wanted to know where they came from and what their backgrounds
were; he wanted to know what sort of music they liked and what
books they read; he wanted to hear stories about their families and

talk to them about their girlfriends, hopefully imparting some of the lessons he had learned from his darker days. Most of all, he wanted to know how they thought and solved problems. Military regulations, born from centuries of experience, required a professional distance between an officer and enlisted personnel, as rank and respect for the chain of command were paramount in warfare, but that didn't mean you couldn't get to know the men around you.

Brian felt that doing so was even more important after his first tour. Men had come in and out of his life so quickly—Lamson, Mcelhinny, Goldsmith, Miller, Hernandez, Gass, Lowe, Robertson—men whose experiences with him were like water over rapids, brief and violent with no time to appreciate the beauty that comes in the stillness of quiet hours. Operational tempo cheated the bonding process, even though bonding was more important now than ever. During the height of the Iraq War, Marine specialists, corporals, and sergeants had a one-in-twelve chance of being injured. They had a one-in-twenty-four chance of being killed.

"Combat is so utterly random that only a fool believes it can be controlled," Brian said. "That is the issue we all faced in Anbar Province. Warriors are purpose-built control freaks. We thrive on order and discipline because we believe both will save lives once the bullets start flying. It is our way to try to control the uncontrollable."

That uncontrollability hit home for him early. A month after he arrived back in Anbar, a roadside bomb went off near the main FOB. A dozen were injured, but none more grievously than Corporal Don Champlin of Natchitoches, Louisiana, a twenty-eight-year-old with a smooth Cajun accent and a knack for being underestimated. He had gotten a degree in medical technology from LSU and worked at Natchitoches Regional Medical Center before enlisting. A day after the explosion, he died in Landstuhl Regional Medical Center in Germany. Don's parents took over the raising of his two-year-old son, Mekhiah.

A month later, on September 24, an insurgent fired an RPG into one of the remote patrol bases. Brian's duties had him leapfrogging all over the region. He wanted to go out with his men as much as possible. In fact, he thrived on those patrol runs and the message his presence sent to the other marines. But this time he had been engaged in other matters. Had he been around, maybe he would have smelled a setup; maybe he would have sensed that the hit-and-run on a heavily armed patrol base was bait, a lure to get the marines out into the open. Certainly he believed he would have ordered the men who went out to carry a device that blocked cell phone signals. Unfortunately, he wasn't there, and when the company commander sent a platoon out to search for the bad guy, the trap was sprung. A large IED was detonated by a cell phone as they went by.

Lance Corporal Rene Martinez, a twenty-year-old kid from Miami who looked about thirteen and who had wanted to be a marine since he was six years old, was blown more than two hundred feet into the air. He died instantly.

When Brian heard about the explosion, he jumped in a Humvee and raced to the scene. The blast had left a five-foot-deep hole in the road and gnarled steel where a vehicle had once been. When he finally got there, he helped load Martinez's body into a vehicle.

He carried Martinez into the morgue at the patrol base. The kid looked even younger in death, his face not yet filled out to match the size of his ears and what stubble of a beard he had coming in thin patches. Alone with the body, Brian allowed himself to cry as he held the young man's hand.

He should have been out there with them, he told himself. He should have saved Martinez.

Chad didn't work with the same group throughout his time with the 2nd Ranger Battalion. One of the problems with protracted wars was the rotations. Unlike World War II, where a core group could invade Normandy and still be together in Berlin, the nature and length of the Afghanistan and Iraq wars made staying with the same men for the entire campaign impossible. There was constant turnover. In order for an NCO to advance in his military career, he needs to take additional training and be part of stateside programs, so new faces were rolling in and out on a monthly basis.

Chad lost Jake Denman in 2006 to just such a scenario. Jake was one of the tougher platoon sergeants in the Rangers, but he had to head home to attend ANOC (Advanced Non-Commissioned Officer Course). It could have been a hard loss for the platoon had his replacement not been an old friend, Zac Dean. Once again it was like old home week, with Chad assuming the role of XO of Bravo Company 2/75 and Zac moving in as a squad leader. Another old friend, First Sergeant Bernie Folino—the man who chewed out his superior officers during the airfield seizure exercise, a speech Chad said was "the second-most inspirational I've ever heard, right behind General Schwarzkopf before the Army-Navy Game"—also joined them.

Zac and First Sergeant Folino provided the stability and leadership at the NCO level that Chad needed. But he also gained some fresh new talent in the form of a twenty-five-year-old genius named Kris Domeij, the first Ranger JTAC ever certified to call in Army, Navy, and Air Force aircraft during combat (calling in assets from other branches was like being able to speak five languages and transition between them while someone was shooting at you). He was also a 13-Fox forward observer, which meant he was the Ranger who called in mortar and artillery fire once an enemy position was established. With billions of dollars' worth of assets at his beck and call and an M4 rifle in his hand, Sergeant Domeij was the most dangerous man on the battlefield.

There were many times throughout the fall and winter of 2006 when Chad needed that experience. The enemy wasn't dumb—he quickly learned the tactics of coalition forces and adjusted accordingly. That meant the Ranger missions were more complex now than ever. Surveillance assets like drones were critical, and every officer and NCO had to be able to analyze intelligence and make good decisions on the field under the hardest of conditions.

Never was that more true than during one of Chad's most dangerous missions, one where he seriously thought his luck had run out. It was another middle-of-nowhere mission in central Iraq, although this area was flat and hard and desolate. Once again they went with a remote insertion so they could walk in and surprise the target without helicopter noise. Intel pinpointed the subject at a small farmhouse on the east side of a blacktop road a couple of kilometers from the LZ. Chad took one platoon—a light force, but large enough to get the job done—up the pavement, spreading out so they could maneuver easily but remain elusive.

"We never bunched up like grapes for tactical reasons," Chad said. "I walked in the back with all the radios, and Zac was up front again."

As they were walking in, they saw a stream of headlights coming in their direction, a "white-light convoy." Chad had no idea what this could be, maybe a coalition convoy on a supply run, or maybe something more nefarious. Either way, the headlights were a problem. A platoon walking up a road would not go unnoticed when bathed in the glow of halogens. On the southeast corner of a T-shaped intersection ahead, Chad saw a dirt hill about twenty feet high, not huge but big enough to provide adequate cover.

"Zac, take us behind that hill and we'll wait until the convoy passes," Chad radioed ahead.

None of them realized how far away the vehicles were. Under NVGs, they looked to be a couple of kilometers out, but because of the lack of depth perception, no one could see that the convoy was actually many miles away.

A lot closer was a group of people moving around in the darkness.

"Sir," Zac radioed back to Chad. "I think I see guys moving on that hilltop."

What, Chad said to himself. It was the middle of nowhere in the middle of the night.

"My spider sense went on high alert," he said. "We figured it was a group of insurgents about to ambush that white-light convoy."

Zac had the same idea. "Sir, I can move a team to the north and ambush them before they can hit the convoy."

"Roger," Chad said.

The platoon began to move in a coordinated pattern on the hill, but as Zac got closer he saw a couple of men behaving strangely. Then, out of nowhere, they yelled and opened fire on the platoon with a barrage of RPGs.

Exposed and with no cover in sight, they went into immediate react-to-contact drills. The closest squad laid down suppressive fire, lighting up the hilltop while a second squad flanked to their left.

As the firing intensified, Chad got a second round of bad news. One of the ISR operators who was providing overhead visual support called Chad and said, "Hey, there's a walled compound to the north-west of your location. Tanks are inside."

"Tanks?" Chad said. That didn't make any sense. This was a wasteland. What sort of compound would be out here? And who on earth had tanks? Not the Muj.

"They appear to be M1A1 Abrams," the ISR operator said, adding to the confusion.

Chad had little time to analyze this new information as the fighting was growing more intense by the second. A two-man fire team went after the RPG-wielding assailants with a Carl Gustav, a recoilless 84 mm shoulder-mounted antitank weapon that fired re-loadable explosive projectiles. They lit up the hilltop with the Gus.

Then Chad saw the distinct red flare off the tail of an RPG as it landed right in the middle of Third Squad. His heart sank. He figured he had just lost at least three men, maybe more. Thankfully, the grenade didn't explode. His guys continued to fire and the squad leader radioed, "All eagles are up."

The next words he heard over the radio stunned him. "The tanks are moving," the air support team said.

Chad was radioing his battalion commander, Lieutenant Colonel Erik Kurilla at the TOC (tactical operations center), when the tanks started firing. The first couple rounds went over his team's heads, but any experienced gunner would correct that mistake right away.

"That was the only time I ever lost radio discipline," Chad said. "I felt pretty sure we were going to be killed, and my voiced showed that."

They might have been wiped out had Air Force JTAC Sergeant Brian Temple not called in a wealth of air support. This was most likely friendly fire. Insurgents didn't have M1A1 tanks or walled compounds just off blacktop roads inside Iraq. Whoever was shooting didn't know they were shooting at guys on their team. Chad had no choice but to fight back. That was one of the problems at this stage of the war. Standing up an Iraqi army presented challenges no one could have expected, not the least of which was the lack of communication and a definitive chain of command. But that overview analysis would have to wait. At the moment, Chad had to do whatever he could to save his men.

There was a four-foot ditch on the east side of the blacktop about three hundred yards south of the hilltop. It was the only cover they could find, but it would be little help if the tanks dialed in their location.

Then Sergeant Temple called in F-16s to do a "show of force." The jets flew over low and fast, hitting the afterburners to warn whoever was shooting. That presented a new problem: the jets flew so low they kicked off their flares. Those flares backlit the platoon. They might as well have painted neon targets on their chests.

Fire from the hillside intensified and became a lot more accurate. Chad couldn't see the tanks, but he knew they were adjusting their turrets. It would take about ten seconds for the rounds to incinerate them in that ditch. At least it would be quick.

Then he saw a light and heard a roar overhead. It was the unmistakable thumping of an Apache helicopter. Bravo 2/75 had some Apaches attached to them from a National Guard unit out of Utah. One of those National Guard pilots turned on his lights, buzzed the hilltop, and landed on the road, putting himself and his gunship between the platoon and the group that was firing on them.

Why the Apache achieved what the F-16s could not was a mystery, but suddenly the firing stopped.

In one of the thousands of acts of heroism that became routine in the Iraq and Afghanistan wars, a National Guard Apache pilot risked his life to save Chad and his platoon from being overrun. The act didn't make the news. No one except the men who were there and their superiors who read the after-action reports knew it had happened. The pilot certainly never got the recognition he deserved. That level of bravery was common in Iraq, so much so that it became routine. For Chad and his men, nothing about that night was routine. They would be forever grateful to the man who undoubtedly saved their lives.

Because of the heroism of one pilot and the quick thinking of Chad, Sergeant First Class Mike Burke, and JTAC Brian Temple, what could have been the worst Ranger disaster of the Iraq War ended without a single casualty.

The compound belonged to a unit of Kurds that had been trained by the Special Forces, but there was no American presence on-site, and no one had any communications with the Kurdish army.

Chad understood how lucky they had been. He also knew their luck couldn't go on forever.

Brian was exhausted by the end of his second tour. From the lost sleep and the constant torment about the decisions he'd made, decisions his superiors assured him were exactly right, he felt an edge that was being rubbed raw. If he'd done everything right, why were mothers back home weeping over folded flags instead of hugging sons? Why were some of his marines gone, never to laugh at a joke or drink a beer or make love to a woman again? And why were so many other men's lives so permanently altered? Brian had lived his life as a protector, a man called to stand up for others. Yet in the heat of combat, he hadn't been able to protect all of his own men.

His time in Iraq had shaken him, but he still had men who counted on him to complete missions and keep them alive. Rather than show doubt, he became even more hypervigilant and intense. Even so, fifteen men from the 3/2 Marines died in Anbar Province while Brian was there. That didn't count the Iraqi translator who was gunned down on his way home for nothing more than making a living.

"It makes it tough," Brian said. "You're getting shot at. They're killing your guys. Your men want to return fire because their buddy has been shot, but you can't tell exactly where the shots have come from or if there are civilians in the area. Now you have to go back to the base with your buddy's body. It's frustrating and tough. And the anger just festers."

That frustration led to misplaced guilt as leaders like Brian blamed themselves for acts that were as random as rain. One bullet hits harmlessly in the dirt while another hits a human heart. One typical fall afternoon in the region, Corporal Mike Brown was manning a 240 Golf in a guard tower. It was brutally hot, and the sandbags and camouflage netting blocked any breeze. Mike was roasting. Late in the day he leaned forward to catch a second of air. No one knew how long the sniper had been waiting for that moment, but he shot Mike in the forehead, killing him instantly.

Then, two days after Christmas 2006, Lance Corporal Willie Koprince of Lenoir City, Tennessee, and Corporal Joshua Schmitz of Spencer, Wisconsin, were on a patrol run at 0245 when an IED exploded, killing both of them. Willie's family could not be immediately found by the Marine contact team. They had recently moved from Lenoir City to Oak Ridge and hadn't left the Corps a forwarding address. When the Marine captain and chaplain finally found them, they were in a restaurant having an early lunch. The scene when the news arrived would never be forgotten by any of the diners who were there.

Willie had been baptized at the First Baptist Church in Lenoir

City. Four days into the New Year, he was memorialized there. He
was twenty-four years old.

Brian understood why they were in Iraq. He had seen the hatred,
not just for the Americans, but for all of Western civilization. These
were people who hanged homosexuals from streetlights; who stoned
rape victims to death for having tempted their rapists; who sent children out as spies, not with bribes of candy or toys, but through death
threats to their parents and siblings. He also wondered if there was
ever going to be a way to win, or a definition of victory that would
make sense of everything he'd seen.

He saw progress, especially in the rebuilding of the Iraqi Army,
but when he left there was still a long way to go. Before flying out
of Anbar Province in March 2007, Brian was attempting to help the
Iraqis establish a National Guard post there. They had open enlist-
ments and scores of Iraqi men came out. After they signed up, Brian
told them they would be loaded on a bus and taken to a U.S. base for
a couple of days before being shipped to Baghdad for basic training.
Five of the new recruits elected not to go to the base. They wanted to
go home to be with their families for two final days before heading
out. Even though Brian told them it was bad idea, the men insisted.

The next morning Brian got a call telling him that five bodies
were in the main intersection of town. When he got there, the five
National Guard recruits who had gone home were lying in the street,
decapitated, their eyes gouged out of their severed heads.

Chad had already talked to Emily about getting out. They wanted
to start a family, and as 2006 slipped into 2007, no one knew how
many more deployments would be in his future if he stayed. The
missions weren't the problem—they were what energized him and
got him excited about putting on the uniform—but military careers
have a certain arc. After serving as a platoon leader and a company
XO, the next phase would be administrative. There would be a lot
of planning and perhaps some lecturing—like the seminars he gave

on the friendly-fire incident with the Kurds, a fight that gained the after-action name "Veterans Hill, Bravo 2.75: Objective Bain"—but his days working a shoot house and leading a platoon into the night were coming to a close. That reality convinced him it was time to call it a career and get home to his wife.

At West Point he had listened to the senior officers talk about the "five-and-fliers," and what a problem it was for the long-term well-being of the Army. A strong Army needed experienced, career officers, men who committed themselves to a military life from start to finish. There was no better breeding ground for those men than West Point. Now Chad was about to be one of those five-and-fliers. Intellectually it was the right decision, but emotionally he would have a hard time letting go.

After dinner one night toward the end of his final deployment in 2007, as his team was heading to the command post for a briefing on the night's operation, First Sergeant Bernie Folino looked at him and said, "Sir, you know you're going to miss this, right?"

"Yeah, FirSarnt, I know," Chad said.

"No, Chad," Bernie said. "You need to understand: Nothing you'll do for the rest of your life will ever touch this. You'll never have this feeling again. You need to accept that before you get out."

Chad looked down and kept walking for a moment. Then he looked at Sergeant Folino and said, "Roger that."

Nothing looked better than Teressa and Camp Lejeune when Brian returned in the spring of 2007, although seeing the families of the fallen was the hardest thing he would ever do in his life. "Nothing in your life is tougher or more gut-wrenching than looking at a mother and explaining to her why she will never see her son again," Brian said. "I think about those families and those moments all the time."

He wasn't home for even three weeks before he had his next fight. The WEC figured out what a marketing boom they had with "the All American" Brian Stann, a light heavyweight at 205 pounds who looked like he'd been cut from central casting: handsome, chiseled, and a war hero who had come straight off the battlefield and into the octagon. If the marketing department couldn't sell that, they needed to close the doors.

Brian was slated on the undercard at the Hard Rock Cafe in Las Vegas against a WEC newcomer from Long Beach, California, named Steve Cantwell. No one knew how Brian would fare after another stint overseas, especially against an opponent who was 3-0 as a professional and devoted to the mixed martial arts game full-time.

Before the fight, Brian spoke to his buddy Travis Manion via satellite phone. Brian asked Travis to stand with him at his and Teressa's formal wedding ceremony, and they talked about things in Iraq. Travis was on his second tour, this time embedded with the Iraqi Army, trying to stand up those troops and turn the country over to them. That was the ultimate goal, which most marines had to remind themselves of when nothing else made sense. The Iraqis would carry on the fight long after the Americans were gone. Guys like Travis were in the field carrying out the most important mission of all.

Brian told him about the Cantwell fight, and Travis said, "Your heart's unbeatable, Brian. Bring that to every fight, and you'll never lose."

When the bell rang in Vegas, Brian came out again with the fury, hammering Cantwell with one combination after another. One of the punches landed squarely on the Californian's chin. Cantwell went down, and Brian pounced, beating him with one hammer blow after another until the referee jumped in.

That one lasted forty-one seconds. Brian was 3-0 and on his way to becoming a brand name in the fight world.

He was still accepting backslaps and congratulations a month after the fight when his phone rang and he heard words that hit him harder than any punch. During a routine patrol of Fallujah with his new crop of Iraqi troops, Travis's platoon fell under ambush by a group of insurgents. One of the vehicles was disabled, and several marines and Iraqi soldiers were wounded. Thinking only of the safety of his men, Travis left his Humvee and ran through heavy machine gun fire, drawing fire to himself and away from the wounded. A sniper killed him instantly.

Travis Manion and J. P. Blecksmith had been two of Brian's best friends at the academy. Both were killed doing their jobs. Both died being who they were: heroes. Whatever Brian did from that point forward, he vowed it would be to honor their memory and sacrifice. No matter what, the message of what those men had done would get out.

At Travis's memorial service in Iraq, one of the Iraqi colonels who served with him called Travis "a brave warrior who did not fear the death." The honor went farther, and the Iraqi Army named their Fallujah operating base Combat Outpost Manion, one of the only Iraqi military facilities named after an American.

He was awarded the Silver Star and Bronze Star for Valor posthumously. Part of the commendation read, "His selfless actions allowed every member of his patrol to survive."

From the time of Travis's death forward, Brian carried a laminated card with Travis's handwritten words on them:

> *Make my lonely grave richer*
> *Sweeter be,*
> *Make this truly the land of the free*
> *And the home of the brave.*
> *I gave my life to save*
> *That I might here lie*
> *Eternally*
> *Forever free.*

Travis wrote that poem on the plane to Brett Harmon's funeral with Brian sitting to his right. The next time Brian heard it was when Joel Sharratt, Travis's wrestling coach at the Naval Academy, read it at his funeral.

During some of their last conversations, Travis had talked about how he would love to get into the MMA world once he got out of the Corps. He wasn't like Brian; he didn't have the energy to fight in his spare time while still a marine.

After Travis's death, Brian didn't, either. When he told his commanding officer that he would be getting out of the Corps at the end of his commitment, e-mails flew around the Marine hierarchy and Brian was offered a position as an instructor at The Basic School, one of the most coveted positions in the service. He could train officers, mold them and make them better, and possibly save lives in the future.

"Sir, you do know what happened to me when I was at TBS, right?" Brian asked. The memories of his court-martial and all the hurt that went with it still stung him.

"Stann, that is so far behind you, no one can see it," his CO said.

Brian could see it. The memories would never leave him. Being wrongfully charged with a heinous crime was the first time Brian had been blindsided by an enemy that he never saw coming, and the first time he felt the sting of what he considered an institutional betrayal. Marines had seen the truth and acquitted him, but others had made his life a living hell.

"Thank you, sir," Brian said. "But I'm going to devote myself to my new career. I think I can honor our guys there as well."

Like Chad, Brian served the minimum commitment, moving on to life as a civilian. But also like Chad, he would never truly leave the fight. It was in their blood.

PART THREE

SURVIVORS

CHAPTER 13

If a man does his best, what else is there?
—GENERAL GEORGE S. PATTON

Young men can't retire. The human psyche won't allow it. It is unnatural for a man hitting his physical and mental prime to be snatched out of a career, especially one that has kept him on the edge of an adrenaline high with constant goals and missions directly ahead. It is why a boxer stays in the ring one fight too long and the quarterback can't see when it is time to walk away from the game.

Former Tampa Bay Buccaneer Kevin Carter opened up about it, saying, "Every NFL player struggles when they first get out of the game. Not only are you in front of cheering fans every week, but you go from waking up every day with a mission, an opponent to plan for or a camp to prepare for, and suddenly that's gone. You're in your thirties, healthy, productive, but everything you've ever known, you can't do anymore. Anybody who tells you they don't struggle with that is lying."

Chad didn't miss football, even though he'd thought he would. After taking a knee to run out the clock in the 2001 Army-Navy Game, he had put away the pads and rarely thought about playing the game again, especially since he knew he had more intense and exciting things ahead of him. There were a few wistful moments, especially sitting around with his buddies and reliving the old days, but they were fleeting. As he had planned from the moment he signed the commitment papers to go to West Point, he transitioned out of sports and into a career without any residual longings.

Leaving the Army, especially the Ranger Regiment, which was where his loyalties had taken root, was a different matter. He could have stayed in the Army and flourished in any number of administrative functions, playing the game, logging his time, writing briefs, and making presentations while waiting for the next promotion. He could easily have advanced to Major Jenkins, and if he'd stuck with it long enough, he could have become Lieutenant Colonel Jenkins before hitting the twenty-year mark. Training jobs would have been plentiful. He could have taught leadership, or even gone back to West Point and worked with the football team. They love their own at the academy and would have welcomed him like the prodigal son, returning to lead the Cadets out of the pigskin wilderness. But after all he'd done and seen, none of those jobs stirred his soul.

Staying in would have also meant more tours. No one knew how long the conflicts in Iraq and Afghanistan were going to continue, but one thing was certain: leaders like Chad would be beating a regular trail back and forth to the other side of the world for years to come. Leading a platoon on nightly missions was worth that sacrifice. Coordinating intelligence and logistics and looking at video monitors inside battalion HQ while sending others into the night— that was not in his DNA. He would rather be stateside with Emily raising a family and starting anew.

He was honorably discharged at the rank of captain with three Bronze Stars and a chest full of what he termed "do-your-job medals," although no one who knew the kind of hero Chad was would ever call them that. None of his personal awards meant much after he left. Like all soldiers during times of war, Chad knew who the real heroes were, and he didn't consider himself among them. He was just a guy in transition, trying for the first time since his senior year in high school to live a life without regiment or formations or uniforms. It was tougher than he thought. He never dipped into full-bore depression, but he experienced a loss of purpose in civilian life.

Chad and Emily moved back to Dublin, Ohio, where he went to work for his dad for a while, selling equipment to the Navy. Dave Jenkins had been in sales Chad's whole life, so it wasn't as though the process was foreign to Chad. He and Emily got a house and converted the spare bedroom into a home office complete with a desk and bookshelves, a fax machine, and a dedicated phone, all the tools an aspiring salesman would need.

His old friends expected as much. "I always figured he'd go back home and get into the family business," his old teammate Gary Bartels said. "There was nobody who loved their family more, so it seemed like the perfect fit."

It felt wonderful living back in his hometown and working with his father. But was this what the rest of his life would be like? Was it his destiny to wade through a morass of Defense Department contracts and spend his days engaged in long, banal conversations with government purchasing agents? He was good at it. He exceeded his quotas almost immediately. He also started going to bars and hanging out with friends, events he should have enjoyed but that he found utterly unfulfilling. He was in the prime of his life, the time when most men are at their peak, and he was wondering if his best days were behind him.

After a few months of making calls for his father, Chad realized that the government purchasing bureaucracy made no more sense from the civilian side than it did from the inside. So he left his dad's firm and went to work with his brother-in-law, Brian, Laura's husband, selling medical devices. The medical device company put him on a monthly draw until he could develop enough clients to get his commissions up—a standard practice for the industry—but Chad attacked the new job with the gusto of a Ranger. Within two months he was on straight commission and was one of the top producers. The infectious smile and easy charm made him a natural. There was no one he couldn't talk to, and nothing he couldn't sell, especially to doctors who were all too eager to hear stories from a former Army officer just back from the front lines.

Sometimes the conversations listed toward uncomfortable topics. Throughout American history it has been hard for combat veterans to talk about their actions and experiences, so in past generations the subject of war was simply not brought up in polite company. For some reason this war was different. Chad was asked all sorts of probing questions about his service—where he had been, what he had done, and most uncomfortably, whom he had killed. One doctor was curious about any guilt he experienced after taking out an insurgent during a raid. "Nothing to feel guilty about," Chad said. "Once you see what the enemy is capable of doing, it doesn't bother you at all when you have to put them down. The guilt comes when they kill civilians that you aren't able to protect."

That chat took place inside Adena Medical Center as Chad and one of his spine surgeon clients waited out a summer thunderstorm. The doctor wanted to know about the Ranger Regiment and how the fire teams worked, details that were still classified, so Chad tap-danced around most of them. He offered just enough nuggets to have the doctor shaking his head in disbelief.

When the storm passed, Chad and the surgeon walked out together. That's when they heard a woman scream.

The doctor looked up in time to see a middle-aged woman in a business suit struggling with a man in his twenties. She fought to keep her purse, but the man was too strong. He grabbed the bag and shoved the woman away. Her knees buckled, but she did not go to the ground.

Then the doctor saw a blur at his side. It was Chad sprinting at the assailant. The kid didn't make it twenty yards. Chad lowered his shoulder and hit him in the side, knocking him off his feet and to the ground. The mugger tried to squirm, but Chad pulled his arm behind his back and put a knee in the young man's throat.

"Call security!" Chad shouted to the doctor, who only then realized he had been too stunned to move.

Chad could have made a great living in medical device sales. It was honorable and lucrative work and he was good at it. But it didn't engage the body and mind the way he had known before. Missing a sale wasn't the same as missing a target during a raid, or missing an IED on a sweep. The consequences for mission failure now were losing an account, not losing a limb or, possibly, a life.

Then an Army buddy called him about an opening at the FBI. "You can still be in the fight, just here at home," his friend said.

Chad put in his application immediately. After one round of interviews in Quantico, he was hired. Within three months, he was raising his hand and taking another oath to defend the Constitution, this time as part of the Counterterrorism Division of the Federal Bureau of Investigation.

One of his options was south Florida. In the previous five years, he'd spent time in the hottest weather imaginable and in the cold winds at the foothills of Mount St. Helens. Warm was better. After consulting with Emily, he accepted south Florida sight unseen. "I had to be one of the luckiest guys in the world," Chad said later. "The main office for the FBI is in an awful part of Miami, but somehow I got assigned to Palm Beach County."

They had moved a total of seven times in seven years when Chad and Emily bought a house in Jupiter, Florida, a mile from the beach and four blocks from a Starbucks where it was commonplace to line up in the drive-through behind a four-hundred-thousand-dollar Lamborghini. He couldn't have been happier in his government-issue Pontiac. The Jenkinses had a daughter and then a son, and they nestled into the life they had never allowed themselves to dream of. Emily gave up her work at GlaxoSmith-Kline to stay home and raise her family. And once again, Chad put on a uniform and carried a firearm in defense of his country. The hints of despair he had felt would never return again.

Ten years after the 2001 Army-Navy Game, neither man could hide his intensity. The way they walked, the way they sat, the unflinching eye contact: these were not men who could interact casually, even when carrying on light conversation. They digested each question before giving fully formed responses, grammatical and complete; even when saying breezy things—telling a joke, razzing a buddy, or heaping compliments on someone—the words came with an unmistakable edge, a warrior cadence that caused anyone in earshot to sit up a little straighter.

Maybe it was the training, or what they had endured in combat; or maybe it stemmed farther back, to their days as children playing Peewee football, suiting up in pads and running over others, reacting to whistles and snap counts and the rants of coaches. Whatever the genesis, Brian and Chad remained men who could not say "good morning" without jarring the relaxed sensibilities of those around them.

Never was that more evident than Memorial Day weekend of 2011. In a twelfth-floor corner suite of the MGM Grand, a tan room with tacky curtains and a view of the Las Vegas airport and the Excalibur hotel, Brian did his best to answer questions about his life and career. He was in Las Vegas to fight Jorge Santiago in UFC 130, a pay-per-view event that wouldn't get under way for another thirty hours. Rather than secluding himself in a room after his mandatory press conference, Brian put on a dress shirt and blazer and hosted a reception for his friend Marcus Luttrell, a former Navy SEAL who was the only member of SEAL Team Ten to make it home alive from Operation Red Wings in Afghanistan.

Marcus's newest role was that of bestselling author and fundraiser. Copies of his book, *Lone Survivor,* the story of his team's final mission and the men who died on a rocky mountain in Afghanistan, sat on a table in the center of the suite, but Marcus preferred to sit away from the books and the windows and the limelight. He was in Las Vegas to see Brian fight and raise money for his Lone Survivor Foundation, a nonprofit group tasked with building a ranch in Texas for troops suffering from post-traumatic stress disorder.

Brian had rearranged his schedule to be with Marcus and raise awareness for the charity. He stood center stage as Marcus moved slowly to a couch, a visible limp in his gait. Marcus's facial scars from the firefight that killed his teammates, including Medal of Honor recipient Michael Murphy, were amplified by having his identical twin brother, Morgan, also a SEAL, sitting across from him. The effect was jarring: Morgan the "before" picture and Marcus the "after."

"I do not celebrate this weekend. I am not happy this weekend," Brian said when the subject inevitably turned to the symbolism of him fighting a man in a cage during Memorial Day weekend. Still ramrod straight with hair cut high and tight, not quite shaved, as it had been during active duty, but short enough, Brian had trimmed down to 185 pounds from his natural weight of 200, so he now had the mean, hungry look of a man who needed a couple of hamburgers. He could still run ten miles in sixty minutes and rip off a dozen chinups without gritting his teeth. But unlike his college years or even his years in active duty, his body fat percentage hovered in the single digits, giving him abs and a core as chiseled as any model's on the cover of a fitness magazine. His current weight was what he needed to maintain to qualify as a middleweight in the UFC. The day before he was to climb into the octagonal cage, Brian's face drew a little tighter.

"There are guys that I miss, guys who aren't coming back," he said, his Scranton accent growing thicker as emotion bubbled closer to the surface. "They are what I think about on this weekend. They are the reason I do what I do. Their memory.

"I love Jorge Santiago. I have so much respect for him. He is a great champion, but I wouldn't want to fight me on Memorial Day weekend. Come Saturday night, I'm going to be ready to fight. I'd fight everybody on the card."

Those were hard words for him to say as reporters milled around and gorged themselves on miniature burgers topped with bleu cheese and cucumbers.

"It's never easy to talk about," he continued. "You never want to come across as if you're saying 'look at me' when talking about your life and especially your military service, because that's not it at all. It's the opposite of that. Being president of a charity that helps veterans find jobs when they get out of the military, it's important for me to continue to leverage the media when I'm fighting. And to raise money for charity is important. Maybe some of the hard-core fans are sick of hearing about my time in the Marine Corps, but I'm not the one asking the questions. Obviously [this] being Memorial Day, it was going to happen before this fight."

He looked out the window and across the Strip to the Excalibur, one of the tackiest examples of Vegas architectural decadence: King Arthur's castle on meth, a $100 million Renaissance fair without the funnel cakes and fried turkey legs.

"Shit bothers you, you know," Brian said in a soft tone, more to himself than to any of the reporters. "Fans can't stand that my military service is brought up all the time, but what people don't understand is that there are men who died or were permanently injured who were under my command. One guy has had three brain surgeries. Another will never walk again. People who think I pound my chest over what I did are out of their minds. I've lost more sleep over decisions I made, thinking, what if I had done this, or what if I'd done that, maybe this guy would still be walking or this guy would able to speak clearly and live a normal life. All of this"—he waved his arm around the room, at Vegas and all it represented—"that shit does not matter to us. None of that shit brings anybody back."

There is a special ringside assistant whose job is to wipe blood off the canvas before a fight goes live. The fights themselves are violent and unpredictable, but between bouts, every UFC event is a finely choreographed ballet, with one man assigned the task of taking a fresh, warm towel soaked with hospital-grade antiseptic into the octagonal cage and cleaning up the inevitable blood splatters that come when men pound on each other with fists, feet, elbows, and knees.

Brian's Memorial Day weekend fight against Santiago had been played to the hilt. In the prefight press conference, UFC president Dana White had smiled and said, "Do you think I'm smart enough to put Brian Stann on the card on Memorial Day?" Then he winked and said, "Don't give me too much credit." But there was nothing subtle about White's marketing strategy. The mixed martial arts world couldn't get enough of "the All American" Brian Stann.

Unlike Chad, Brian hadn't struggled with his career transition, because he had already established himself in one arena before letting go of the other. The rush of a fight still didn't match the intensity of combat, but it was a lot closer than any other job he could have had. The lights, the crowd, and the intensity of being locked in a cage with another human being intent on beating you unconscious kept the juices flowing, but cage fights didn't wake you up in the middle of the night in a cold sweat; they didn't haunt you with screams that you could never unhear; they didn't visit you in the stillness like the faces of the dead. Brian now made his living as a fighter, but the warriors were the men he saw when he closed his eyes.

After his Cantwell victory, a fight that earned Brian six thousand dollars, the WEC had put him on the fast track, setting him up for another bout less than three months later with a former University of New Mexico football player and ex-boxer named Craig Zellner, an impressive fighter with a 4-1 record and a ground game that made everyone sit up and take notice. Zellner won most of his fights by flinging his opponents to the mat and forcing them into submission.

They had met in the cage at an event titled "WEC 28 Wreckage" in Las Vegas, a televised bout where the league played up Brian's active-duty service to the hilt. It was an uncomfortable period for him. Fight promotion was part of the business, and the fighters were supposed to take every media opportunity to hype the upcoming event. The WEC came up with the "All American" nickname, putting it on every press release and promotion card they sent out. Brian was on CNN and the Howard Stern show as well as local stations. The cameras barely started rolling before the subject of Anbar Province and Al Qa'im came up. At first Brian tried to deflect and change the subject, but the questions came back again. He could sense that the producers wanted him to brag or at least to outline the things he had done during combat. That wasn't going to happen. He would cut off the interviews and walk away from the fight before he would take credit for anything that took place on those battlefields.

After talking it over with Teressa and several of his fellow marines, he realized this might be the only opportunity to tell the stories of the fallen. He owed it to the real heroes of Al Qa'im to use this platform. He owed it to men like Sergeant Francis, whom Brian saw on a flight line not six weeks after Operation Matador as Francis returned to Iraq after treatment at Landstuhl Regional Medical Center. The burn scars couldn't be missed, but neither could Francis's smile. "Hey, sir, I'm back," he'd said to Brian.

Then there was Sergeant Robertson, the man who had been at Brian's side as they pulled the wounded from a burning tank near the Ramana Bridge. He had returned home and become a drill instructor: unheralded and unsung, but a hero worthy of more praise than Brian could ever give him. And there was his boundary-pusher, Corporal Lamson, the man who did so many remarkable things during the firefight at Al Qa'im that Brian welled up thinking about him. He had gone home to Indiana and resumed a normal life. Those and others—Robert Gass, Jonathan Lowe, and the fallen, Rene Martinez, Willie Koprince, Don Champlin, as well as his classmates and teammates Brett Harmon, Ron Winchester, and his buddies J. P. Blecksmith and Travis Manion—were the ones he had to promote. If he could use his notoriety in martial arts fighting to tell their stories, then he would be in the cage every day.

When the bell rang for WEC 28, Zellner came out and immediately went for Brian's legs, but Brian slid away and counterpunched to force the bigger man to keep his distance and stay upright. On his feet was where Brian held an advantage. Brian couldn't charge in and flail away during this fight. Zellner was a very large man. He had to be approached with care. Brian jabbed and moved until Zellner exposed his chin. Then Brian landed a combination that sent him back.

In the middle of the first round, Zellner opened himself up again, and Brian nailed him on the cheek, knocking him out cold.

That victory had earned Brian a shot at the WEC Light Heavyweight Championship against Doug Marshall in March 2008. Once again Brian came out with a flurry of punches, taking the initiative and keeping the fight off the mat. When it came to punching and kicking, Brian was virtually unstoppable in the 205-pound weight class. Once it went to the mat, he still needed work.

Fists, knees, and feet flew, and in the first round it appeared as though Brian was in trouble. Marshall came at him with a flurry after the two traded blows for the first half of the round. Brian covered up to avoid any serious damage while Marshall hammered his shoulders and forearms.

Then Brian dropped his guard and counterpunched. The two men went after each other in a brawl that brought the fans to their feet and had the announcers yelling into their microphones. For a full ten seconds, it looked like a back-alley street fight. Brian took one blow to the jaw that almost downed him, but he came back with two quick counterpunches, a right that grazed the side of Marshall's face and then a left hook that landed squarely on the champion's jaw.

Marshall went down. Still stung from the earlier blow, Brian wasn't sure what had happened. His arms went out to his sides as if to say, "What are you doing?" Then he realized that this was his chance to end it. With Marshall on the mat, Brian landed two more quick jabs. Marshall's head bounced twice and his arms went limp. He was out.

Brian leaped around the ring twice, but then fell to a knee and cried. He was a title holder, an MMA champion, and a standard-bearer.

The WEC eventually folded into the UFC, and Brian continued to work his way up the ladder, trimming down to fight as a middle-weight and becoming far more proficient at the technical aspects of the sport. White exploited the marketing potential he had with Brian, but the relationship was mutual. Brian had endorsement deals with Xtreme Couture (an MMA-centric clothing line) and Gaspari Nutrition (a supplement company). He was a regular public speaker and guest on CNN, and White sent him all over the country to sign autographs and attend promotional shows.

These were not things Brian did to enrich himself. After returning home, he used his celebrity to create Hire Heroes USA, a non-profit placement agency for returning combat veterans. When he was not in the cage or in the gym, Brian could be found in the charity's Atlanta offices, lobbying CEOs to hire returning servicemen and training his fellow veterans in resume writing and interviewing for the next phase of their lives.

Saturday night of Memorial Day weekend, 2011, Jorge Santiago came into the ring first to a blast of heavy-metal music that rever-berated through the chests of everyone in the MGM Garden Arena. Crowds at UFC fights are not dissimilar to what you would find at a Megadeth concert: young, loud, and tattooed, awash in energy and disenfranchisement, silicone and testosterone. Brian didn't fit the UFC mold. He kept his hair cut and conducted himself as the consummate professional. In the prefight interviews, he showed up in a jacket and slacks while Dana White, sporting a three-day beard, wore jeans and a Hugo Boss golf shirt. A stranger would have thought that the president of the UFC was the fighter and the fighter the president.

"That's the one thing about this guy," White said about Brian. "Everything that comes out of his mouth is perfect. He is an easy guy to like, and a very good fighter."

When Brian walked into the arena, there was no doubt who the crowd wanted. Chants of "U-S-A" started within seconds. The tenth anniversary of 9/11 made this Memorial Day especially poignant as stories from America's most recent conflict filled the airwaves and stayed near the forefront of everyone's mind. Santiago wasn't a bad guy, and he was a very good fighter. In Asia he had gone undefeated and was thought to be a shoe-in for an eventual title shot. But he was Brazilian, and he was up against the All American. Jorge might as well have been a member of the Taliban as far as the fans were concerned.

Brian and Santiago felt each other out, but Jorge made the mistake of believing he could stand up and fight against Brian.

A cadre of camera people climbed like Spider-Man onto the cage to film the action from every possible angle. Pay-per-view was the golden egg of the UFC, and the weekend's take totaled in the tens of millions. The highlights and replays would generate even more, especially with it being "the Marine hero," as the cage-side announcers said over and over.

Brian pushed the pace, "slinging leather," UFC analyst Joe Rogan called it. His pacing was more precise and his movement much more efficient than in his WEC days. Advanced training in Albuquerque with the game's best, Greg Jackson and Mike Winkeljohn, had transformed him from a brawler into a sculpted fighter. But to the untrained eye, Brian still appeared to be a raging bull, charging and punching in a whirlwind of aggression. He harbored no ill will toward Santiago and had praised him in every prefight interview, but when the battle began, Brian went into combat mode.

Santiago, who seemed wounded that he was being cast as the villain in this drama—"I love America, too," he said prior to the fight—

absorbed some of the hardest blows Brian had ever thrown. Those punches were not for Jorge. They were for his dear friend Travis Manion, who had been with him at the start of his MMA journey. The student quarters at The Basic School, a large brick building in Quantico that housed future Marine officers, had been named Manion Hall, and Brian hoped every marine who entered would learn about the man whose name was over the door. Travis had never lived his MMA dream, so Brian had to fight for both of them.

Moving, punching, kicking: three minutes and fifteen seconds into the first round Brian landed a left hook to Santiago's jaw and the Brazilian went down. Brian swarmed on top of him, landing blow after blow, attempting to put it away, but Santiago recovered, wrapping Brian up and holding him on the canvas for a minute and a half until the bell rang.

The second of three rounds began with a ring girl in a bikini and full makeup carrying a placard with the number 2. When the official gave the signal to fight, Brian moved in and took control. Santiago landed a few kicks, but his movements were much slower than they had been before the knockdown.

Santiago spun and caught Brian in the side of the head with the back of his hand, but Brian didn't flinch. It was as if he'd been hit with a Ping-Pong ball. Two minutes and numerous body kicks later, Santiago dropped his left hand a fraction of an inch. Maybe fatigue got the best of him, or maybe it was the start of a punch that developed too slowly. Whatever the reason, Brian saw the opening and threw a right hook into Santiago's temple.

The head snapped as he went down. Before Santiago hit the floor, Brian had moved in and hit him twice more. Santiago's jaw went slack and his eyes rolled back in his head. The referee jumped in front of Brian. It was over.

Brian threw up his hands in victory as the crowd erupted in cheers and chants of "U-S-A . . . U-S-A." Then he knelt down and made sure Santiago was okay, an act the ringside announcers praised as "the classiest" they had seen from a fighter. As the chants intensified—"U-S-A . . . U-S-A"—Brian fell to his knees, covered his head, his back heaving and his arms quivering as he wept openly and freely.

Rogan, a tattoo-laden announcer with a week-old beard who hosted the show *Fear Factor* and had starred as a baseball player on the Fox comedy *Hardball* before becoming a commentator for the UFC, jumped into the octagon and shoved a microphone in Brian's face.

"How important is this victory, especially since we're here on Memorial Day weekend?" Rogan said.

"It's just vital," Brian said, blinking away tears. "I use this as a symbol. All you families out there who have lost somebody in combat, this weekend is all about you. So, everyone, please, remember those who made the ultimate sacrifice for freedom."

A row of marines in their dress blue uniforms in the front row raised their hands and yelled "OoooRAH!" as loudly as they could. Next to them, standing and cheering, was Marcus Luttrell, who gave his friend a crooked smile and thumbs-up.

In the row behind Luttrell, a group of hard men slapped each other on the backs and joined the chorus of cheers. They too looked out of place, although no one could say exactly why. Nobody recognized them. No one was supposed to. They were members of SEAL Team Six. As always, they slipped in and out unnoticed.

CHAPTER 14

Never give in. Never, never, never, never, in nothing
great or small, large or petty, never give in except to
convictions of honor and good sense.

—Winston Churchill

On December 10, 2011, Washington, D.C., was thirty-five degrees
colder than Philadelphia had been on this weekend ten years before.
Still, the pageantry and traditions of the Army-Navy Game marched
on unabated by the weather. At 0700 that Saturday morning, Cadet
Brigade Operations Officer David Adamic, a firstie, called the West
Point Corps of Cadets to formation, and four thousand students
dressed in gray shivered in silent unison on cold metal bleachers in
the Platinum parking lot of FedExField.

It was thirty-four degrees. The game didn't start for seven hours.

Fifty yards away from the cadet formation, Mike Erwin, West
Point Class of 2002, smiled and laughed and told everyone at his
tailgate party how thrilled he was to have them eating his chicken
and burgers, even as his hand shook uncontrollably. The cold air
was partly to blame for the shivering, but exhaustion also played a
role. Erwin and five of his buddies had just finished running 197
miles in two days. Fifteen klicks of that (military jargon for fifteen

kilometers, or just over thirteen miles) had come that very morning.

"The original idea was to run from the Flight 93 Memorial in Shanksville, Pennsylvania, to Arlington National Cemetery," Erwin said. "Then when I got up this morning, I realized it was just another thirteen-point-one miles to the stadium, so I said, 'What the heck, that's a half marathon. You've run this far, might as well finish it off.'"

He spoke in a matter-of-fact, clinical voice, as if he were describing a round of golf. Erwin didn't get excited by much. Almost all the males at the party had seen combat, so conversations about a brisk run were nothing to get worked up over, even if it was almost two hundred miles. To put it into perspective, the Badwater Ultramarathon, which bills itself as "the world's toughest footrace," is 135 miles from Death Valley to the trailhead of Mount Whitney. The record for that one is just under twenty-three hours. Erwin, along with Gary Bartels, Sam Linn, John Faunce, and Blake Saksa, ran almost half again that far in forty hours, without first-aid or watering stations; without time bands on their ankles or television cameras capturing their every step; they did it without volunteers lining the route or family and friends cheering them along the way. All they had was snow, ice, and an American flag, the standard five-foot version on a wooden pole. They took turns carrying it every ten miles.

"It was amazing to run through all that farm country and not see a car or a person for a lengthy spell," Bartels said. "But it was just as awesome to run through towns and have people yell 'Way to go!' or 'Thank you!' They stopped their cars and took pictures of us."

Then quietly, almost as if he were admitting some transgression, Bartels said, "Pain builds character. I prayed and cried and sang patriotic songs and talked to my grandfather, who served in France and Austria during World War II in the Third Infantry Division. He passed away two days after I got back from Iraq in 2003. So, I think of this as the most rewarding run of my life."

They all considered the run a fitting tribute to the ten-year anniversary of the attacks that had changed their lives and the lives of most Americans. Mike accepted a few quiet accolades, a "great job" or two, and a lot of knowing nods when the subject of his near-two-hundred-mile run came up. Only a few people, mostly spouses and outsiders who were not a part of the culture, raised eyebrows and said things like "You guys did what?"

They were in their early thirties now, a stage in their lives when they were most comfortable in their own skin, and it embarrassed them if you made a big deal out of them running absurd distances before a football game. They hadn't done it to get their names in *Runners World;* they did it as personal tributes to fallen friends and personal tests to make sure that, a few years removed from combat, they still had the right stuff. Could you finish? Were you man enough? Those questions rarely popped into the minds of most thirty-two-year-olds, but they hung like an unfinished verse in this atmosphere. Even though most of these men had put the uniform away and moved on with their lives, theirs remained a culture of certitude, a place where life was experienced through the pursuit of physical, intellectual, and moral clarity.

Chad wasn't part of the run, but he was at the tailgate festivities and would be attending the game. He and Emily had flown into Washington from West Palm Beach on Friday night. Their wedding anniversary happened to coincide with the tenth anniversary of the 2001 Army-Navy Game. Emily understood how important it was for Chad to be there, though this wasn't exactly the sort of romantic getaway she had envisioned.

"She's a trouper when it comes to stuff like this," Chad said as Emily chatted with other Army wives away from the beer keg and the increasing testosterone that flowed with it. His hair was longer than it had been when he was on active duty, not long enough to touch the tops of his ears, and short by civilian standards; it receded slightly at the corners of his temples. He hadn't gained any weight. The eyes were still sharp and focused and he carried himself with the calm swagger of a leader.

By noon he had been asked a dozen questions about his job. Ten years after accepting his commission as an officer in the U.S. Army, Chad found excitement and fascination in his post as an FBI special agent in the elite Counterterrorism Division, even though he couldn't go into too many details about the specifics of what he did. Just as was the case in the 2nd Ranger Battalion, most of what Chad did with the bureau was classified.

None of his friends seemed to mind when he evaded mission-specific questions or flat-out said, "I can't talk about it." He did tell them about running into Coach Berry just seven days ago. One of the parts of Chad's job that he could share was the security he occasionally provided at football games. It was no secret that Al Qaeda encouraged its followers to target sporting events. FBI counterterrorism forces were charged with making sure venues were safe and local security was doing a good job of protecting civilians. On December 3, 2011, Chad volunteered to check the security at Florida Atlantic University Stadium in Boca Raton during the Owls' final home game. He didn't do it because he loved FAU football—he didn't even know the school's record prior to that game—but because the Owls were hosting Louisiana-Monroe, coached by Todd Berry.

Berry spent two seasons at LoMo, as Louisiana-Monroe was called, working as offensive coordinator for Charlie Weatherbie. Then in 2006 he spent one season as the quarterbacks coach at the University of Miami before heading to the Nevada desert to work as offensive coordinator at the University of Nevada, Las Vegas under head coach Mike Sanford. After the 2009 season, Weatherbie was released at LoMo after amassing a record of 31-51, and Berry was called back into head coaching.

No one other than the players who were on those Army and Navy teams in 2000 and 2001 appreciated the synergy of Weatherbie's and Berry's career tracks. College coaching could seem like musical chairs at times, with the same men showing up on the sidelines of several different schools in just a few short years. But Weatherbie and Berry shared a special experience no others had, having coached the first Army-Navy Game after 9/11.

Chad left his home in Jupiter and got to Boca early so he could be waiting outside the visitors' locker room when Berry arrived. A team manager showed up to guard the door before any of the players or coaches arrived. Chad introduced himself and asked if he could say hello to Coach Berry before the game. In less than a minute, Berry charged down the hallway and gave Chad a hug. They talked about family and football and how their lives had changed in the past decade.

"You're with the FBI now?" Berry asked.

"Yes, sir, if you can believe it."

"How many tours overseas?"

"Four, all in Iraq, three with the Second Ranger Battalion," Chad said.

Berry shook his head and looked at the concrete floor outside the locker room for a second before saying, "God bless you, man."

The former players at the tailgate party in Washington hung on every word as Chad recounted the story.

"Who won?" one of them finally asked.

"LoMo won twenty-six to nothing," Chad said. "Coach Berry's got a good team. They're young, so he should be in good shape next year." Minutes later the party waned and some of the crowd began migrating toward FedExField. Chad hurried to finish his beer before heading inside so he could be in his seat when the corps and brigade marched onto the gridiron.

Just as he took the last sip and threw the plastic cup into a nearby trash bag, the soft, staccato thumping of helicopter rotors grew louder overhead, and all eyes look up to see two UH-60 Black Hawks beating a path toward the north parking lot. The one carrying the president was Marine One.

Chad smiled and said to one of his buddies, "Now, there's something you won't see at the Alabama-LSU game."

Then he stared quietly at the sky for a second, still as a winter night.

"Hard to believe it's been ten years," he finally said.

* * *

Between the parking lot and the gate, Chad took Emily by the arm and showed her to an area where the Navistar military contractor had parked an MRAP, an IED-resistant, ambush-protected transport vehicle with high clearance and no windows.

"We sure could have used more of those on my first tour," he said.

Emily didn't smile. She had pushed away those memories into dark corners where they should remain.

Then Chad and Emily meandered through the gates and made their way to the club level, where Rick Dauch, a former Army defensive back from the class of 1984, had a suite.

Dauch was the president and CEO of Accuride, makers of wheels for commercial vehicles. He was also the immediate past president of the Army Football Club, a fraternity of former players, some still active-duty and others, like Dauch, highly successful businessmen. John Garrison, president and CEO of Bell Helicopter, who played with Dauch in 1981 and '82, and Tommy Morgan, free safety, helicopter pilot, and West Point Class of 1983, who became a successful investment banker and ultimately bought the Thayer Hotel, the grand stone structure that serves as the meeting spot for all returning West Pointers, were both part of the group.

Four months prior to this Army-Navy Game, Dauch, Garrison, Morgan, and 150 other former players from the Classes of 1949 through 2005 showed up at the post to tell jokes, drink beer, play a round of golf, and have dinner in the meeting room above the end zone of Michie Stadium, where head coach Rich Ellerson came in to talk about the team.

"You all want to know specifics, and I'll be happy to tell you what I can," Ellerson had said that night. "I understand what's expected of us."

"Beat Navy!" someone from the back of the room shouted.

"I know," Ellerson said. "I know."

Beating Navy hadn't happened enough. Even though Dauch's

suite, located at the forty-yard-line of FedExField, was filled with generals and colonels and more than a few CEOs, Chad was the most popular celebrity there because of a record he didn't want to hold. Ten years later, he was still the last Army quarterback to beat Navy. There was nothing he wanted more than for that torch to be passed.

After Paul Johnson's first year as Navy's head coach (and Brian's last as a player), the Mids went on a tear, going to eight straight bowl games: five under Johnson, who left Navy in 2007 to take the head coaching job at Georgia Tech; and three under head coach Ken Niumatalolo, the former Hawaii Rainbows quarterback who played for Johnson in 1989 when Hawaii went to their first bowl game. Niumatalolo worked for Johnson as offensive coordinator before assuming the head job in Annapolis, and between them, Johnson and Niumatalolo were a combined 76-50 at Navy coming into this game. They were 9-0 against Army.

Both the president and vice president were there, one of the few times that both had attended a sporting event of any kind. After escorting Emily to her seat, Chad pointed out the Secret Service snipers in the top corners of the stadium. Everyone had passed through metal detectors on the way in, which was standard procedure at any event the president attended even before 9/11. All the Secret Service agents were affable and apologetic for the inconvenience they were causing.

The Brigade of Midshipmen marched in first, followed a few minutes later by the cadets. Both student bodies wore overcoats and gloves, and both remained standing for the rest of the afternoon. The Naval Academy glee club sang a moving a cappella version of the National Anthem. Then President Obama came to midfield with the captains. They saluted and he tossed the coin to the cheers of the Washington crowd. Once his official duties were complete, the president walked along the edge of the stadium shaking hands with the crowd. Then he went upstairs to the CBS booth for an interview with Verne Lundquist and Gary Danielson, who, along with sideline reporter Tracy Wolfson, made up the network's college football A-team.

"They're smart, dedicated, tough, love their country, and do an incredible job," the president said of the players from both teams as the first quarter got under way. "And that's what gives this game such resonance. What we're reminded of is that as important as sports are, these guys are going to be in life-or-death situations voluntarily protecting our country. They're going to be on the same team. It constantly makes you grateful for being here in America and these incredible young people. They are the best we have to offer.

"It's a reminder that these games, as much fun as these things are, part of what we celebrate is the dedication and the sacrifice that all these young men and young women who are in the stands are going to be making for our country day in and day out."

President Obama and Vice President Joe Biden would spend time with both student bodies throughout the afternoon, but they did their best not to be a distraction. Nobody wanted to disrupt this game.

Under normal circumstances the game ball would have come from the sky, delivered by Navy SEALs who would parachute in, landing on the fifty-yard line. But because FedExField wasn't the normal venue, wires for suspension cameras stretched from sideline to sideline, so the ball was walked out and placed on a tee.

Once it got airborne, fans were treated to a great one. Navy jumped out to a quick 14–0 lead after two Army fumbles in the first quarter. Chad tried not to show his early disappointment, but as he got up from his seat to get a drink and some buffalo wings, he looked at a friend and said, "What the hell? Not again."

Beach balls began being volleyed through the end zone section where the brigade was chanting "Why so quiet?" to their cadet counterparts on the other side of the stadium.

Army answered with back-to-back scoring drives, with quarterback Trent Steelman leading the attack. Steelman executed the triple option to perfection after the first two miscues. He pulled the ball in and ran around his right tackle for thirty-four yards and Army's first score. Then he executed a perfect two-minute drill, moving the ball sixty-three yards in just over a minute and a half to tie the game at fourteen going in for the half.

At halftime, President Obama, Vice President Biden, and Biden's wife, Jill, came down to greet wounded warriors who were in attendance. The three met and posed for pictures with forty-nine soldiers, eighteen sailors, two marines, and one airman, all of whom had been wounded in Iraq and Afghanistan. Then country music star Lee Greenwood walked to midfield and led the crowd in his most famous song, "God Bless the U.S.A."

The game went down to the wire. As is often the case in rivalry games, the difference was turnovers and special teams, and Navy won on both counts.

"Offensively and defensively it was pretty much back and forth," Coach Niumatalolo said afterward. "But special teams, we won outright."

The stats bore that out. Rushing yards (and both teams were ground-oriented) were almost identical. Army ran for 298 yards to Navy's 296. Neither team threw much, but Army won what little air game there was, with Trent Steelman going four-for-six for seventy-seven yards and a touchdown, and Navy's quarterback, Kriss Proctor, completing only one pass for thirteen yards. But Proctor also led the Mids in rushing with ninety-seven yards.

In the second half Navy took the opening kickoff and plowed into Army territory, shortening the field for Proctor, who took advantage by orchestrating a five-play drive that ended in a touchdown.

Steelman responded by leading Army down the field and scoring another touchdown with a twenty-five-yard pass, only the fifth touchdown pass Army quarterbacks had thrown all season.

The game was tied with twelve minutes left in the fourth quarter, but then Navy pulled ahead by three with a field goal from their reliable kicker, Jon Teague.

On the ensuing kickoff, Army fans saw their hopes and dreams dashed as return specialist James Whittington fumbled the ball deep in his own territory. Navy recovered and appeared to be ready to walk in for another score. But the Army defense held and the Mids had to settle for another field goal to go up by six.

With time running out, Army needed a touchdown to tie and an extra point to win. Steelman looked like he might just pull it off. The quarterback ran the option and worked the clock, moving the ball down to the Navy twenty-five-yard line. But that was where the Mids stiffened. After barely gaining three yards on three plays, Steelman ran another option to his right and pulled the ball in to run it himself. It was the same play he had run for thirty-four yards and a touchdown in the first half. This time, Navy linebacker Matt Warrick read it perfectly and met Steelman at the line of scrimmage, driving the quarterback backward for a one-yard loss.

Navy took over on downs and ran out the clock. As close as they came, Army lost another one.

"[The Midshipmen] are a good football team," quarterback Kriss Proctor said afterward. "To beat Army for a decade is unheard-of. To do anything for a decade is pretty remarkable, especially in a rivalry like this."

"They are very good," Niumatalolo said of the Army squad. "Just look at this game. That was a battle, a great football game with two teams battling to the end."

Then Niumatalolo had to pause as soft pools welled in his eyes. "This is my fourteenth Army-Navy Game, but this one was different," he said. "The seniors knew it was their last game, and so everything—the emotion, the atmosphere, the attitude—it was just different. Our country is in good hands. With those seniors who will be leading men very soon, our country is in very good hands."

Chad's streak hadn't been broken. Right after the game, Brian Zickefoose sent him a text that read: "The legend lives."

"When I was at West Point, I lived Army football," Chad said. "It was the most important thing in the world to me, and a game like this: man, that would have been tough to stomach. But once you get out, and you lead men in the real fight, the good fight, that's when you're able to put things like this in perspective."

As he and Emily were leaving Rick Dauch's suite, saying good-bye to the officers who had treated him like royalty all day, Chad took one last look at the field and shook his head. "We just turned the ball over too much," he said. "You can't turn it over like that and win."

And then, as if the words he'd spoken mere seconds before had vanished from his memory, he said, "Man, I hate losing to those guys. I just hate it."

EPILOGUE

This nation will remain the land of the free only so long as it is the home of the brave.
—ELMER DAVIS

Brian lost three consecutive fights after beating Jorge Santiago in Las Vegas on Memorial Day weekend in 2011. The first loss was perhaps the most devastating, a first-round submission in October 2011 to Chael Sonnen, a great wrestler and the man many considered to be the best middleweight fighter in the UFC. UFC president Dana White did not hide the fact that the winner of the Stann-Sonnen fight would be given a middleweight title shot, so Brian's loss was a huge setback.

Plus, the bout was a legitimate good guy/bad guy matchup. Sonnen arrived in Houston having just come off a suspension for steroid use and still serving probation after pleading guilty to money-laundering in a federal mortgage fraud case, a crime that carries a maximum penalty of twenty years in prison. A former Realtor, Sonnen admitted to falsifying documents as part of a broader scam. He was given probation as part of a plea agreement in return for testifying against his partners in crime.

"Nothing surprised me," Brian said immediately after the loss.

"I trained with world-class guys to try to simulate Chael both wrestling and on top of me, and that's the hard part. You train with guys and do the right things and hope that carries over into the fight. But there is a reason Chael is so good and why he has been doing so well over the body of a very long career. I didn't have him in the practice room to train with me."

The Houston crowd was certainly on Brian's side. The fight had been under way ten seconds when chants of "U-S-A" reverberated through the Toyota Center. Thirty seconds after that, it was over. Sonnen got onto Stann's back and worked an arm underneath his neck. His face growing redder, Stann tapped out.

"Each loss I've become a better fighter for it, and more importantly a better person," Brian said. "This won't be any different. I've always tried to fight the best. This is a matchup most other guys in my weight division would have run from and I took it without a second's delay. That's about the only thing I'm proud of."

Brian's next two bouts were overseas as part of the UFC's initiative to broaden the sport. He fought well in both, losing one in a decision and then getting knocked out by former champion Wanderlei Silva in Japan on May 3, 2013, a bloody slugging match that experts called one of the best fights of the year. Scored on points, Brian was winning until Silva landed one mammoth left hook to the temple that reeled him and sent him to the ground. Silva then moved in and knocked Brian unconscious.

Thankfully, Brian was an atypical fighter who understood the limited shelf-life of athletes in the sport and planned accordingly. He opened a gym in Atlanta called Warrior Legion Academy and began training students in 2012. Clippings and memorabilia of Brian's fight career and Marine service adorn the walls, but there are also reminders—photos of Travis Manion and J. P. Blecksmith—that he wants everyone to see. The words on the wall of the gym are "Honor, Courage, Confidence, and Discipline," all traits that accurately describe the owner.

When Fox bought the television rights to the UFC, Brian found a home in the broadcast booth providing fight commentary for the Fuel Network. His expertise and articulate analysis made him an instant hit.

He and Teressa moved into a new house in Alpharetta, Georgia, a northern suburb of Atlanta, and in March 2013 the Stanns announced that they were expecting their third child.

On May 1, 2013, Chad Jenkins left his job as an FBI special agent to open his own security consulting firm specializing in national security and terrorism. His decision was made prior to the terrorist attack at the Boston Marathon in April 2013, but the bombings in Boston illustrated why he chose to go out on his own. Police and FBI agents can't be everywhere, nor can they train every event organizer on threat assessment and proper security measures. That is a role only the private sector can fill. Chad left the bureau hoping to fill it.

"It's a frightening proposition," he said. "But I also see the national security needs that the FBI simply cannot fill. On my own, I believe I can assemble a team to solve problems and make our nation safer, make the citizens safer. That's why I've gone out on my own. That's why I get up in the morning."

As of November 2013, Chad was still the last Army quarterback to beat Navy. In the 2012 matchup, Army gained more yards than Navy and had more first downs, but they also had more turnovers, none more crucial than on the last possession when senior quarterback Trent Steelman lost a handoff to his fullback on the Navy fourteen-yard line when it looked like Army would drive in for the winning score.

The Mids ran out the clock to win their eleventh Army-Navy Game in a row and capture the Commander-in-Chief Trophy.

The indelible image of the game was Steelman sobbing in the arms of General Ray Odierno after the loss.

"That's what the game does to you," Chad said. "That's what it means."

AUTHOR'S NOTE

I never served. In my family I am a coward among heroes, as both my grandfathers were World War II vets, my father was an Army artillery officer (when I was one month old he was on a ship to Cuba after the Russians decided to park some nukes down there); my younger brother also served in the Army, and my oldest son was in the 6th Motor T Battalion of the 8th Marine Corps Reserves. That is why this story is told in the words and from the perspective of a civilian. Like many, I am awed by men like Chad and Brian and honored to call them friends. Any mistakes in these pages are mine alone, as the list of those who helped in this process is long and far more distinguished than my talents deserve.

When I first stumbled upon the idea of writing about America's latest greatest generation, my goal was to find two men who went to the military academies to play football in a time of peace, but who left in a time of war with far more important goals than winning a game. Because of my background as a sportswriter, I started with the sports information directors. Navy's SID, Scott Strasemeier, got back to me first and said, "I have the perfect guy for you." He introduced me to Brian Stann, and we were off.

Throughout the process Scott was just a phone call or e-mail away. He and his staff went to great lengths to make sure I had everything I needed from the Naval Academy, including a new friend in Brian Stann, whom I am honored and privileged to know.

Once Brian was in place, I called Brian Gunning, the SID at Army, and said, "Hey, Brian, Navy really came through for me: what have you got?" He put on a full-court press that ultimately included generals at the highest level. But when they got back to me with Chad Jenkins, it was certainly worth it.

Emily Jenkins and Teressa Stann are also deserving of great thanks. They are responsible for the men in this story, and their service, while different, is just as important as that of their husbands.

Also, special thanks to: Rick Dauch; Lieutenant Mark Kurtz; General Buck Kernan (ret.); General David Huntoon; Honorable Senator John McCain; the late General Normal Schwarzkopf; Tommy Morgan; Lance Barrow; Bonnie Bernstein; Tracy Bailey; Dana White and the entire staff at the UFC; Lee and Dave Jenkins; John Manley; Sherri Reed; Gary Bartels, Jr.; Jake Denman; Michael Erwin; Teri Jenkins Kirk; Laura Jenkins Watson; John G. Bond; Jeffrey Schroeder; Jeff Winstead; Candice Scott; Robin Brendle; Brian Zickefoose; Clint Dodson; Debra J. Weierman; Rachael Dean; Scott Tolley; Mr. and Mrs. Jack W. Nicklaus; the entire staff and student body at the United States Military Academy and United States Naval Academy; Colonel Tim Maxwell and the East Battalion, Wounded Warrior Regiment, Camp Lejeune, North Carolina; and the entire staff at the 75th Ranger Regiment, Fort Benning, Georgia.

Also a special thanks to my agent, Dan Conaway, and my editor, Henry Ferris, for believing in this idea, these men, and my ability to pull it off.

Most of all, thanks to all who serve and have served. And to the families of those who sacrificed in the course of that service, a special and humble God bless you.